PRENTICE HALL

Language Teaching Methodology Series

Applied Linguistics
General Editor: Christopher N. Candlin

Communicative Language Testing

Other titles in this series include:

CANDLIN, Christopher and MURPHY, Dermot
Language learning tasks

ELLIS, Rod
Classroom second language development

ELLIS, Rod
Classroom language acquisition in context

FRANK, Christine and RINVOLUCRI, Mario
Grammar in action

GOLEBIOWSKA, Aleksandra
Getting students to talk

KENNEDY, Chris
Language planning and English language teaching

KRASHEN, Stephen
Second language acquisition and second language learning

KRASHEN, Stephen
Principles and practice in second language acquisition

KRASHEN, Stephen
Language acquisition and language education

McKAY, Sandra
Teaching grammar

NUNAN, David
Understanding language classrooms

PECK, Antony
Language teachers at work

STEVICK, Earl
Success with foreign languages

SWALES, John
Episodes in ESP

STEMPLESKI, Susan and TOMALIN, Barry
Video in action

TAYLOR, Linda
Teaching and learning vocabulary

WALLACE, Catherine
Learning to read in a multicultural society

WENDEN, Anita and RUBIN, Joan
Learner strategies in language learning

YALDEN, Janice
The communicative syllabus

Communicative Language Testing

CYRIL J. WEIR

University of Reading, UK

ENGLISH LANGUAGE TEACHING

Prentice Hall

New York   London   Toronto   Sydney   Tokyo   Singapore

First published 1988 by the University of Exeter
This edition published 1990 by
Prentice Hall International (UK) Ltd
66 Wood Lane End, Hemel Hempstead
Hertfordshire HP2 4RG
A division of
Simon & Schuster International Group

Typeset in 10 pt Times
by MHL Typesetting Ltd, Coventry

Printed and bound in Great Britain at
Dotesios Printers Ltd, Trowbridge, Wiltshire

Library of Congress Cataloging-in-Publication Data

Weir, Cyril J.
    Communicative language testing / Cyril J. Weir.
        p. cm. — (Language teaching methodology series) (English
    language teaching)
        ISBN 0-13-155284-8
        1. English language — Study and teaching — Foreign speakers.
    2. English language — Ability testing. I. Title. II. Series.
    III. Series: English language teaching.
    PE1128.A2W395   1990
    428'.0076 — dc20   89-29167
                                                                      CIP

British Library Cataloguing in Publication Data

Weir, Cyril J.
    Communicative language testing. — (Language teaching
    methodology series)
    1. Non-English speaking students. Education. Curriculum
    subjects : English language. Examinations and tests
    I. Title II. Series
    428.2'4'076

    ISBN 0-13-155284-8

---

1 2 3 4 5   94 93 92 91 90

*To Hilya and
to my parents*

Contents

General Editor's Preface

There is no doubt that the development of what has become known as a 'communicative' approach to language teaching poses serious issues for language test designers, researchers and administrators. These issues extend over the entire gamut of validity, encompassing content, construct, face, washback and criterion-related questions. They also invoke important concerns for test administration and impose substantial demands on the various aspects of test reliability.

At a time when local institutions as well as extensive public educational systems concerned with language learning are required to meet unfamiliar and hitherto inexplicitly stated performance goals for their learners, and where learners themselves are increasingly demanding evidence of their own communicative achievement, the requirement on language testing to be equally explicit and accountable is very great. Moreover, where dominant paradigms of instruction and learning exercise in part countervailing forces against the imposition of such centrally determined standards, as with the learner-centred movement implicit for many in communicative theory, testing has an additional problem of determining where its ideological commitment and its loyalties must lie.

Communicative language testing, therefore, is no easy option. It has several masters to serve, linguistic, pedagogic, administrative, acquisitional, and ideological, all of which are in essence free to define their own interests without paying heed to the subject-specific constraints of testing theory and practice.

Given this minefield, therefore, it is perhaps surprising that testers do not throw in the towel. Many have, in the sense that they have proposed easy nostrums which sit comfortably within the constraints of testing and only acknowledge those external demands we have indicated where it is easy and politic for them to do so. We see their products in many of the simplistic so-called 'communicative tests' where the subject matter of language and the contextual requirements of language use have been sacrificed to well-worn testing paradigms, item-types and familiar sets of items.

What makes Cyril Weir's contribution to the **Language Teaching Methodology Series** so refreshing in this climate is the extent and the carefulness of his argument. Drawing from the writing of a range of testing specialists concerned with these issues, he constructs a model of what constitutes communicative demand, setting it within the history of language test development in the recent past and the basic considerations on test design. From this background he sets out a number of exemplary testing methods, skill focused, which serve different aspects and different goals of communicative testing. These methods he then illustrates from established and current tests, including the most recent, for example, the International English Language Testing System (IELTS) developed in the UK and Australia. These examples and his extensive bibliography offer the non-specialist but concerned reader a demonstration of the field, its current objectives and the practical difficulties that lie in wait. Not that the book is negative; it does offer considerable practical assistance and guidance to the language teacher. But equally, it doesn't fudge the difficulties of communicative language testing but meets them head on, thereby providing a valuable agenda for the more specialised readership.

As a consequence, Cyril Weir's book is both useful for the practising language teacher and for the administrator. At the same time, in establishing the framework for decision-making, it offers for the testing specialist an admirably clear and succinct statement of the challenge of communication and how, albeit yet imperfectly, it may be met.

Professor Christopher N. Candlin
General Editor
National Centre for English Language Teaching and Research
Macquarie University, Sydney, Australia

Acknowledgements

The author wishes to acknowledge his gratitude to the following examination boards for their permission to reproduce samples of tests:

The Associated Examining Board (Test in English for Education Purposes);
University of Cambridge Local Examinations Syndicate/Royal Society of Arts Examinations Board (UCLES/RSA);
The British Council/University of Cambridge Local Examinations Syndicate (International English Language Testing Service);
International Development Program of Australian Universities and Colleges (IDP); and
The Joint Matriculations Board (Test in English Overseas).

The author and publisher acknowledge that material in parts of Chapter 4 draws upon the Commonwealth of Australia copyright publication, *Language Proficiency Testing for Migrant Professionals: New Directions for the Occupational English Test* (Council for Overseas Professional Qualifications, AGPS, Canberra, 1986), written under a consultancy arrangement with the Institute of English Language Education, University of Lancaster, which included the participation of the author.

Chapter One

Approaches to Language Test Design: A Critical Review

1.1 Introduction

To help decide on the most suitable formats for inclusion in a test, it is useful to be aware of the alternative approaches to language testing and their limitations in terms of the criteria of validity, reliability and efficiency.

Validity is concerned with whether a test measures what it is intended to measure. Reliability is concerned with the extent to which we can depend on the test results. Efficiency is concerned with matters of practicality and cost in test design and administration.

These glosses should be sufficient to follow the review of approaches to language testing in this chapter. Readers requiring a more detailed treatment before continuing are referred to Chapter Two where a full discussion of these concepts can be found.

Davies (1978) argued that by the mid-1970s, approaches to testing seemed to fall along a continuum stretching from 'discrete' item tests at one end, to integrative tests such as cloze at the other. He took the view that in testing, as in teaching, there was a tension between the analytical on the one hand and the integrative on the other, and considered that (p. 149) 'the most satisfactory view of language testing and the most useful kinds of language tests, are a combination of these two views, the analytical and the integrative.' He went on to say that it was probable, in any case, that no test could be wholly analytical or integrative (p. 149):

> The two poles of analysis and integration are similar to (and may be closely related to) the concepts of reliability and validity. Test reliability is increased by adding to the stock of discrete items in a test; the smaller the bits and the more of these there are, the higher the potential reliability. Validity, however, is increased by making the test truer to life, in this case more like language in use.

Oller (1979), on the other hand, felt that testing should focus on the integrative end of the continuum. He made a strong case for following the swing of the testing pendulum away from what Spolsky (1976) had described as the 'psychometric—structuralist era', or the so-called 'discrete point' approach to testing, to what he termed 'the psycholinguistic—sociolinguistic era': the age of the integrative test.

In the description of these approaches below, they are treated as if they were 'distinct' or 'pure' types. It is recognised that, in practice, most tests contain elements of the discrete and the integrative, either in the test format or the assessment procedures adopted, but, while the distinction between the two is neither real nor absolute, it is nevertheless felt that approaches to testing can be usefully described in terms of the particular focus they represent.

1.2   The psychometric—structuralist era

The clear advantages of testing 'discrete' linguistic points are that they yield data which are easily quantifiable, as well as allowing a wide coverage of items. Tests which focus on 'discrete' linguistic items are efficient and have the usual reliability of marking associated with objectively scored tests, but both the 'discrete point' approach and the various formats employed in it suffer from the defects of the construct they seek to measure.

The problem with this approach to the measurement of proficiency is that it depends on proficiency being neatly quantifiable in this fashion. Oller (1979, p. 212) outlined the deficiencies in terms of the construct validity of a hypothetically pure form of this approach:

> Discrete point analysis necessarily breaks the elements of language apart and tries to teach them (or test them) separately with little or no attention to the way those elements interact in a larger context of communication. What makes it ineffective as a basis for teaching or testing languages is that crucial properties of language are lost when its elements are separated. The fact is that in any system where the parts interact to produce properties and qualities that do not exist in the part separately, *the whole is greater than the sum* of its parts ... organisational constraints themselves become crucial properties of the system which simply cannot be found in the parts separately.

Oller is on fairly safe ground here as most people would probably agree that testing a candidate's linguistic competence is a necessary, but not sufficient, component of a test battery. In another context, people taking a driving test are required to demonstrate that they can perform the task. The licensing authority does not depend solely on a pencil and paper test to inform about the extent of examinees' knowledge concerning the principles of driving. Similarly, those who have to make assessments about a piece of music will make them on the piece as a whole, not on selected parts of it. Chaplen (1970a, p. xxvii) criticised isolated skills tests from this point of view, arguing that: 'It seems unlikely that measurements of the component skills most commonly isolated can provide either singly or in aggregate, a satisfactory measurement of the gestalt.' This is a view shared by Savignon (1972) who found that grammatical competence was not by itself a good predictor of communicative skills.

Kelly (1978) argued that if the goal of applied linguistics was seen as the applied analysis of meaning, e.g., the recognition of the context-specific meaning of an utterance as distinct from its system-giving meaning, then applied linguists should be more interested in the development and measurement of ability to take part in specified communicative performance, the production of and comprehension of coherent discourse, rather than in linguistic competence. This echoed Spolsky's (1968) earlier point that perhaps instead of attempting to establish a person's knowledge of a language in terms of a percentage mastery of grammar and lexis, we would be better employed in testing that person's ability to perform in a specified socio-linguistic setting.

Rea (1978, p. 51) has expressed a similar view:

> although we would agree that language is a complex behaviour and that we would generally accept a definition of overall language proficiency as the ability to function in a natural language situation, we still insist on, or let others impose on us, testing measures which assess language as an abstract array of discrete items, to be manipulated only in a mechanistic way. Such tests yield artificial, sterile and irrelevant types of items which have no relationship to the use of language in real life situations.

Morrow (1979) argued that if we are to assess proficiency, i.e., potential success in the use of the language in some general sense, it would be more valuable to test for a knowledge of and an ability to apply the rules and processes by which these discrete elements are synthesised into an infinite number of grammatical sentences and then selected as being appropriate for a particular context, rather than simply to test knowledge of the elements alone. Morrow (1979, p. 145) argues the point that:

> knowledge of the elements of a language in fact counts for nothing unless the user is able to combine them in new and appropriate ways to meet the linguistic demands of the situation in which he wishes to use the language.

1.3 The psycholinguistic–sociolinguistic era

In response to a feeling that 'discrete point' tests were insufficient indicators of language proficiency, the testing pendulum on the whole swung in favour of global tests in the 1970s, into what Spolsky (1976) termed the psycholinguistic–sociolinguistic era, an approach to measurement that was in many ways contrary to the allegedly atomistic assumptions of the 'discrete point' tests (see Davies, 1978).

It was claimed by Oller (1979) that global integrative tests such as cloze and dictation went beyond the measurement of a limited part of language competence achieved by 'discrete point' tests with their bias towards testing the receptive skills; that such tests could measure the ability to integrate disparate language skills in ways which more closely approximated the actual process of language use. Oller's view (1979, p. 37) was that:

> The concept of an *integrative* test was born in contrast with the definition of a discrete point tests. If discrete items take language skill apart, integrative tests put it back together. Whereas discrete items attempt to test knowledge of language one bit at a time, integrative tests attempt to assess a learner's capacity to use many bits all at the same time, and possibly while exercising several presumed components of a grammatical system, and perhaps more than one of the traditionally recognized skills or aspects of skills [author's italics].

Read (1981a, p. x) succinctly described the psycholinguistic—sociolinguistic era:

From a psycholinguistic perspective, language came to be seen as less of a well-defined taxonomic structure and more of a dynamic, creative, functional system. It was recognised that natural language contains a considerable amount of redundancy, so that it is difficult to show that any single linguistic unit is indispensable for communication . . . . The sociolinguistic contribution centres on the concept of communicative competence, which represents a broadening of Chomsky's notion of competence to cover not only knowledge of rules for forming grammatical sentences but also rules for using those sentences appropriately with different contexts . . . . Thus the psycholinguistic and sociolinguistic perspectives have enlarged the basis on which the validity of a test is to be judged. New criteria have become introduced that cannot be measured by the standard 'objective' methods.

Oller maintained that provided linguistic tests such as cloze require 'performance' under real life constraints, e.g., time, they are at least a guide to aptitude and potential for communication, even if they do not test communication itself. They are also practicable to administer, economical to set and mark, and have respectable reliability figures associated with them.

Work by Alderson (1978a), however, raised serious questions about the validity of these integrative measures as testing devices. He demonstrated that there is no such thing as '*the* cloze test' and even in using the same passage, results are affected by altering the point where the deletions are started from, or by using a different n/th rate deletion. (The cloze procedure is examined in more detail in Section 4.1.3 where consideration is given to the construction and the potential advantages and disadvantages of this test method.)

A major cause of concern is the assumption made by Oller (1976, 1979, 1980) that General Language Proficiency (GLP), the grammar of expectancy his integrative tests are aimed at, is a single principal factor underlying all language skills. His concept of 'overall proficiency' has inevitably merged into a hypothesis of an underlying unitary competence.

This is a view implicit in Oller's concept of the internalised expectancy grammar and, though it is one which is seductive for the purpose of those having to take administrative decisions, as Davies (1981b) points out, it conflicts with substantial evidence in favour of at least two competences, namely reception and production (see Vollmer, 1981). The differences between knowing how to analyse input and knowing how to construct output would seem to outweigh the correspondence between the two processes. Pedagogical experience would also suggest that the different performance tasks an individual is faced with result in a variety of different proficiencies being exhibited in the completion of these tasks.

Davies (1981b) emphasised that although Oller has claimed that his integrative tests represent total language proficiency better than any other single test or combination of tests, this is not in itself an argument in favour of the unitary competence hypothesis, as measures such as cloze and dictation are so integrative that they contain most or all language abilities anyway. High correlations between cloze and other measures may only reflect that they are measuring different skills which are highly correlated among individuals; however, this does not mean that there will be no individuals whose performances in the various skills differ considerably.

A group of examinees may have scores in two tests which correlate very highly, in the sense that both tests put the individuals in more or less the same rank order, but since correlational measures take little or no account of mean scores, the group's scores may be centred on very different means in the two tests, indicating quite different levels of performance overall. In other words, correlational data do not provide evidence about standards.

The empirical evidence that has been marshalled in favour of the 'unitary competence hypothesis' is open to some doubt and there is a growing body of evidence favouring a divisibility hypothesis (see Vollmer, 1979; Bachman and Palmer, 1981a; Hughes, 1981a; Vollmer, 1981; and Porter, 1983).

Principal component analysis is often used to substantiate the 'unitary competence hypothesis', but this method is essentially designed to simplify data, and would be expected to produce one factor from a battery of seemingly different language tests (see Porter, 1983). More crucially, this general language proficiency factor does not necessarily explain all the variance in the results, and the percentage of variance explained differs from study to study (see Vollmer, 1981). Because of the existence of factors other than the principal component, which explain reasonable proportions of the remaining variance, it is often possible by pursuing further factor analysis, for example Varimax rotation of the factor structure, to obtain a number of independent factors each of which makes a sizeable contribution to the total variance.

There is also evidence in the literature that the format of a task can unduly affect the performance of some candidates (see Boniakowska, 1986; Murphy, 1978, 1980; and Weir, 1983a). This makes it necessary to include a variety of test formats for assessing each construct rather than rely on a single overall measure, such as cloze.

Though the tests Oller has advocated are global in that they require examinees to exhibit simultaneous control over different aspects of the language system, they are nevertheless indirect. Although the tests might integrate disparate language skills in ways which more closely approximate actual language use, one would argue that their claim to the mantle of communicative validity remains suspect, as only direct tests which simulate relevant authentic communication tasks can claim to mirror actual communicative interaction (see Kelly, 1978; Morrow, 1979). As Moller (1982b, p. 25) pointed out, the indirect tests Oller has advocated do not: 'require subjects to perform tasks considered to be relevant in the light of their known future use of the language.'

Advocates of communicative language testing would argue that Oller's view pays insufficient regard to the importance of the productive and receptive processing of discourse, arising out of the actual use of language in a social context with all the attendant performance constraints, e.g., the interaction-based nature of discourse, unpredictability and behavioural outcomes (see Morrow, 1979; Moller, 1981b). Both Rea (1978) and Morrow (1979) have emphasised that although indirect measures of language abilities claim extremely high standards of reliability and concurrent validity as established by statistical techniques, their claim to other types of validity remains suspect.

Morrow (1979) cited as evidence for this the fact that neither cloze nor dictation offers the opportunity for spontaneous production by the candidate and the language norms which are followed are those of the examiner (or original author of the text), not of the student himself. Neither testing procedure offers the possibility for oral or non-controlled written production and since the oral and written skills are generally held to be highly important, some means of assessing them reliably in communicative situations should be found. Although integrative measures appear to correlate highly with other similar measures of general language proficiency, there is empirical evidence that cloze correlates only moderately with tests of written production (see Weir and Ormiston, 1978) and with spoken production (see Vollmer, 1981). Given that the tests concerned are reliable, this would suggest the possibility that proficiency in these areas cannot be adequately predicted by a test of overall proficiency.

Morrow also claimed both cloze and dictation to be fundamentally suspect since they are tests of underlying ability (competence) rather than actual performance. In other words, they depend basically on a knowledge of the language system rather than the ability to operate this sytem in authentic settings. B.J. Carroll (1980b, p. 9) reached the same conclusion: 'this (cloze test) is still essentially usage based. The task does not represent genuine interactive communication and is, therefore, only an indirect index of potential efficiency in coping with day-to-day communicative tasks.'

Even if it were decided that indirect tests such as cloze were valid in some sort of derived fashion, it still remains true that performing on a cloze test is not the same sort of activity as reading. The pedagogical consequences of including this type of test measure in a battery might be harmful if it results in candidates being taught specifically to handle indirect assessment tasks in preference to teaching them to cope with more realistic tasks.

Kelly (1978, p. 241) made the further point that some candidates may manage to succeed in the indirect task by training of a certain kind and thus invalidate the test: 'indirect tests are subject to attacks on their validity in those cases where it is possible to bypass the ability in question and develop proficiency in the assessment task alone.' He also noted (1978, pp. 245−6) that:

> Analysis of a student's responses to an indirect test will not provide any relevant information as to the reasons for the student's difficulties in the authentic task, of which one assumes, the indirect test is a valid and reliable measure. By their very nature, indirect tests can provide evidence for *level* of achievement, but cannot diagnose specific areas of difficulty in relation to the authentic task.

Integrative tests such as cloze only tell us about a candidate's linguistic competence. They do not tell us anything directly about a student's performance ability, and their main value in their unmodified form is in designating competence levels rather than relating candidates' performance to any external criteria. They are perhaps only of limited use where the interest is in what the individual student can or cannot do in terms of the various language tasks he may face in real life situations.

The deficiencies in the type of information the 'discrete point' approaches of the psychometric−structuralist era and the more integrative approaches of the psycholinguistic−sociolinguistic era can provide bring about a need to investigate the 'communicative paradigm' to see whether this approach might prove more satisfactory.

1.4 The communicative paradigm

1.4.1 Terminology

There is a potential problem with terminology in some of the literature on communicative approaches to language testing. References are often made in the literature to testing communicative 'performance', e.g., B.J. Carroll's book (1980b) is entitled *Testing communicative performance*. It seems reasonable to talk of testing performance if the reference is to an individual's performance in one isolated situation, but as soon as we wish to generalise about ability to handle other situations, 'competence' as well as 'performance' would seem to be involved, or more precisely 'capacity' in the Widdowsonian sense (Widdowson, 1983). Bachman's use of the term 'communicative language ability' which includes both knowledge, or competence, and the capability for implementing that competence in language use would seem to be consistent with Widdowson's term in providing a more inclusive and satisfactory definition of language proficiency.

Strictly speaking, a performance test is one which samples behaviour in a single setting with no intention of generalising beyond that setting — otherwise a communicative language test is bound to concern itself with 'capacity' (Widdowson, 1983) or 'communicative language ability' (Bachman, 1989). The very act of generalising beyond the setting actually tested, implies some statements about abilities to use the language and/or knowledge of it. Conversely it is difficult to see how competence (knowing about using a language) might be evaluated except through its realisation in performance. Only performance can be directly observed and hence evaluated. All linguistic behaviour, even completing multiple choice tests of phoneme discrimination, necessarily involves performance. In practice a clear distinction between performance and competence will be difficult to maintain.

In testing communicative language ability we are evaluating samples of performance, in certain specific contexts of use, created under particular test constraints, for what they can tell us about a candidate's communicative capacity or language ability. Skehan (1988) points out that while such tests may not replicate exactly the performance conditions of a specific task in the target situation they are likely to replicate to some degree conditions of actual performance.

Skehan summarises the current position succinctly:

> What we need is a theory which guides and predicts how an underlying communicative competence is manifested in actual performance; how situations are related to one another, how competence can be assessed by examples of performance on actual tests; what components communicative competence actually has; and how these interrelate .... Since such definitive theories do not exist, testers have to do the best they can with such theories as are available.

1.4.2 The theoretical base

The validity of tests which claim to be communicative is a function of the degree of understanding of communication and communicative ability on the part of the test constructor. It is naïve to asssume that one can develop valid tests of communicative language ability without reference to the construct which one is attempting to measure, arguments relating to the state of the available descriptions of language in use not withstanding.

Agreement on what components should be included in a model of communicative language ability is by no means unanimous (see Courchene and de Bagheera, 1985, p. 49). Indeed relatively little is known about the wider communicative paradigm in comparison with linguistic competence per se and adequately developed theories of communicative language use are not yet available. This is not to say we must wait for completion of such theories before appropriate testing procedures can be developed. Rather we need to investigate systematically some of the available hypotheses about language use and try to operationalise these for testing purposes. In this way the constructs and processes of applied linguistics may be examined empirically and their status evaluated.

Canale and Swain (1980) provided a useful starting point for a clarification of the terminology necessary for forming a more definite picture of the ability to use language communicatively. These authors took communicative competence to include grammatical competence (knowledge of the rules of grammar), sociolinguistic competence (knowledge of the rules of use and rules of discourse) and strategic competence (knowledge of verbal and non-verbal communication strategies). The model was subsequently updated by Canale (1983), who proposed a four-dimensional model comprising linguistic, sociolinguistic, discoursal and strategic competences; the additional distinction being made between sociolinguistic (sociocultural rules) competence and discoursal competence (cohesion and coherence).

The framework proposed by Bachman (1989) is consistent with these earlier definitions of communicative language ability:

> Communicative language ability consists of language competence, strategic competence, and psychophysiological mechanisms. Language competence includes organisational competence, which consists of grammatical and textual competence, and pragmatic competence, which consists of illocutionary and sociolinguistic competence. Strategic competence is seen as performing assessment, planning and execution functions in determining the most effective means of achieving a communicative goal. Psychophysiological mechanisms involved in language use characterise the channel (auditory, visual) and mode (receptive, productive) in which competence is implemented.

Language competence is composed of the specific knowledge and skills required for operating the language system, for establishing the meanings of utterances, for employing language appropriate to the context and for operating through language beyond the level of the sentence. Strategic competence consists of the more general knowledge and skills involved in assessing, planning and executing communicative acts efficiently. Skehan (1988) suggests that the strategic component is implicated when communication requires improvisation because the other competences are in some way insufficient. The final part of Bachman's model deals with skill and method factors which are meant to handle the actual operation of language in real situations and so locate competence in a wider performance framework.

Models such as these provide a potentially useful framework for the design of language tests, but it must be emphasised that they are still themselves in need of validation (see

Brindley, 1986; Swain, 1985). The existence of the components of the model even as separate entities has not been established. Skehan (1988) rightly points out that the relationship between the various competences is not entirely clear, nor is the way they are integrated into overall communicative competence. Nor is it made clear how this communicative competence is translated into communicative performance. Candlin (1986) also outlined some of the problems to be faced in testing communicative competence and argued that their solution depends first on our description of this construct.

To date a limited amount of research has been carried out on investigating the measurement of language competence and method factors but very little has been done on the specific measurement of communication strategies or its relationship to the other competences. This in itself may be an indication of the inherent difficulties in this area. There is a pressing need for systematic research to illuminate all of these unresolved issues.

To help clarify what is meant by communicative testing we are forced to resort to available pretheoretical data from the literature relating to the concept of communicative competence. Since Hymes's two-dimensional model of communicative competence, comprising a 'linguistic' and a 'sociolinguistic' element, most subsequent models have included consideration of a sociolinguistic dimension which recognises the importance of context to the appropriate use of language and the dynamic interaction that occurs between that context and the discourse itself.

For Hymes (1972), communicative competence had included the ability to use the language, as well as having the knowledge which underlay actual performance. Morrow (1979) felt that a distinction needed to be made between communicative competence and communicative performance, the distinguishing feature of the latter being the fact that performance is the realisation of Canale and Swain's (1980) three competences and their interaction: 'in the actual production and comprehension of utterances (under general psychological constraints that are unique to performance).' (Morrow, 1979.)

Morrow (1979) and Canale and Swain (1980) argued that communicative language testing, as well as being concerned with what the learner knows about the form of the language and about how to use it appropriately in contexts of use (competence), must also deal with the extent to which the learner is actually able to demonstrate this knowledge in a meaningful communicative situation (performance), i.e., what he can do with the language, or as Rea (1978, p. 4) put it: 'his ability to communicate with ease and effect in specified sociolinguistic settings.'

The capacity or ability (see Widdowson, 1983; Bachman, 1989) to use language communicatively thus involves both competence and demonstration of the ability to use this competence. It is held that the performance tasks candidates are faced with in communicative tests should be representative of the type of task they might encounter in their own real-life situation and should correspond to normal language use where an integration of communicative skills is required with little time to reflect on, or monitor language input and output. The criteria employed in the assessment of performance on these tasks should relate closely to the effective communication of ideas in that context.

This perspective is consistent with the work of language testers generally supportive of a broadly based model of communicative language ability where there is a marked shift in emphasis from the linguistic to the communicative dimension. The emphasis is no longer on linguistic accuracy, but on the ability to function effectively through language in particular contexts of situation.

Cooper's (1968) view that existing test frameworks, because they concentrated on linguistic competence, might fail to assess a person's communicative ability, was taken up by Morrow (1979, p. 149) who argued that traditional tests did not give:

> any convincing proof of the candidate's ability to actually use the language, to translate the competence (or lack of it) which he is demonstrating into actual performance 'in ordinary situations', i.e., actually using the language to read, write, speak or listen in ways and contexts which correspond to real life.

B.J. Carrol (1989b, p. 1) adopted a similar line:

> the prime need of most learners is not for a theoretical or analytical knowledge of the target language, but for an ability to understand and be understood in that language within the context and constraints of particular language-using circumstances.

His opinion (1989b, p. 7) is that: 'the ultimate criterion of language mastery is therefore the learner's effectiveness in communication for the settings he finds himself in.'

Rea (1985) argued that all tests can be seen as tests of performance that are to varying degrees communicative or non-communicative, or (in Widdowson's dichotomy) use- or usage-based. Rea further distinguishes between items as meaning-dependent or meaning-independent, and describes how the former can be subdivided according to whether they involve a context determined response or not.

Moller (1981b) felt that communicative performance relates to the transmission and reception of particular meanings in particular contexts, and what can be tested is the quality and effectiveness of the performance observed in these circumstances. Kelly (1978, p. 350) had argued in a similar vein:

> To take part in a communicative event is to produce and/or comprehend discourse in the context of situation and under the performance conditions that obtain. It is the purpose of a proficiency test to assess whether or not candidates are indeed capable of participating in typical communication events from the specified communication situation(s).

These statements reflect an emphasis in language teaching and, more recently, testing that has been placed on *use* and the concern that has been shown with communicative functions rather than with the formal language patterns of *usage* (see Campbell and Wales, 1970; Hymes, 1972 and Widdowson, 1978 and 1983). Such theoretical descriptions are essential for describing the broad parameters within which communicative language testing should fall but practitioners need more tangible attributes to ascertain the degree of communicativeness of a test or to make their tests as communicative as possible within the constraints obtaining. What does a communicative test look like? How does it differ from other tests? These are questions which we need to address.

1.4.3 Distinguishing features of communicative language tests

Only a few of the currently available theories of language use seem amenable to the demands of language testing. It is therefore essential to be as precise as possible about the skills and performance conditions for any tests which claim to assess communicative language ability. Test constructors must closely identify those skills and performance conditions (see Skehan, 1988) that are the most important components of language use in particular contexts. The incorporation of these features, where appropriate, would indicate the degree to which the test task reflected the attributes of the activity in real life that it was meant to replicate. Unless steps are taken to identify and incorporate such features it would seem imprudent to make statements about a candidate's ability to function in normal conditions in his or her future target situation.

We also have to ensure that the sample of communicative language ability in our tests is as representative as possible. What and how to sample with our tests is a key issue in language testing. Many of the available descriptions of use are now both detailed and quite extensive, but are not always called on by testers. We need to make good this deficiency. If we are to extrapolate from our test data and make statements about communicative language ability in real life situations, great care needs to be taken over the texts and tasks we employ in our tests. These should accord as far as possible with the general descriptive parameters of the intended target situation particularly with regard to the skills necessary for successful participation in that situation. Additionally, tests should meet the performance conditions of that context as fully as possible. The difficulties of achieving this match with real life and the resultant implications for generalisability from communicative test data are discussed in the final section of this chapter.

In the testing literature there is a strong emphasis on the importance of test purpose, and it is held that no one solution can accommodate the wide variety of possible test scenarios. It is argued that appropriately differentiated tests in different skills areas need to be made available for evaluating different groups of examinees with different target situation needs. To measure language proficiency adequately in each situation, account must now be taken of: where, when, how, with whom, and why the language is to be used, and on what topics, and with what effect. The fact that communicative performance is affected by prior knowledge/experience/abilities is accepted along with the implications of this for test specificity (see Alderson and Urquhart, 1985b).

The important role of context as a determinant of communicative language ability is stressed and an integrative approach to assessment as against a decontextualised approach is advocated. Language can not be meaningful if it is devoid of context (linguistic, discoursal and sociocultural). For Oller (1973, 1979) the higher the level at which language is contextualised, the more effective language perception, processing and acquisition are likely to be. The variability in performance, according to the discourse domain or type of task involved, is recognised with the attendant implications this might have for test length and the types of text and formats to be included in a test battery (see Douglas and Selinker, 1985; Skehan, 1987).

The authenticity of tasks and the genuineness of texts in tests is regarded as something worth attempting to pursue despite the problems involved both in the definition of this and in its realisation. If inauthentic tasks are included in tests of communicative language ability there is a real danger that the method employed could interfere with the measurement of the construct we are interested in. We could end up measuring ability to cope with the method rather than the ability to read, listen, write, speak or deal with a combination of these skills in specified contexts. The more authentic the tasks the less we need to be concerned about this. If certain techniques only occur in tests, e.g., cloze or multiple choice, why should we ever contemplate their use? Tests of communicative language ability should be as direct as possible (attempt to reflect the 'real life' situation) and the tasks candidates have to perform should involve realistic discourse processing.

Unsimplified language, i.e., non doctored, 'genuine' texts should be used as inputs (see Widdowson, 1983) and due reference made to the referential and functional adequacy of these. In addition attention needs to be paid to other task dimensions such as the size of the text to be understood or produced and to processing in real time.

The net result of these considerations is that different tests need to be constructed to match different purposes and these instruments are no longer uniform in content or method. A variety of tests is now required whereas within previous orthodoxies authors were satisfied with a single 'best test'.

In assessing the ability to interact orally we should try to reflect the interactive nature of normal spoken discourse and attempt to ensure that reciprocity is allowed for in the test tasks included. The tasks should be conducted under normal time constraints and the element of unpredictability in oral interaction must be recognized, for authentic communication may lead the participants in unforeseen directions. Candidates may also be expected in certain tasks such as group discussion to demonstrate an ability to manage the interaction and/or to negotiate meaning with interlocutors. In short what we know from the theory of spoken interaction should be built into tasks which purport to test it (see Bygate, 1987).

The legitimacy of separate skills testing is being questioned, however, and indeed the more innovatory testing of skills through an integrated story-line set of procedures (see Low, 1986) is gaining favour. The discredited holy grails of the psycholinguistic—sociolinguistic era, such as cloze, are still seen to have a minor role to play in adding to the reliability of test batteries and assessing the more specifically linguistic skills, but centre stage is now given to more direct attempts to operationalise the integrated testing of communicative language ability.

Direct testing requires an integrated performance from the candidate involving communication under realistic linguistic, situational, cultural and affective constraints. Candidates have to perform both receptively and productively in relevant contexts. The focus is on the expression and understanding of functional meaning as against a more limited mastery of form. The move to direct testing has been further encouraged by a concern among language testers about the problems of format effect.

Format effect relates to the possibility that test results may be contaminated by the test format employed, i.e., a different estimate of a skill such as reading might be obtained if a different format is employed. This possible influence of test method on trait estimation is increasingly recognised if not yet fully understood (see Bachman and Palmer, 1982; Bachman, 1989). There is some evidence (Murphy, 1978, 1980; Weir, 1983a) to suggest that multiple choice format may be particularly suspect in this respect.

In order to elicit the student's best performance it is important to minimise any detrimental effect of the techniques of measurement on this performance. It is felt that the type of performance elicited by certain assessment methods may be qualitatively different from real life language use and to the extent that this is the case it is difficult to make statements about candidates' language proficiencies.

In the area of marking, the holistic and qualitative assessment of productive skills, and the implications of this for test reliability, need to be taken on board. The demands of a criterion-referenced approach to testing communicative language ability (where statistical analysis is likely to be more problematic) and the establishment of meaningful cut off scores demand attention (see Brindley, 1986; Cziko, 1981; and Hauptman *et al.*, 1985). At the final stage of the testing process the profiling of test results has to be addressed as we abandon the notion of a single general proficiency.

Though it is accepted that linguistic competence must be an essential part of communicative competence, the way in which they relate to each other, or indeed how either relates to communicative ability (in the performance sense), has not been clearly established by empirical research. A good deal of work needs to be done in comparing results obtained from performance on non-communicative, linguistically-based tests with those which sample communicative ability through instances of performance, before one can make any positive statements about the former being a sufficient indication of likely ability in the latter or in real life situations. No realistic comparisons are possible until reliable and effective, as well as valid, methods are investigated to assess proficiency in performing relevant communicative tasks.

For testers operating within the communicative paradigm there is greater pressure to validate tests because of an expressed desire to make the tests as direct as possible both in terms of task and criteria. Claims made for tests being able to measure or predict real life language performance adequately must be tentative until the validity of the measures used is substantiated. There is a pressing need to establish the theoretical and empirical validity of measures conceived within this paradigm.

The use of introspection studies to investigate the validity of a skills approach to the testing of reading is an example of one way validation studies might develop in the future. Candidates taking a reading test might be asked to verbalise how they answer each item and the results of these investigations could then be compared with the tester's intentions in setting each item. This might shed light on the nature of the reading construct itself and the way suspected component skills relate to each other (or not) (see also Candlin, 1986).

The commitment to making tests communicative thus entails a high degree of explicitness both at the test design stage where one is concerned with the required result and at the evaluation stage where one is estimating the acquired result (see Hawkey, 1982). It is not necessarily the case that communicative tests will look radically different from some existing tests; but there may be strong pragmatic reasons for trying to demonstrate any difference in either the test content, the marking schemes to be applied and the way results are reported.

In the present state of uncertainty the effect of the test on the teaching that precedes it should receive serious consideration. If our communicative tests have a beneficial backwash effect in encouraging the development of communicative capacity in the classroom (see Swain, 1985; Hughes 1989) then we can be less worried about the theoretical or empirical shortcomings of our knowledge of language in use. Similarly if we can include in our tests what is considered to be most appropriate and best practice from the language classroom the match between teaching, testing and reality is that much enhanced. The procedures adopted by the Royal Society of Arts/UCLES in the design of their Certificates in Communicative Skills in English are worthy of note in this respect (see Appendix III).

1.4.4 An acceptable paradigm?

In a recent Test of English as a Foreign Language (TOEFL) conference entitled 'Toward Communicative Competence Testing', the theme was to explore ways in which the TOEFL test might be made more 'communicative' without seriously impairing its present psychometric attributes (see Stansfield, 1986). Bachman (1986) investigated the lack of context associated with many of the TOEFL items and concluded (p. 86) that: 'the majority of the tasks measure only grammatical competence ... with only a handful tapping illocutionary or sociolinguistic competence.'

Douglas (1986) argued for learning from interlanguage studies which had shed light on the variability of performance occasioned by the elicitation procedures employed (task) and by the discourse domain (context) in which the tasks are carried out (see Douglas and Selinker, 1985; Selinker and Douglas, 1985; and Skehan, 1984, 1987). Douglas argued that if the TOEFL and the Test of Spoken English (TSE) were revised in the direction of domain-specific tasks they would fit more easily into a framework of communicative competence. Consideration was also given to the authenticity of the language used (see Bachman 1986; Douglas, 1986) and it was agreed that in the then current TOEFL not enough attention was given (in the listening section) to replicating the normal features of spontaneous spoken discourse, e.g., hesitations, nor to incorporating normal features of interaction such as the negotiation of shared meaning.

What is significant about these discussions at the Educational Testing Service (ETS) at Princeton is that an organisation which had hitherto been operating firmly in the psychometric−structuralist tradition was now concerned in making its tests more communicative. The conference was a limited indication of acceptance of the principles of communicative language testing.

In the language classroom, however, the majority of commercially available tests are still predominantly structure-based (see Archer and Nolan-Woods, 1976; Fowler and Coe, 1978; and Allen, 1982). Most language teaching coursebooks and accompanying teacher manuals, if they contain any advice on testing at all, usually offer vague theoretical generalisations far removed from the practical needs of the teacher who has to construct achievement tests for use in the classroom. Equally unpalatable is the outdated and overly specific advice that is sometimes provided on various discrete point, non-communicative, atomistic approaches, which pay scant regard to any of the insights gained through testing research in the last two decades.

Very little help is normally provided in relating test task to test purpose or in selecting appropriate formats for testing more communicatively. There is an almost total silence on how to interpret test results once the data has been generated.

There is an urgent need for ELT publishers to take account of the developments in the field of communicative language teaching and testing if new initiatives are not to be stifled.

The promising field of Action Research has much to offer in this respect. Cumulative, informal, small-scale investigations by teachers, in a variety of classroom contexts, could help advance our understanding of a whole range of communicative techniques for assessing language proficiency (see Brindley, 1989).

There are strong arguments for following the lead of the UCLES/RSA in this respect. In the design of their certificates in Communicative Skills in English, the test constructors drew heavily on what EFL teachers thought to be sound practice in the classroom. The communicative tests that resulted are in essence classroom-proven teaching techniques which are convertible to elicitation techniques in a test situation (see Appendix III for a full description of this test).

The only necessary difference between teaching and testing within the communicative paradigm relates to the amount of help that is available to the candidate from his teacher or his peers. The help that is normally available in the teaching situation e.g. prompts, reformulation of questions, encouragement, correction and the opportunity to try again, is removed in a test for reasons of reliability of measurement. In this sense the test might be viewed as an intermediate stage between the world of the classroom and the future target situation where the candidate will have to operate unaided.

1.4.5 The promised land?

So far in this chapter the development of a communicative approach to testing language has been outlined and, in general, a positive view has been taken of these developments. There are, however, a number of outstanding problems in adopting an approach within this paradigm that need to be addressed. In order to try and draw these problems together they are considered in relation to the central issue of generalisability of test results. This is an unavoidable issue, whatever approach to testing we adopt.

1.5 The problem of extrapolation

Other than serious marker reliability problems, associated with the assessment of performance (see Section 4.3), the major issue affecting an adoption of a 'communicative' approach to language testing is the generalisability of the results produced by a test.

Any test can be seen as a sampling instrument that provides evidence on which to base inferences that extend beyond the available data. For most purposes the evidence provided by test performances has to be relevant to the whole domain of interest, that is, the test has to be valid; it also has to be capable of allowing stable predictions to be made about a candidate's performance in any part of the domain, in other words, the test has to be reliable.

A communicative test implies the specification of performance tasks closely related to the learner's practical activities, that is, to the communicative contexts in which he would find himself. This creates a problem of generalisability of tasks to be selected. For Kelly (1978, p. 225) the possibility of devising a construct valid proficiency test, i.e., one that measured ability to communicate in the target language, was dependent on the prior existence of 'appropriate objectives for the test to measure'.

There is an often expressed demand in the literature on performance-based tests for a systematic and thorough specification of the communicative demands of the target situation (see Wesche, 1985). Advocates of performance-based tests (see Morrow, 1977, 1979; Carroll, 1980b, 1981b; and Wesche, 1981) seem to be arguing that it is only necessary to select certain representative communication tasks, as we do not use the same language for all possible communication purposes. In the case of proficiency tests, these tasks are seen as inherent to the nature of the communication situation for which candidates are being assessed. Caution, however, demands that we wait until empirical evidence is available before making such confident statements concerning the identification of these tasks. It is only after examining if it is feasible to establish suitable objectives, through empirical research based on real people coping with real situations, that there would be any grounds for claiming to have selected a representative sample of operational tasks to assess performance ability. Even when empirical research is conducted to establish suitable objectives, viz., to identify relevant communicative tasks and underlying constituent enabling skills for a target population, the problems of sampling, practicality, reliability and validity still remain.

The problems associated with establishing such specifications empirically, the methods to use and the ranking of needs are discussed by Wesche (1981) and Weir (1983a). A factor that emerges clearly is that the very increase in specificity brought about by the needs analysis (particularly of the Munby variety) in itself serves to decrease the possibility of generalisability. The more specific the tasks one identifies the less one can generalise from performance on its realisation in a test. This type of needs analysis is in any case unable to specify the relative importance of the variables. If, as Rea (1978) and Morrow (1979) suggest, the aim should be to construct simulated communication tasks which closely resemble those a candidate would face in real life and which make realistic demands on him in terms of language performance behaviour, it might be difficult to do so reliably or validly. Communication is not conterminous with language and much communication in non-linguistic. Often the conditions for actual real-life communication are not replicable in a test situation, which is unavoidably artificial and idealised and, to use Davies's (1978) phrase, Morrow and others are perhaps fruitlessly pursuing the chimera of authenticity.

Further, even if the sample of communicative tasks possessed content and face validity, might it not still lack generalisability in terms of the other communicative tasks which are not included? Are assessments of performance on these tasks made under particular linguistic and social constraints and thus not relatable to competence as 'characteristic abilities'? In other words, if a selection is made, if a sample is taken from a domain, how can it be ascertained that it is an adequate sample?

Kelly (1978, p. 226) observed that any kind of test is an exercise in sampling and from this sample an attempt is made to infer students' capabilities in relation to their performance in general:

> That is, of all that a student is expected to know and/or do as a result of his course of study (in an achievement test) or that the position requires (in the case of a proficiency test), a test measures students only on a selected sample. The reliability of a test in this conception is

the extent to which the score on the test is a stable indication of candidates' ability in relation to the wider universe of knowledge, performances, etc., that are of interest.

He pointed out (p. 230) that even if we had a clear set of communication tasks:

> the number of different communication problems a candidate will have to solve in the real world conditions is as great as the permutations and combinations produced by the values of the variables in the sorts of messages, contexts of situation and performance conditions that may be encountered.

Thus, on the basis of performance on a particular item, one ought to be circumspect, to say the least, in drawing conclusions about a candidate's ability to handle similar communication tasks.

Morrow (1977, p. 53) was also aware of the problems of extrapolation. He succinctly set out the problem like this:

> The very essence of a communicative approach is to establish particular situations with particular features of context, etc., in order to test the candidate's ability to use language appropriate in terms of a particular specification. While it is hoped that the procedures discussed will indeed be revealing in those terms, they cannot strictly speaking reveal anything of the candidate's ability to produce language which is appropriate to a situation different in even one respect from that established.

Alderson (Alderson and Hughes, 1981, p. 59) also accepted that to follow the communicative paradigm one needed to define what it was that students had to do with language in a specific situation or series of situations, but recognized that by specifying performance in this manner: 'one might end up describing an impossible variety of situations, which one cannot encompass for testing purposes.'

In order to make stable predictions of student performance in relation to the indefinitely large universe of tasks, it would seem necessary to sample candidates' performances on as large a number of tasks as is possible, which conflicts immediately with the demands of test efficiency. The larger the sample of tasks and the more realistic the test items, the longer the communicative test will have to be. However, as Alderson noted:

> it may be that the issue of extrapolation is not (yet) of crucial importance: even if we cannot generalise from performance in one situation to performance in a variety of situations, if we can say something about performance in *one* situation, then we have made progress, and if we can say something important about performance in the target situation so much the better. Ultimately the student will have to perform, despite the statistical evidence of the relationship between predictor and predicted, or the theoretised relationship between competence and performance.

It may not, however, be all that easy to identify this 'one situation' on which to base our predictions. Let us take as an example the development of an EAP reading test. Here an additional problem for sampling in a test may well occur in the selection of texts on which a candidate has to demonstrate his or her comprehension skills. There is some evidence in the literature that a number of students might be disadvantaged by being tested on their comprehension of texts outside their academic field (see Weir, 1983a; Alderson and Urquhart, 1985a, 1985b). The implication of this might be that different tests are necessary for audiences which are clearly identifiable as different. There is an urgent need for further investigation into language testing for specified purposes.

Morrow (1977) observed that in the case of conventional language tests aimed at measuring mastery of the language code, extrapolation would seem to pose few problems. The grammatical and phonological systems of a language are finite and manageable and the lexical resources can be delimited. The infinite number of sentences in a language is made up of a finite number of elements, and tests of the mastery of these elements are extremely powerful from a predictive point of view. Thus, Davies (1978, p. 225) remarked: 'What remains a convincing argument in favour of linguistic competence tests (both discrete point and integrative) is that grammar is at the core of language learning . . . . Grammar is far more powerful in terms of generalisability than any other language feature.'

Kelly (1978) provides an interesting argument against this viewpoint. It is not known, for example, how crucial a complete mastery of English verb morphology is to the overall objective of being able to communicate in English, or how serious a disability it is not to know the second conditional. We still do not possess what Kelly (1978, p. 17) described as a: 'reliable knowledge of the relative functional importance of the various structures in a language.'

Given this failing, it would seem ill-advised to make any claims about what students should be able to do in a language on the basis of scores on discrete point tests of syntax or lexis. The construct 'ability to communicate in language' involves more than a mere manipulation of certain syntactic patterns with a certain lexical content. In consequence, it would appear that there is still a need to attempt to devise measuring instruments which can assess performance ability.

As a way out of the extrapolation quandary, Kelly (1978, p. 239) suggested a two-stage approach to the task of devising a test that represents a possible compromise between the conflicting demands of the criteria of validity, reliability and efficiency:

> The first stage involves the development of a direct test that is maximally valid and reliable, and hence inefficient. The second stage calls for the development of efficient, hence indirect, tests of high validity. The validity of the indirect tests is to be determined by reference to the first battery of direct tasks. Clearly, where valid and reliable but inefficient tests already exist for the construct in question, then the research strategy calls for the development of efficient indirect tests whose results correlate highly with those of the existing test.

Thus, retreat from direct evaluation of performance may be acceptable, *provided* relationships or even correlations between data from competence testing and predicted behaviour have been established.

As far as large scale proficiency testing is concerned, another viable solution might be to focus attention on language use in individual and specified situations while retaining, for purposes of extrapolation, tests of the candidate's ability to handle those aspects of language which are generalisable to all language use situations, namely the grammatical and phonological systems. Or it may be the case that the former make the latter unnecessary (see Weir, 1983a) as was the case in the TEEP research, *where the grammar test was abandoned because it offered no additional information to that provided by the more use based components.*

Morrow (1979, p. 152) saw a third way out of the extrapolation quandary. His argument is that a model (as yet unrealised) for the performance of global communicative tasks may show, for any task, the enabling skills which have to be mobilised to complete it:

> The status of these enabling skills vis-à-vis competence : performance is interesting. They may be identified by an analysis of performance in operational terms, and thus they are clearly, ultimately performance-based. But at the same time, their application extends far beyond any one particular instance of performance, and in this creativity they reflect an aspect of what is generally understood by competence. In this way they offer a possible approach to the problem of extrapolation.

He asserted that (p. 153): 'Analysis of the global tasks, in terms of which the candidate is to be assessed, will usually yield a fairly consistent set of enabling skills' and argues that assessment of ability in using these skills would therefore yield data which are relevant across a broad spectrum of global tasks, and are not limited to a single instance of performance.

For Morrow (1979, p. 153), a working solution to the problem would be the development of tests which measure both overall performance in relation to a specified task and the strategies and skills which have been used in achieving it:

> Written and spoken production can be assessed in terms of both these criteria. In task-based tests of listening and reading comprehension, however, it may be rather more difficult to see just how the global task has been completed. . . . it is rather difficult to assess why a particular answer has been given and to deduce the skills and strategies employed. In such cases, questions focusing on specific enabling skills do seem to be called for in order to provide the basis for convincing extrapolation.

He is aware, though, that there exists in tests of enabling skills a fundamental weakness in the relationship between the whole and the parts, as a candidate may prove quite capable of handling individual enabling skills, yet still not be able to communicate effectively.

Another problem is that it is by no means easy to identify these enabling skills; nor are there any guidelines for assessing their relative importance for the successful completion of a particular communicative task, let alone their relative weighting across a spectrum of tasks. Morrow would appear to assume that we are not only able to establish these enabling skills, but also to describe the relationship that exists between the part and the whole in a fairly accurate manner (in this case, how 'separate' enabling skills contribute to the communicative task). He appears to be saying that there is a prescribed formula; possession and ability to use enabling skills $X + Y + Z = $ successful completion of communicative task (1), whereas it would seem likely that the added presence of a further skill or the absence of a named skill might still result in successful completion of the task in hand.

A pragmatic way out of this dilemma of how to know what we are testing would be to pursue an ethnographic validation approach as outlined in Section 2.1.2. Data could be collected from student introspections on the processes they are utilising to complete items. This could be used to help determine which items best fitted the required specification (see Aslanian, 1985; Cohen, 1985; and Jones and Friedl, 1986).

In addition, advice could be taken from professionals who coﬁ. ʳol the content and the language of purposive interactions in the target domain of proficiency test candidates. They could be asked to comment on the appropriateness of test items for the intended populations (see Douglas and Pettinari, 1983). The recent IELTS revision project has adopted this useful strategy.

The extrapolation problem faced by those adopting a more communicative approach to language test design seems to relate to the wider issue of the status of laws in the behavioural sciences. In the physical sciences, laws are extrapolations of replicable phenomena. Researchers in these domains can directly confront what they wish to investigate, formulate hypotheses and repeat experiments as many times as they wish to verify or falsify their hypotheses. Because of problems associated with the infinite variability of language in use and the problems involved in population sampling, the scientific paradigm is a difficult one to follow in educational measurement.

Hawkey (1982) described the classical scientific paradigm as a hypothetico-deductive methodology formulating quantifiable, narrow, parsimonious hypotheses, tested through the observation of the behaviour of a random sample of the target population, followed by a statistical analysis of the results according to pre-ordained procedures. This approach is not suitable for large scale proficiency testing where candidates might be operating in a variety of contexts and at a variety of levels. Account may need to be taken of a large number of variables, some of which are not predictable, all interacting in socio-cultural contexts. Thus there is a task sampling problem, a validity problem.

Unlike the scientific paradigm described by Hawkey there might also be serious problems in terms of population sampling. If the target population of students is transient, widely dispersed and varied in terms of accessibility, the sampling might of necessity have to be opportunistic. This is a population sampling problem, a reliability problem.

The concern might have to be, of necessity, with what Hawkey (1982, p. 16) described as an 'illuminative evaluation' paradigm, where the focus was on the description of complex phenomena, the resolution of significant features, and the comprehension of relationships. Initial research in this area might have to limit itself to providing a descriptive framework for establishing communication tasks of relevance to students in a specified context, prior to test construction (see Weir, 1983b). No definitive claims could be made (without empirical validation studies) about how the language user operates when involved in these communication tasks or how he learns to perform such tasks (see Kelly, 1978). What might be provided is a specification, coarse but robust, of the general communicative tasks facing target students in their specified context.

Irrespective of the problematic nature of the exercise, the need for specifying as clearly as possible what it is that is to be tested seems axiomatic for testing within the communicative paradigm. The current interest in ESP is a reflection of this and the acronym might better be regarded as English for Specified Purposes rather than specific or special. This would emphasise the belief that all teaching and testing is to varying extents specified and never totally general.

However, the nature and shortcomings of target-situation analysis for arriving at specifications of language needs for tests have been discussed extensively in the literature (see Weir, 1983a). There are dangers in analyses being too specific, e.g., they may not be operationalisable in a test, as well as in being too general, e.g., they may disadvantage certain candidates. Perhaps the biggest danger is that there is a tendency for needs analysis to claim a disproportionate amount of the time and resources available for research, often at the expense of test development.

A comprehensive description of the specification stage of a test design can be found in Weir (1983a, 1983b), where the extensive research and development behind the Associated Examining Board's Test in English for Educational Purposes (TEEP) is fully documented (see also Appendix I). The careful reader can see how the results of the needs analysis influenced the adoption of certain test formats (dictation, the integration of reading, listening and writing activities) and clarified the range of skills to be tested and the assessment criteria to be employed. The recent IELTS revision project has forsaken such needs analysis and instead intends to rely on post hoc 'expert' comment to judge the 'authenticity' and other aspects of the products of the test writing teams, who were not to be constrained by any a priori specifications (see Appendix V).

In the development of tests in the future the balance of attention must be paid to translating specifications into test realisations and validating the latter (in the ways to be discussed in Chapter Two), though the need to specify in advance of item writing the construct that is to be measured is ignored at one's peril. The emphasis, however, should be on test development and validation rather than on the analysis of needs for creating test specifications. For this reason the discussion of needs analysis has been limited, and instead the focus in Chapters Three and Four will be on test construction and in particular on examining a range of possible formats for testing language skills within a communicative framework.

The crucial stage in any test development occurs when the specification is translated into a test realisation. The test that results should exhibit the qualities of validity, efficiency and reliability which are examined next in Chapter Two. These qualities need to be determined both qualitatively a priori and empirically a posteriori.

Chapter Two

Basic Considerations in Test Design

The concepts of validity, reliability and efficiency affect all aspects of test design, irrespective of the prevailing linguistic paradigm. In Chapter One the relative importance of these concepts in recent approaches to language testing was reviewed. In this chapter the nature of these key concepts is examined in more detail. The status of the various types of validity, and how the concept of validity relates to those of efficiency and reliability are examined. Chapters Three and Four are more practically oriented; they examine the specification and realisation of the theoretical foundations discussed in the first two chapters.

2.1   The concept of validity

2.1.1   Construct validity

The concept of validity (does the test measure what it is intended to measure?) can be approached from a number of perspectives; the relationship between these is interpreted in a number of ways in the literature.

The most helpful exegesis regards construct validity as the superordinate concept embracing all other forms of validity. Anastasi (1982, p. 153) is of the opinion that: 'content, criterion-related and construct validation do not correspond to distinct or logically co-ordinate categories. On the contrary, construct validity is a comprehensive concept which includes the other types.'

Cronbach (1971, p. 463) commented that: 'Every time an educator asks "but what does the instrument really measure?" he is calling for information on construct validity.' Anastasi (1982, p. 144) defined it as:

> the extent to which the test may be said to measure a theoretical construct or trait .... Each construct is developed to explain and organise observed response consistencies. It derives from established inter-relationships among behavioral measures .... Focusing on a broader, more enduring and more abstract kind of behavioral description ... construct validation requires the gradual accumulation of information from a variety of sources. Any data throwing light

on the nature of the trait under consideration and the conditions affecting its development and manifestations are grist for this validity mill.

She argued that the theoretical construct, trait or behaviour domain measured by any test can be defined in terms of the operations performed in establishing the validity of the test. She was careful to emphasise that the construct measured by a particular test (1982, p. 155): 'can be adequately defined only in the light of data gathered in the process of validating that test . . . . It is only through the empirical investigation of the relationship of test scores to other external data that we can discover what a test measures.'

The view expressed below differs only insofar as external empirical data are seen as a necessary but not a sufficient condition for establishing the adequacy of a test for the purpose for which it was intended. Though there is a lack of an adequate theoretical framework for the construction of communicative tests, this does not absolve test constructors from trying to establish a priori construct validity for a test conceived within the communicative paradigm. A test should always be designed on a principled basis, however limited the underlying theory, and, wherever possible after its administration, statistical validation procedures should be applied to the results to determine how successful the test has been in measuring what it intended to measure.

In the past little attention has been accorded to the non-statistical aspects of construct validity. In the earlier psychometric-structuralist approach to language testing (see Section 1.2) the prevailing theoretical paradigm lent itself easily to testing discrete elements of the target language and little need was seen for much a priori deliberation on the match between theory and test. Additionally the empiricism and operationalism of those working in educational measurement made the idea of working with non-objective criteria unattractive. The notions of concurrent and predictive validity, more consistent with the principles of operationalism and the desire for an objective external criterion, took precedence.

Construct validity is viewed from a purely statistical perspective in much of the recent American literature (see Palmer *et al.* 1981; Bachman and Palmer, 1981a). It is seen principally as a matter of the a posteriori statistical validation of whether a test has measured a construct which has a reality independent of other constructs. The concern is much more with the a posteriori relationship between a test and the psychological abilities, traits and constructs it has measured than with what should have been elicited in the first place.

To establish the construct validity of a test statistically, it is necessary to show that it correlates highly with indices of behaviour that one might theoretically expect it to correlate with and also that it does not correlate significantly with variables that one would not expect it to correlate with. An interesting procedure for investigating this is the convergent and discriminant validation process first outlined by Campbell and Fiske (1959) and later used by Bachman and Palmer (1981b). The latter argue that the strong effect of test method that they discovered points to the necessity of employing a multi-trait multi-method matrix as a research paradigm in construct validation studies. They found that the application of confirmatory factor analysis to these data enabled them to quantify the effects of trait and method on the measurements of proficiency employed and provided a clearer picture of this proficiency than was available through other methods.

The experimental design of the multi-trait/multi-method matrix has been criticised (see Low, 1985) especially in relation to more direct tests of language proficiency, but nevertheless is deserving of further empirical investigation as so few studies have been reported, particularly from this side of the Atlantic. It is a potentially useful, additional measure for clarifying what it is that we have measured in a particular application of a test. The only difficulty in employing this technique is that to be effective a high degree of test reliability is essential as error variance is likely to confound the results.

In contrast to this emphasis on a posteriori statistical validation there is a body of opinion which holds that there is an equally important need for construct validation at the a priori stage of test design and implementation.

Cronbach (1971, p. 443) believes that: 'Construction of a test itself starts from a theory about behaviour or mental organisation derived from prior research that suggests the ground plan for the test.' Davies (1977, p. 63) argued in a similar vein: 'it is, after all, the theory on which all else rests; it is from there that the construct is set up and it is on the construct that validity, of the content and predictive kinds, is based.' Kelly (1978, p. 8) supported this view, commenting that: 'the systematic development of tests requires some theory, even an informal, inexplicit one, to guide the initial selection of item content and the division of the domain of interest into appropriate sub-areas.'

It would seem self-evident that the more fully we are able to describe the theoretical construct we are attempting to measure, at the a priori stage, the more meaningful might be the statistical procedures contributing to construct validation that can subsequently be applied to the results of the test. Statistical data do not in themselves generate conceptual labels. We can never escape from the need to provide clear statements concerning what is being measured, just as we are obliged to investigate how adequate a test is in operation, through available statistical procedures.

2.1.2 Content validity

Because we lack an adequate theory of language in use, a priori attempts to determine the construct validity of proficiency tests involve us in matters which relate more evidently to content validity. The more a test simulates the dimensions of observable performance and accords with what is known about that performance, the more likely it is to have content and construct validity. We can often only talk about the communicative construct in descriptive terms and, as a result, we become involved in questions of content relevance and content coverage. Thus, for Kelly (1978, p. 8) content validity seems 'an almost completely overlapping concept' with construct validity, and for Moller (1982b, p. 68): 'the distinction between construct and content validity in language testing is not always very marked, particularly for tests of general language proficiency.'

Given the restrictions on the time and resources available to those involved in test construction, especially for use in the classroom, it is often only feasible to focus on the a priori validation of test tasks. In these cases, particular attention must be paid to content validity in an attempt to ensure that the sample of activities to be included in a test is as representative of the target domain as is possible.

A primary purpose of many communicative tests is to provide a profile of the student's proficiency, indicating in broad terms the particular modes where deficiencies lie. Content validity is considered especially important for achieving this purpose as it is principally concerned with the extent to which the selection of test tasks is representative of the larger universe of tasks of which the test is assumed to be a sample (see Bachman and Palmer, 1981a).

Anastasi (1982, p. 131) defined content validity as: 'essentially the systematic examination of the test content to determine whether it covers a representative sample of the behaviour domain to be measured.' She (p. 132) provided a set of useful guidelines for establishing content validity:

1. 'the behaviour domain to be tested must be systematically analysed to make certain that all major aspects are covered by the test items, and in the correct proportions';

2. 'the domain under consideration should be fully described in advance, rather than being defined after the test has been prepared';

3. 'content validity depends on the relevance of the individual's test responses to the behaviour area under consideration, rather than on the apparent relevance of item content.'

The directness of fit and adequacy of the test sample is thus dependent on the quality of the description of the target language behaviour being tested.

J.B. Carroll (1961) pointed to the importance of and the difficulties involved in defining the area of language from which the sample is to be taken and the resultant problems this has for sampling. Moller (1982b, p. 37) also referred to the problems involved: 'In the case of a proficiency test, however, the test constructors themselves decide the "syllabus" and the universe of discourse to be sampled. The sampling becomes less satisfactory because of the extent and indeterminate nature of that universe.'

Establishing content validity is problematic, given the difficulty in characterising language proficiency with sufficient precision to ensure the representativeness of the sample of tasks included in a test. Additional threats to validity may arise out of attempts to operationalise real-life behaviour in a test especially where some sort of quantification is necessary either in the task or the method of assessment. These difficulties do not, however, absolve the test constructor from attempting to make tests as relevant in terms of content as is possible.

The procedure of designing a test from a skills specification (see the list drawn up by Munby, 1978 and its attempted implementation by B.J. Carroll, 1981b) may lead to variability in opinions as to what is being tested by specific items. There is a need to establish clear procedures that might reduce this variability.

Further, there is a need to look closely at test specifications to make sure that they describe adequately what ought to be tested. A close scrutiny of the specification for a proficiency test by experts in the field (or colleagues in the case of classroom achievement tests) and the relating of the specification to the test as it appears in its final form is essential (see Weir, 1983a). This would provide useful information as to what the test designer was intending to test and how successful the item writers had been in implementing the specification in the test realisation.

Mere inspection of the modules in the test, even by language and subject experts, does not necessarily guarantee the identification of the processes actually used by candidates in taking them. In addition, it would be valuable to employ ethnographic procedures to establish the validity of items in a test.

A useful procedure is to have a small sample of the test population introspect on the internal processes that are taking place in their completion of the test items (see Aslanian, 1985; Cohen, 1985). This would provide a valuable check on experts' surface-level judgements on what was being tested and would contribute to the establishment of guidelines for the conduct of this type of methodological procedure in future investigations of test validity.

It is crucial for a test supposedly based on specified enabling skills to establish that it conforms to the specifications, especially if claims are made for these being representative of the domain in question. To the extent that the content is made explicit the concern also becomes one of face validity which Porter (1983) describes as perhaps the most contentious validity that might be invoked.

2.1.3   Face validity

Anastasi (1982, p. 136) pointed out that face validity:

> is not validity in the technical sense; it refers, not to what the test actually measures, but to what it appears superficially to measure. Face validity pertains to whether the test 'looks valid' to the examinees who take it, the administrative personnel who decide on its use, and other technically untrained observers. Fundamentally, the question of face validity concerns rapport and public relations.

Lado (1961), Davies (1965), E. Ingram (1977), Palmer (1981) and Bachman and Palmer (1981a) have all discounted the value of face validity. Bachman and Palmer (1981a, p. 55) argue as follows:

> Since there is no generally accepted procedure for determining whether or not a test demonstrates this characteristic, and since 'it is not an acceptable basis for interpretative inferences from test scores', we feel it has no place in the discussion of test validity.

If a test does not have face validity though, it may not be acceptable to the students taking it, or the teachers and receiving institutions who may make use of it. If the students do not accept it as valid, their adverse reaction to it may mean that they do not perform in a way which truly reflects their ability. Anastasi (1982, p. 136) took a similar line:

> Certainly if test content appears irrelevant, inappropriate, silly or childish, the result will be poor co-operation, regardless of the actual validity of the test. Especially in adult testing, it is not sufficient for a test to be objectively valid. It also needs face validity to function effectively in practical situations.

The usual empirical caveat of course applies (Anastasi, 1982, p. 136): 'To be sure, face validity should never be regarded as a substitute for objectively determined validity . . . . The validity of the test in its final form should always be directly checked.'

Stevenson (1985b) expresses a similar concern that construct and content validities should not be sacrificed at the altar of an increased lay acceptance of non-technical face validity.

2.1.4 *Washback validity*

The difficulties of precisely determining what it is that needs to be measured perhaps argues for a greater concern with what has recently been termed 'washback validity' (Morrow, 1986) or more commonly (Porter, 1983 and Weir, 1983a) the washback of the test on the teaching and learning that precedes it.

Given that language teachers operating in a communicative framework normally attempt to equip students with skills that are judged to be relevant to present or future needs, and to the extent that tests are designed to reflect these, the closer the relationship between the test and the teaching that precedes it, the more the test is likely to have construct validity.

In other circumstances the tail may wag the dog in that a communicative approach to language teaching is more likely to be adopted when the test at the end of a course of instruction is itself communicative. A test can be a very powerful instrument for effecting change in the language curriculum as recent developments in language tests in Sri Lanka have shown.

A suitable criterion for judging communicative tests in the future might well be the degree to which they satisfy students, teachers and future users of test results, as judged by some systematic attempt to gather quantifiable data on the perceived validity of the test. If the test passes the first a priori validity hurdle it is then worthwhile establishing its validity against external criteria, through confirmatory a posteriori statistical analysis. If the first stage, with its emphasis on construct, content, face and washback validities, is bypassed then we should not be too surprised if the type of test available for external validation procedures does not suit the purpose for which it was intended.

For construct, content, face and washback validity, knowing what the test is measuring is crucial. There is a further type of validity which we might term criterion-related validity where knowing exactly what a test measures is not so crucial.

2.1.5 *Criterion-related validity*

This is a predominantly quantitative and a posteriori concept, concerned with the extent to which test scores correlate with a suitable external criterion of performance: what Ingram (1977, p. 18) termed 'pragmatic validity'. Criterion-related validity divides into two types (see Davies, 1977), concurrent validity, where the test scores are correlated with another measure of performance, usually an older established test, taken at the same time (see Kelly, 1978; Davies, 1983) and predictive validity, where test scores are correlated with some future criterion of performance (see Bachman and Palmer, 1981a).

For many authorities, external validation based on data is *always* superior to the 'armchair speculation of content validity'. Davies (1983, p. 1) has argued forcefully that external validation based on data is always to be preferred: 'The external criterion, however hard to find and however difficult to operationalise and quantify remains the best evidence of a test's validity. All other evidence, including reliability and the internal validities is essentially circular.' And he quotes Anastasi on the need for independently gathered external data: 'Internal analysis of the test, through item-test correlations, factorial analysis of test items, etc., is never an adequate substitute for external validation.'

Though this concept of criterion-related validity is more in keeping with the demands of an empiricist-operationalist approach, the problem remains that a test can be valid in this way without our necessarily knowing what the test is measuring, i.e., it tells us nothing directly about its construct validity. Morrow (1979, p. 147) drew attention to the essential circularity of employing these types of validity in support of a test:

> Starting from a certain set of assumptions about the nature of language and language learning will lead to language tests which are perfectly valid in terms of these assumptions but whose value must inevitably be called into question if the basic assumptions themselves are challenged.

For Jakobovits (1970, p. 75) the very possibility of being able to construct even one communicative test appeared problematic: 'the question of what it is to know a language is not well understood and, consequently, the language proficiency tests now available and universally used are inadequate because they attempt to measure something that has not been well-defined.'

Even if it were possible to construct a valid communicative test there would still be problems in establishing sufficiently valid criterion measures against which to correlate it. Hawkey (1982, p. 153) felt this to be particularly problematic for tests conceived within a communicative paradigm: 'At this developmental stage in communicative testing, other tests available as criteria for concurrent validation are likely to be less integrative/communicative in construct and format and thus not valid as references for direct comparison.'

There is a distinct danger that one might be forced to place one's faith in a criterion measure which may in itself not be a valid measure of the construct in question. One cannot claim that a test has criterion-related validity because it correlates highly with another test, if the other test itself does not measure the criterion in question.

It seems pointless to validate a test conceived within the communicative paradigm against tests resulting from earlier paradigms if they are premised on such different constructs. Similarly if equivalent but less efficient tests are not available against which to correlate, other external non-test criteria might need to be established.

Establishing these non-test criteria for validating communicative tests could well be problematic. Even if one had faith in the external criterion selected, for example, a sample of real life behaviour, the quantification process which it might be necessary to subject this behaviour to in order for it to become operational might negate its earlier direct validity.

Though caution is advocated in the interpretation of these criterion-related validity measures, they are still considered to be potentially useful concepts. For example, one might be very wary of tests that produced results seriously at variance with those of other tests measuring the same trait, especially if the latter had been found to have construct validity.

It is particularly important to try to establish criterion-related validity for a test through empirical monitoring whenever the candidates' futures may be affected by its results. For example, given the variety of language qualifications currently acceptable as evidence of language proficiency for entry into tertiary-level study in Britain (see Weir, 1983a), there is some cause for concern about the equivalence of such a broad spectrum of tests. Where is the empirical evidence for the equivalence of one entry qualification with another?

In the case of predictive validity, it may be that in certain circumstances the predictive power of the test is all that is of interest. If all one wants is to make certain predictions about future performance on the basis of the test results, this might entail a radically different test from that where the interest is in providing information to allow effective remedial action to be taken. If predictions made on the basis of the test are reasonably accurate then the nature of the test items and their content might not be so important.

Incidentally, both validity and reliability estimates based on correlational data must be treated with caution. A high correlation may indicate the measurement of two different attributes which are themselves quite highly correlated among the population of examinees. On the other hand, a low correlation may indicate that two quite different attributes are being measured or may merely reflect a high level of error variance in one or both of the tests.

2.1.6 How should a test be known?

Most GCSE examinations and existing language proficiency examinations, e.g., the University of Cambridge Local Examinations Syndicate (UCLES) Certificate of Proficiency in English (CPE) and the Joint Matriculation Board (JMB) Test in English (Overseas), because of their public, operational nature, are not over interested in concurrent or predictive validity, whereas, as Davies (1982) has pointed out, these are matters of major concern for most standardised, closed EFL tests. Correlating the results of one year's examination with other examinations or against some future criterion is perhaps viewed as a pointless exercise when a new set of examinations is already in preparation for the following year and results already issued for current candidates.

Only closed tests, such as the Associated Examining Board's Test in English for Educational Purposes, the TEEP test (see Appendix I), or UCLES and the British Council's English Language Testing Service's (ELTS) battery (see Appendix V), feel obliged to concern themselves with a posteriori validation procedures. Open examinations which are held annually tend to rely more heavily on construct (non-statistical), content and face validity.

In situations where the test is to have a diagnostic function a high degree of explicitness at the a priori stage of test construction is felt to be necessary. This is particularly so where the aim is to provide meaningful statements on a candidate's performance which would be of use to those providing remedial support for candidates with known difficulties.

If the concern is to collect appropriate information on a candidate's performance for the purposes of profile reporting rather than to establish a test's predictive validity, then there is more obligation to improve the content/construct validity of the test by identifying, prior to test construction, appropriate communicative tasks which it should include. This a priori validation is essentially a first, though crucial, step in the total validation process of a test.

Having made rigorous attempts at an a priori stage to make the test as valid as possible, there is then a need to establish the validity of the test against external criteria. If the first stage with its emphasis on content validity is bypassed, then the type of test available for external validation procedures would not, in all likelihood, suit the purpose for which the test is intended.

To illustrate the recent awakening of interest in a priori validation of tests it might be useful to take a concrete example of the construction of a test for a particular purpose. Let us assume the task is to construct a proficiency test in English for Academic Purposes (EAP) which can also provide through profiling some diagnostic information on the language-related study skills candidates are weak in.

A test of discrete grammatical items constructed for this purpose might be found to correlate highly with an external criterion, e.g., another established test concurrently administered or a measure taken at a later date, such as final academic grades. That is, it might possess criterion-related validity. It would, however, be of less value to those providing remedial English language support, who, rather than a single score, require information about the particular study modes in which a student has difficulty operating, i.e., they might be better served by a test exhibiting construct, content and face validity. One would not be able to allocate students effectively to remedial language programmes on the basis of performance in a discrete-point structuralist test lacking these validities.

The a priori validation of an EAP proficiency test with diagnostic potential would seem to demand that we test integrated macro-skills rather than micro-elements in isolation. If the aim is to test the communicative competence of overseas students in an EAP setting, it is doubtful whether tests of linguistic competence alone are appropriate because the constructs for such tests are necessarily based on discrete linguistic levels, not on integrative work samples. Since the essence of communication is an ability to combine discrete linguistic elements in a particular context it seems essential that this ability should be assessed by tests of integrated skills rather than by tests of discrete linguistic levels in isolation.

The content of an EAP proficiency test based on work samples from the target situation would be qualitatively different from the content of a test of linguistic competence based upon discrete linguistic items. In the case of the EAP proficiency test which aims at assessing communicative competence the main justification for item selection would be a careful sampling of the communicative tasks required of students in English-medium study. In the case of a test of linguistic competence a test may be considered valid if its content is based on an adequate sample of 'typical' discrete linguistic elements.

According to Canale and Swain (1980, p. 34) communicative testing: 'must be devoted not only to what the learner knows about the second language and about how to use it (competence) but also to what extent the learner is able to actually demonstrate this knowledge in a meaningful communicative situation.'

The proficiency tester today is influenced by what Moller (1981b) has described as the sociolinguistic–communicative paradigm. The nature of communicative testing was discussed in Section 1.4 above. Briefly a test within this communicative paradigm might be expected to exhibit the following features:

- There would be an emphasis on interaction between participants, and the resultant intersubjectivity would determine how the encounter evolves and ends.
- The form and content of the language produced would be to some extent unpredictable.
- It would be purposive in the sense of fulfilling some communicative function.

- It would employ domain-relevant texts and authentic tasks.
- Abilities would be assessed within meaningful and developing contexts and a profile of performance on these made available.
- Where deemed appropriate and feasible, there might be an integration of the four skills of reading, listening, speaking and writing.
- The appropriateness of language used for the expression of functional meaning would have high importance.
- It would use direct testing methods, with tasks reflecting realistic discourse processing.
- The assessment of productive abilities would most probably be qualitative rather than quantitative, involving the use of rating scales relating to categories of performance.

Thus a good deal more attention will have to be paid to content and face validity than was the case within previous orthodoxies. However, given the rudimentary state of the art in communicative approaches to language testing, some authorities still feel it would be prudent to retain a number of components which sample major linguistic categories, for, as Moller (1981b, p. 44) argued:

> It is clear that communicative testing does test certain aspects of proficiency. But it is important to be aware that testing language proficiency does not amount just to communicative testing. Communicative language performance is clearly an element in, or a dimension of, language proficiency. But language competence is also an important dimension of language proficiency and cannot be ignored. It will also have to be tested in one or more of the many ways that have been researched during the past thirty years. Ignoring this dimension is as serious an omission as ignoring the re-awakening of traditional language testing in a communicative setting.

The revision of the British Council/UCLES ELTS Test 1986−89, which has resulted in the new IELTS battery (see Appendix V), had originally planned to include a test of lexis and grammar in the General Component. In the earlier trials of the TEEP test 1979−82 a discrete item multiple-choice test of grammar had been included in the trial battery and proved to be a robust and valid indicator of General Language Proficiency. The TEEP research (Weir 1983a) indicated clearly, however, that the grammar component added no additional information to the picture of a candidate's language ability already available from the more communicative, use-based components. For this reason it was dropped from the battery. For similar reasons the tests of lexis and grammar have been dropped from the IELTS battery.

So far we have concentrated on examining ways of improving the validity of tests and neglected the crucial fact that unless a test is reliable it cannot be valid. The need for reliability in order to guarantee the validity of our tests is the next issue we address.

2.2 The concept of reliability

A fundamental criterion against which any language test has to be judged is its reliability (see Anastasi, 1982; Guilford, 1965). The concern here is with how far can we depend on the results that a test produces or, in other words, could the results be produced consistently.

Three aspects of reliability are usually taken into account. The first concerns the consistency of scoring among different markers, e.g., when marking a test of written expression. The degree of inter-marker reliability is established by correlating the scores obtained by candidates from marker A with those from marker B. The consistency of each individual marker (intra-marker reliability) is established by getting them to remark a selection of scripts at a later date and correlating the marks given on the two occasions. (See Anastasi, 1982 for a clear and accessible introduction to the necessary statistics. Also of use are Crocker, 1981 and more recently Woods *et al.*, 1986.)

The concern of the tester is how to enhance the agreement between markers by establishing, and maintaining adherence to, explicit guidelines for the conduct of this marking. The criteria of assessment need to be established and agreed upon and then markers need to be trained in the application of these criteria through rigorous standardisation procedures (see Murphy, 1979). During the marking of scripts there needs to be a degree of cross-checking to ensure that agreed standards are being maintained.

It is also considered necessary to try and ensure that relevant sub-tests are internally consistent in the sense that all items in a sub-test are judged to be measuring the same attribute. The Kuder-Richardson formulae for estimating this internal consistency are readily available in most statistics manuals (see Anastasi, 1982, pp. 114−6).

The third aspect of reliability is that of parallel-forms reliability, the requirements of which have to be borne in mind when future alternative forms of a test have to be devised. This is often very difficult to achieve for both theoretical and practical reasons. To achieve it, two alternative versions of a test need to be produced which are in effect clones of each other. The reliability of the versions is directly proportional to the similarity of the results obtained when administered to the same test population. Less frequently reliability is checked by the test-retest method where the same test is readministered to the same sample population after a short intervening period of time.

The concept of realiability is particularly important when considering language tests within the communicative paradigm (see Porter, 1983). For as Davies (1965, p. 14) stressed: 'reliability is the first essential for any test; but for certain kinds of language test may be very difficult to achieve.'

2.3   Validity and reliability — an inevitable tension?

Given the normal limitations affecting test development (especially of achievement tests in the classroom), concern usually centres on validation at the test construction stage and only to a lesser extent with a posteriori validation at the performance stage. The resources to do large-scale concurrent and predictive validity studies, such as conducted by Moller (1982b) and by the Institute of Applied Language Studies at the University of Edinburgh, on the ELTS battery, are not normally available.

The concern is often by necessity with content, construct and face validity though the predictive and concurrent validity of tests should always be examined as far as circumstances allow. Validation might prove to be a sterile endeavour, however, unless care has also been taken over test reliability.

The problem is that while one can have test reliability without test validity a test can only be valid if it is also reliable. There is thus sometimes said to be a reliability—validity tension (see Guilford, 1965 and Davies, 1978). This tension exists in the sense that it is sometimes essential to sacrifice a degree of reliability in order to enhance validity. If, however, validity is lost to increase reliability we finish up with a test which is a reliable measure of something other than what we wish to measure. The two concepts are, in certain circumstances, mutually exclusive, but if a choice has to be made, validity 'after all, is the more important'. (see Guilford, 1965, p. 481).

Rea (1978) argued that simply because tests which assess language as communication cannot automatically claim high standards of reliability in the same way that discrete-item tests are able to, this should not be accepted as a justification for continued reliance on highly reliable measures having very suspect validity. Rather, we should first be attempting to obtain more reliable measures of communicative abilities. This seems a less extreme and more sensible position than that adopted by Morrow (1979, p. 151), who argued polemically that: 'Reliability, while clearly important, will be subordinate to face validity. Spurious objectivity will no longer be a prime consideration.'

Rea's viewpoint was shared by Read (1981a, p. x—xi), who reported that a recurring theme at the April 1980 RELC Seminar on 'Evaluation and Measurement of Language Competence and Performance' was that: 'subjective judgements are indispensable if we are to develop testing procedures that validly reflect our current understanding of the nature of language proficiency and our contemporary goals in language teaching.'

Read went on to emphasise that: 'this does not mean a return to the old pre-scientific approach. It is generally accepted that a substantial, verifiable level of reliability must also be attained, if test results are to have any meaning.' Moller adopted a similar approach (1981a, p. 67):

> While it is understood that a valid test must be reliable, it would seem that in such a highly complex and personal behaviour as using a language other than one's mother tongue, validity could be claimed for measures that might have a lower than normally acceptable level of reliability.

He argued that, although reliability is something we should always try to achieve in our tests, 'it may not always be the prime consideration' and offers a possible compromise position (p. 67):

> In constructing test batteries that contain different types of task, for example, certain of the sub-tests may be required to exhibit a high degree of reliability. Other sub-tests, particularly tests of communicative use, may quite properly exhibit lower reliability without adversely affecting the overall validity of the battery.

Hawkey (1982, p. 149) commented in a similar vein:

> the reliability of a test cannot be ignored without a harmful effect on the validity of the instrument. But it is likely that, if the construct validity of communicative tests is to be ensured, the reliability question is going to have to be accepted as subordinate, though worked at fairly hard by item analysis and correlational operations.

Validity is important also because it is related to the way in which test performance levels are defined. Houston (1983) describes the difference between norm- and criterion-referenced methods of defining levels and discusses some of the difficulties of specifying appropriate performance criteria when the latter method is chosen. Popham (1978, p. 2) provided the following functional definitions of these approaches:

> a criterion-referenced test is designed to produce a clear description of what an examinee's performance on the test actually means. Rather than interpreting an examinee's test performance in relationship to the performance of others as is the case with many traditional tests, a good criterion-referenced test yields a better picture of just what it is that the examinee can or cannot do.

Davies (1978, p. 158) made the connection with language testing and expressed certain reservations about criterion-referenced tests:

> there are difficulties in using criterion-referenced tests for language: there is no finite inventory of learning points or items; there are very many behavioural objectives; there are variable (or no) external criteria of success, fluency, intelligibility, etc; there is no obvious way of establishing adequate knowledge, of saying how much of a language is enough.

Thus some of the difficulties referred to later by Houston (1983) are put in a language testing context. Clearly, criterion-referencing of performance levels is possible only to the extent that the test has a high degree of content validity.

2.4   Test efficiency

A valid and reliable test is of little use if it does not prove to be a practical one. This involves questions of economy, ease of administration, scoring, and interpretation of results. The longer it takes to construct, administer and score, and the more skilled personnel and equipment that are involved, the higher the costs are likely to be.

The duration of the test may affect its successful operation in other ways, e.g., a fatigue effect on the candidates, administrative factors such as staff to invigilate and the availability of rooms in which to sit the examination; all have to be taken into consideration. It is thus highly desirable to make the test as short as possible, consistent with the need to meet the validity and reliability criteria referred to above. If the aim is to provide as full a profile of the student's abilities as is possible then there is obviously a danger of conflict, for although hard-pressed administrators seem to want a single overall grade, remedial language teachers would prefer as much information as possible (see Moller, 1977; Alderson and Hughes, 1981; and Porter, 1983).

To provide profiles rather than standard scores, each part of the profile will need to reach an acceptable degree of reliability. To achieve satisfactory reliability, communicative tests may have to be longer and have multiple scoring. The difficulties in ensuring that the test contains a representative sample of tasks may also serve to lengthen it. To enhance validity by catering for specific needs and profiling, more tests will be needed, thus further raising the per-capita costs as compared to those of single general tests available for large populations.

Efficiency in the sense of financial viability, may prove the real stumbling block in the way of the development of communicative tests. Tests of this type are difficult and time consuming to construct, require more resources to administer, demand careful training and standardisation of examiners and are more complex and costly to mark and report results on. The increased per-capita cost of using communicative tests in large-scale testing operations may severely restrict their use.

However problematic, there is clearly an imperative need to try and develop test formats and evaluation criteria that provide the best overall balance among reliability, validity and efficiency in the assessment of communicative skills. In the survey of developments in language testing in Chapter One we noted that the pendulum of change had swung several times and differing emphases had been given in test design and implementation to the demands of reliability, validity and efficiency. In this chapter these concepts have been examined from a deeper, theoretical perspective.

In Chapter Three we return to more practical concerns and the stages in the development of a test are briefly outlined to give an idea of the processes that are normally followed in the design and implementation of a language test. This is followed in Chapter Four by an examination of a range of formats available for testing language skills within the communicative paradigm and an assessment is made of their advantages and disadvantages in the light of the discussion in Chapters One and Two.

Chapter Four is intended to be of immediate practical use to the reader faced with the problem of selecting appropriate test formats. It outlines what might be the best choices given the uncertain state of the art in communicative testing and a desire, nevertheless, to make a test as communicative as possible within the constraints imposed by considerations of practicality and reliability.

Chapter Three

Test construction

In this chapter the stages in the development of a test are briefly examined. Many of the external, large scale language tests students are prepared for in language classes will have an important effect on their lives and it is important to evaluate how rigorously these tests have been developed and how far they meet the criteria of reliability, efficiency and validity discussed in Chapter Two.

There are four stages which are currently accepted as the 'best practice' in test construction and validation, namely: design, development, operation and monitoring (see Courchene and de Bagheera, 1985; Carroll and Hall, 1985).

3.1   Test design

In Chapter One we examined briefly what might be involved in the design of a test within the communicative paradigm and indicated certain criteria that such a test might be expected to exhibit, e.g., it should be interactive; direct in nature with tasks reflecting realistic discourse processing activities; texts and tasks should be relevant to the intended situation of the target population; ability should be sampled within meaningful and developing contexts and the test should be based on an explicit a priori specification. In Chapter Two we discussed how the validity of the test would need to be established, the potential reliability of test options assessed and the practicality of the procedures ascertained.

In order to pursue the communicative paradigm, tasks should, as far as possible, be included in the testing operation with due regard to their directness of fit with criteria which accurately and adequately describe the significant aspects of the target activities and the conditions under which they are normally performed.

The starting point for testing within this paradigm is the specification of the general descriptive parameters of the target test population's context of situation, irrespective of differing views on the most appropriate methodology for doing so. These parameters are useful to the tester as a checklist against which the appropriacy of performance based test taks can be evaluated. If the intention is to simulate in the testing situation those events and component activities students are to be faced with in the real world then it is necessary to have a systematic basis for describing these. If a set of general descriptive parameters applicable to events in the target situation are established these can then be used to evaluate the degree of similarity between the test tasks and the activities candidates are involved in, or are likely to be involved in, in their real-world situations.

The parameters that it would be important to collect information on include:

Activities — the sub-tasks students have to cope with while participating in events.

Setting — the physical and psycho-social contexts of the events.

Interaction — the role set and social relationships candidates are involved in.

Instrumentality — the medium, mode and channel of the activities within events.

Dialect — the dialects and accents candidates are exposed to.

Enabling skills — the underlying skills which appear to be necessary to enable students to operate in the various activities.

Empirical data could be generated on the frequency of, and difficulty encountered in, the performance of the relevant activities in the target situation under the various constraints that are operative. More crucially, steps should be taken to establish the relative importance of these to satisfactory operation in the target situation.

In communicative approaches to language testing there would seem to be an emphasis not on linguistic accuracy, but on the ability to function effectively through language in particular settings and contexts. This involves the notion that linguistic activity in the test should be of the kinds and under the conditions which approximate to real life.

Davies (1978) argued that we need to do little more than ensure that we have a test of context as well as grammar, in the sense of making our test items more realistic. Rea (1978) took a stronger line and argued the case for constructing tests that involved simulated communicative tasks which directly resemble those which examinees would encounter in real life and which made realistic demands on them in terms of language performance behaviours.

The issue would seem to be whether there are dimensions of language use that are not part of existing tests and which from a communicative perspective need to be incorporated, since it is important that examinees be exposed to them. While appreciating that the conditions for real life communication are not replicable in test situations we should still try and make tests as realistic as possible in terms of that situation.

Only if we try to make tests simulate as closely as possible the tasks students face in the target context and the conditions under which these are normally performed, are we in a position to judge whether less direct measures of the same abilities can furnish us with similar information about student performance. There is a need to make tests as direct as possible in the first instance in order to compare the relative effectiveness of more traditional discrete point and integrative tests which purport to measure the same construct. In communicative tests we should aim to provide the opportunity for what Widdowson (1978, p. 80) termed 'authentic' language use, i.e., putting the learner in positions where 'he is required to deal with . . . genuine instances of language use' in a way that corresponds to 'his normal communicative activities'. If testers are committed to recreating as many of the conditions of real communication as is feasible in their tests, Hawkey argues (1982, p. 164) that they need to describe what happens 'when the parameters of communicative events trigger each other off.'

The characteristics listed below are illustrative rather than definitive. However, given the unlikelihood of our arriving at an adequate theory of language in use, in the near future, we are at present forced to heed those characteristics identified as important by practitioners in the language teaching field.

No claim is made for the comprehensiveness of the list nor for the discreteness of the categories in it. In addition some of the characteristics are more appropriate to one medium than another. What is evident is that the more a test reflects the dynamic communicative characteristics appropriate to target activities, then the more relevant the language behaviour that might result. Even if it were not possible, for practical reasons, to incorporate all of these features into a test, reference to these characteristics would still provide a rough yardstick whereby the test might be judged and compared with other tests which were designed to elicit the same performance behaviour.

Listed below are communicative characteristics which are considered important in the design of communicative tests. They derive from a questionnaire administered to language school teachers (see Weir, 1983a) and from the work of Roger Hawkey (1982) and Keith Morrow (1977, 1979). The characteristics that might be expected are:

Realistic context — the test tasks should be regarded as appropriate to the candidate's situation.

Relevant information gap — candidates should have to process new information as they might in the real-life situation.

Intersubjectivity — the tasks should involve candidates both as language receivers and language producers. In addition the language produced by the candidates should be modified in accordance with what their expectations of the addressee are perceived to be.

Scope for development of activity by the candidates — the tasks should give candidates the chance to assert their communicative independence and allowance should also be made for the creative unpredictability of communication in the tasks set and the marking schemes that are applied.

Allowance for self monitoring by candidates — the tasks should allow candidates to use their discourse processing strategies to evaluate their communicative effectiveness and make any necessary adjustments in the course of an event.

Processing of appropriately sized input — the size and scope of the activities should be such that they are processing the kind of input they would normally be expected to.

Normal time constraints operative — the task should be accomplished under normal time constraints.

Hawkey (1982) provides a further checklist for task design in his set of descriptors for specifying the dimensions of particular events. Establishing test task dimensions provides a description in more objective linguistic, stylistic terms whereby the target test task can be related more closely to the dimensions of the equivalent target language activity and, secondly, it enables the testers to plot their performance evaluation criteria against the dimensions inherent in the task itself. Test task dimensions might usefully take into account the following:

Size of text — the length of the text, receptive or productive, that is involved in the event.

Grammatical complexity and range of cohesion devices required in the event.

Functional range — the degree of variety of illocutionary acts involved in the event.

Referential range — the breadth and depth of lexical knowledge required to handle activities in the event.

In the construction of communicative tests to date, establishing the general descriptive parameters of the situation the target population has to operate in has received the most emphasis. Collecting information on the dynamic communicative characteristics is more problematic given the current state of theories of communication and there are serious practical and to a lesser extent theoretical difficulties in establishing task dimensions other than size.

A fuller account of establishing a framework of categories for the description of communicative test events can be found in Hawkey (1982) and Weir (1983b). An attempt to provide a specification for the design of a Test in English for Educational Purposes and its realisation is documented in Weir (1983a).

The rigorous procedures advocated in this section may not be realisable in many institutional situations. It may not be possible to carry out a comprehensive analysis of the target situation involving observation, interview and questionnaire (see Weir, 1983a and b). The actual method for preparing a content specification and the breadth and depth of its coverage will obviously depend on practical matters such as the amount of time and the number and expertise of staff available. The needs analysis might have to be limited to a short questionnaire or a conference of representatives drawn from the target situation to elicit the most important situations and enabling skills required.

In certain well-researched domains the experience and judgement of professionals might be an equally valid source of data for a needs analysis and the drawing up of a test specification. The dangers of this type of armchair needs analysis should not be ignored, however.

3.2 Test development

Once a satisfactory specification has been drawn up it has to be developed into test items with appropriate accompanying texts (the questions of specificity and authenticity of texts should have been resolved in the design stage). Formats should be selected and items written to reflect as closely as possible the discourse processing activities of the target situation.

The pilot test should undergo a further validation check at this stage by inviting professionals in the field, (language and subject) to comment on the suitability of texts, formats and items. Any necessary amendments should be made in the light of this scrutiny. Methods for training test administrators and markers need to be formalised and tried out before the trialling of the test.

The test then needs to be trialled and great care should be exercised to ensure that the sample of candidates in the trial is adequate for the degree of precision required and as representative of the target population as is feasible. Opinion also needs to be elicited from test takers, lay advisers and professionals with regard to content (appropriateness, level, etc.) and perceived problems in test taking (see Weir 1983a, p. 346).

Empirical evidence of the external validity of the test needs to be established through concurrent validation procedures (see Section 2.1). Reliability needs to be estimated in the ways described above (see Section 2.2). Analysis at the item, task and construct level needs to be carried out to ensure that items and tasks are working satisfactorily. The test then needs to be revised in the light of the qualitative and quantitative data generated concerning its reliability, validity and efficiency.

3.3   Operation

This stage is concerned with preparing for and conducting the first actual operation of a new test. It involves the preparation, printing and distribution of appropriate information manuals for candidates, receiving institutions, invigilators and markers.

Decisions have to be taken in advance on how candidates are to be familiarised with test formats, especially if the new test represents a radical departure from previous test types (as communicative tests might in some countries). Sample tests could be made available to enable candidates to familiarise themselves in advance with test procedures.

They might include examples of test formats and information on how answers have to be recorded (the handbooks prepared for the IELTS Test are noteworthy in this respect and an example has been included at Appendix V). If these cannot be made available in advance it might be necessary to give candidates practice beforehand on the day of the test.

3.4   Monitoring

The results of each administration of the test should be carefully monitored and ideally stored on a data base. Consideration needs to be given to ongoing and future revisions of the test.

It is necessary to monitor the washback of the new test on the teaching that has preceded it in the classrooms. There should be predictive studies where appropriate to see if a proficiency test is identifying those who can and those who cannot. The impact of a new test on the general public should also be monitored as well as the reception of the test by the receiving institutions who are to make use of the information contained in test results.

Obviously not all of these procedures are within the scope of normal classroom practice. They do serve to illustrate, however, the complex and lengthy processes that need to be observed to guarantee that tests are made as valid, reliable and efficient as possible. The hard-pressed classroom teacher does not usually have the time or the resources to conform fully to the stages outlined above and may well ask if it is possible to achieve anything worthwhile within the constraints imposed by the school situation.

The simple answer is that at the very least it is possible to be more rigorous in test task design and if effort is expended in this initial but crucial construction stage of test development, much can be achieved. Given that this is the stage the classroom teacher is likely to be in a position to do most about we concentrate in Chapter Four on what we feel the main alternatives to be in the testing of language skills and outline the advantages and disadvantages of adopting particular test formats.

Chapter Four

Test Methods

Methods are used to construct tests but are not in themselves tests. Though it is possible to talk of a good or a bad test, or a valid or invalid test, this is obviously not possible for methods. The multiple choice procedure might produce a valid test in one realisation but not in another. This is the case for all methods and should be borne in mind when following the discussion on the potential advantages and disadvantages of the various test methods below.

The different approaches to language testing were outlined above in Chapter One and reference was made to the possible effect of test method on test scores. There is some evidence in the literature (see Murphy, 1978, 1980; Porter, 1983; Weir, 1983a; Boniakowska, 1986; and Alderson and Urquhart, 1985a) that test format might affect student performance. Given the limited state of knowledge concerning the effect of test formats, the only practical approach at present is to safeguard against possible format effect by spreading the base of a test more widely through employing a variety of valid, practical and reliable formats for testing each skill.

We have not yet discussed in any detail the different test methods currently in use. This chapter, therefore, gives a brief account of the main kinds of test formats and highlights some of their potential advantages and disadvantages. This is intended to provide a reference and set of guidelines for future test construction.

As a general rule it is best to assess by a variety of test formats, the scores on which are taken as a composite for reporting purposes. The main proviso for testing within a communicative framework is that the test tasks should as far as possible reflect realistic discourse processing and cover the range of contributory enabling skills that have been identified (see Appendix I for an example of this approach in the TEEP test). It is important that tests developed within this paradigm should have a strong washback effect on practice in the language classroom. What follows is an outline of some of the available options along the discrete point/integrative continuum.

4.1   Testing reading comprehension

4.1.1   *Multiple-choice questions (MCQs)*

The advice on the construction of multiple-choice items in this section is also applicable to the construction of tests of listening comprehension, structure and vocabulary. These are referred to later in this chapter.

   A multiple-choice test item is usually set out in such a way that the candidate is required to select the answer from a number of given options, only one of which is correct. The marking process is totally objective because the marker is not permitted to exercise judgement when marking the candidate's answer; agreement has already been reached as to the correct answer for each item. Selecting and setting items are, however, subjective processes and the decision about which is the correct answer is a matter of subjective judgement on the part of the item writer.

Advantages

1. In multiple-choice tests there is almost complete marker reliability. Candidates' marks, unlike those in subjective formats, cannot be affected by the personal judgement or idiosyncrasies of the marker. The marking, as well as being reliable, is simple, more rapid and often more cost effective than other forms of written test.

2. Because items can be pre-tested fairly easily, it is usually possible to estimate in advance the difficulty level of each item and that of the test as a whole. Pre-testing also provides information about the extent to which each item contributes positively towards what the test as a whole is measuring. Ambiguities in wording of items may also be revealed by analysis of the pre-test data and can then be clarified or removed in the test proper.

3. The format of the multiple-choice test item is such that the intentions of the test compiler are clear and unequivocal; the candidates know what is required of them. In open-ended formats ambiguities in the wording of questions may sometimes lead to the candidates submitting answers to questions different from those which the examiner had intended to ask.

4. In more open-ended formats, e.g., short answer questions, the candidate has to deploy the skill of writing. The extent to which this affects accurate measurement of the trait being assessed has not been established. Multiple-choice tests avoid this particular difficulty.

Disadvantages

1. There are however a number of problems associated with the use of this format. If a candidate gets a multiple-choice item wrong because of some flaw in the question, the answer sheet on which he records his answer will not reveal this fact. In addition, we do not know whether a candidate's failure is due to lack of comprehension of the text or lack of comprehension of the question. A candidate might get an item right by

eliminating wrong answers, a different skill from being able to choose the right answer in the first place.

2. The scores gained in multiple-choice tests, as in true-false tests, may be suspect because the candidate has guessed all or some of the answers. This has the effect of narrowing the range of scores. The format of these tests encourages the candidate to guess and it is sometimes considered necessary to take steps to discourage candidates from doing so. It may also be possible to complete some items without reference to the texts they are set on, and, if this is so, whatever it is that is being tested, it cannot be comprehension of the text.

3. Multiple-choice tests take much longer and are more expensive and difficult to prepare than more open-ended examinations, e.g., compositions. A large number of items have to be written carefully by item writers who have been specially trained and these then have to be pre-tested before use in a formal examination. Each item has to be rigorously edited to ensure that:

   - There is no superfluous information in the stem.
   - The spelling, grammar and punctuation are correct.
   - The language is concise and at an appropriate level for candidates.
   - Enough information has been given to answer the question.
   - There is only one unequivocally correct answer.
   - The distractors are wrong but plausible and discriminate at the right level.
   - The responses are homogeneous, of equal length and mutually exclusive and the item is appropriate for the test.

4. It is extremely time-consuming and demanding to get the requisite number of satisfactory items for a passage, especially for testing skills such as skimming. A particular problem lies in devising suitable distractors for items testing the more extensive receptive skills. Heaton (1975) noted that, for these activities, it is more helpful to set simple open-ended questions rather than multiple-choice items; otherwise students will find it necessary to keep in mind four or five options for each item while they are trying to process the text.

5. A further objection to the use of multiple-choice format is the danger of the format having an undue effect on measurement of the trait. There is some evidence that multiple-choice format is particularly problematic in this respect. This has been evidenced by low correlations both with alternative reading measures and with other concurrent external validity data on candidates' reading abilities (see Weir, 1983a).

6. There is considerable doubt about their validity as measures of language ability. Answering multiple-choice items is an unreal task, as in real life one is rarely presented with four alternatives from which to make a choice to signal understanding. Normally, when required, an understanding of what has been read or heard can be communicated through speech or writing. In a multiple-choice test the distractors present choices that otherwise might not have been thought of. If a divergent view of the world is taken it might be argued that there is sometimes more than one right answer to some questions

particularly at the inferential level. What the test constructor has inferred as the correct answer might not be what other readers infer, or necessarily be explicit in the text.

4.1.2 Short answer questions

These are questions which require the candidates to write down specific answers in spaces provided on the question paper. The technique is extremely useful for testing both reading and listening comprehension and the comments made below in reference to reading are, for the most part, also applicable to the testing of listening.

Advantages

1. Short answer questions require the candidate to write down answers in spaces provided on the question paper, allowing the candidate some freedom of expression.

2. Answers are not provided for the student as in multiple-choice: therefore if a student gets the answer right, one is more certain that this has not occurred for reasons other than comprehension of the text.

3. With careful formulation of the questions a candidate's response can be brief and thus a large number of questions may be set in this format, enabling a wide coverage.

4. If the number of acceptable answers to a question is limited it is possible to give fairly precise instructions to the examiners who mark them.

5. Activities such as inference, recognition of a sequence, comparison and establishing the main idea of a text, require the relating of sentences in a text with other items which may be some distance away in the text. This can be done effectively through short answer questions where the answer has to be sought rather than being one of those provided.

6. A strong case can be made in appropriate contexts, e.g., in EAP tests, for the use of long texts with short answer formats on the grounds that these are more representative of required reading in the target situation, at least in terms of length. They can also provide more reliable data about a candidate's reading ability (see Engineer, 1977 for evidence on the increased reliability resulting from the use of longer texts and Appendix I below for an example of this approach in the TEEP test).

Disadvantages

1. The main disadvantage to this technique is that it involves the candidate in writing and there is some concern, largely anecdotal, that this interferes with the measurement of the intended construct. Care is needed in the setting of items to limit the range of possible acceptable responses and the extent of writing required.

2. In those cases where there is more debate over the acceptability of an answer, e.g., in questions requiring inferencing skills, there is a possibility that the variability of answers might lead to marker unreliability. However, careful moderation and standardisation of examiners should help to reduce this.

4.1.3 Cloze

In the cloze procedure words are deleted from a text after allowing a few sentences of introduction. The deletion rate is mechanically set, usually between every fifth and eleventh word. Candidates have to fill each gap by supplying the word they think has been deleted. Alderson's research (1978a) established that more difficult texts were better measures of the lower order skills which cloze tests, than were easy texts. He found the semantically acceptable scoring procedure to be superior to any other.

In comparison of cloze and multiple-choice, Engineer (1977) concluded that the two techniques were measuring different aspects of the reading activity — namely that a timed cloze measured the *process* of reading, i.e., the reader's ability to understand the text while he is actually reading it; multiple-choice, on the other hand, measures the *product* of reading, namely the reader's ability to interpret the abstracted information for its meaning value.

There is a good deal of supportive evidence in the literature for using the cloze format. Klein-Braley (1981, p. 229) commented that: 'Up to now, in the main, the results of research with cloze tests have been extremely encouraging. They have shown high validity, high reliability, objectivity, discrimination and so on.' She quoted J.D. Brown (1979, p. 13): 'As demonstrated in this and other studies, it can be a valid and reliable test of overall second language proficiency.'

Alderson (1978a, p. 2) described how: 'The last decade, in particular, has seen a growing use of the cloze procedure with non-native speakers of English to measure not only their reading comprehension abilities but also their general linguistic proficiency in English as a Foreign Language.' He added (p. 39):

> The general consensus of studies into and with cloze procedure for the last twenty years has been that it is a realiable and valid measure of readability and reading comprehension, for native speakers of English .... As a measure of the comprehension of text, cloze has been shown to correlate well with other types of test on the same text and also with standardised testing of reading comprehension.

He pointed out that though this evidence is not available for non-native speakers (p. 63): 'it does seem cloze procedure is a potentially interesting measure of language proficiency for non-native speakers.'

The term 'cloze' was first introduced by W.L. Taylor (1953) who took it from the gestalt concept of 'closure' which refers to the tendency of individuals to complete a pattern once they have grasped its overall significance. Taylor (p. 416) described it as follows: 'A cloze unit may be defined as: any single occurrence of a successful attempt to reproduce accurately a part deleted from a "message" (any language product), by deciding from the context that remains, what the missing part should be.' The reader comprehends the mutilated sentence as a whole and completes the pattern. Alderson (1978a, p. 8) pointed out that: 'the cloze procedure becomes a measure of the similarity between the patterns that the decoder is anticipating and those that the encoder had used.'

Taylor first applied the procedure to gauging the readability of a text but later it came to be highly regarded as a measure of testing reading comprehension and even as a measure of overall language proficiency. For Bormuth (1962, p. 134): 'cloze tests are valid and uniform measures of reading comprehension ability.' Heaton (1975, p. 122) thought that: 'cloze tests measure the reader's ability to decode interrupted or mutilated messages by making the most acceptable substitutions from all the contextual clues available.'

Engineer (1977) found that a cloze test given under timed conditions provided valid and reliable indices of students' proficiency if two conditions were met: first, that the textual material used was of the appropriate level of difficulty for the population and second, that it contained a sufficient number of deleted items.

Advantages

1. Cloze tests are easy to construct and easily scored if the exact word scoring procedure is adopted. They are claimed to be valid indicators of overall language proficiency (see Bormuth, 1962; Brown, 1979; Engineer, 1977, and Oller, 1979).

2. With a fifth word deletion rate a large number of items can be set on a relatively short text and these can exhibit a high degree of internal consistency, in terms of Kuder-Richardson coefficients. This consistency may vary considerably, though, dependent on text selected, starting point for deletions and deletion rate employed.

3. In the literature cloze tests are often feted as valid and uniform measures of reading comprehension.

Disadvantages

1. Despite the arguments adduced in favour of cloze procedure, a number of doubts have been expressed, largely concerning its validity as a testing device. It has been shown to be irritating and unacceptable to students and doubt has been thrown on the underlying assumption that it randomly samples the elements in a text. Klein-Braley and Raatz (1984) in investigating its construct validity found that it fails to ensure random deletion of elements in a text.

2. Alderson (1978a, p. 392) had discovered that:

   cloze procedure is not a unitary procedure, since there is a marked lack of comparability among the tests it may be used to produce. The fact emerges clearly that different cloze tests, produced by variations in certain of the variables, give unpredictably different measures, particularly of proficiency in English as a foreign language.

   If one changes the text, changes the deletion rate, starts at a different place or alters the scoring procedure, one gets a different test in terms of reliability and validity coefficients and overall test difficulty.

3. The evidence is contradictory about the differing scoring methods to be adopted in marking a cloze procedure. It has been suggested (Klein-Braley, 1985) that a cloze test is a much less effective measure for assessing 'general proficiency' in that it correlates less well with other established general proficiency measures when used on monolingual as against multilingual groups. In addition it seems that cloze is not suitable for restricted range groups (Klein-Braley, 1985); weak relationships have been found between cloze and teachers' judgements (Klein-Braley, 1981; 1985); cloze does not seem to correlate well with productive tests of speaking and writing and scores on cloze

cannot easily be related to native speaker performance since native speaker performance varies considerably from one cloze test to another (Alderson, 1978a).

4. The cloze procedure seems to produce more successful tests of syntax and lexis at sentence level than of reading comprehension in general or of inferential or deductive abilities, what might be termed higher order abilities (see Darnell, 1968).

5. This would seem to accord with Alderson's (1978a, p. 99) findings that:

> cloze is essentially sentence bound . . . . Clearly the fact that cloze procedure deletes words rather than phrases or clauses must limit its ability to test comprehension of more than the immediate environment, since individual words do not usually carry textual cohesion and discourse coherence (with the obvious exception of cohesive devices like anaphora, lexical repetition and logical connectors).

6. Perhaps the most crucial reservation is the question of what performance on a cloze test really tells us about a candidate's language ability.

4.1.4 *Selective deletion gap filling*

In the light of recent negative findings on mechanical deletion cloze, increasing support has developed for the view that the test constructor should use a 'rational cloze', selecting items for deletion based upon what is known about language, about difficulty in text and about the way language works in a particular text. Linguistic reasoning is used to decide on deletions and so it is easier to state what each test is intended to measure (see Alderson, 1978a, p. 397; Klein-Braley, 1981, p. 244; and Weir, 1983a). This technique is better referred to as selective deletion gap filling as it is not 'cloze' in the proper sense.

Advantages

1. Selective deletion enables the test constructor to determine where deletions are to be made and to focus on those items which have been selected a priori as being important to a particular target audience.

2. It is also easy for the test writer to make any alterations shown to be necessary after item analysis and to maintain the required number of items. This might involve eliminating items that have not performed satisfactorily in terms of discrimination and facility value.

Disadvantages

1. It is important to stress that this technique restricts one to sampling a much more limited range of enabling skills (i.e., those abilities which collectively represent the overall skill of reading) than do the short answer and multiple-choice formats (see Weir, 1983a).

2. Whereas short answer and multiple-choice questions allow the sampling of the range of reading enabling skills, gap filling is much more restrictive where only single words are deleted. Gap filling only normally allows the testing of sentence bound reading skills.

3. If the purpose of a test is to sample the range of enabling skills including the more extensive skills such as skimming, then an additional format to gap filling is essential.

4.1.5 C-Tests

Recently an alternative to cloze and selective deletion gap filling has emerged for testing comprehension of the more specifically linguistic elements in a text. An adaptation of the cloze technique called the C-test has been developed in Germany by Klein-Braley (1981, 1985; Klein-Braley and Raatz, 1984) based on the same theoretical rationale as cloze, viz., testing ability to cope with reduced redundancy and predict from context.

In the C-test every second word in a text is partially deleted. In an attempt to ensure solutions students are given the first half of the deleted word. The examinee completes the word on the test paper and an exact word scoring procedure is adopted.

Advantages

1. With C-tests a variety of texts are recommended, and given the large number of items that can be generated on small texts this further enhances the representative nature of the language being sampled.

2. Normally a minimum of 100 deletions are made and these are more representative of the passage as a whole than is possible under the cloze technique. The task can be objectively scored because it is rare for there to be more than one possible answer for any one gap.

3. Whereas in cloze the performance of native speakers on the test is highly variable, according to Klein-Braley (1985) it is much more common for native speakers to be able to score 100 per cent on C-tests. This may be of some help in setting cutting scores, e.g., what percentage constitutes a pass.

4. The C-test is economical and the results obtained to date are encouraging in terms of reliability and internal and external validity. It would seem to represent a viable alternative to cloze procedure and selective deletion gap filling.

Disadvantages

1. Given the relatively recent appearance of the technique in this form there is little empirical evidence of its value. Most concern has been expressed concerning its public acceptability as a measure of language proficiency. It is interesting to note that Davies (1965) has a version of this technique in his battery where the first letter of a word is given.

2. This technique suffers from the fact that it is irritating for students to have to process heavily mutilated texts and the face validity of the procedure is low.

4.1.6 Cloze elide

A technique which is generating interest recently is where words which do not belong are inserted into a reading passage and candidates have to indicate where these insertions have been made. There is in fact nothing new about this technique and Davies was using it much earlier (Davies, 1965). In its earlier form it was known as the intrusive word technique.

Advantages

1. In comparison with multiple-choice format or short answer questions the candidate does not have the problem of understanding the question. It has approximately the same item yield as a cloze test.

Disadvantages

1. Scoring is highly problematic as candidates may, for example, delete items which are correct, but redundant.

4.1.7 *Information transfer*

In testing both reading and listening comprehension we have referred to the problem of the measurement being 'muddied' by having to employ writing to record answers. In an attempt to avoid this contamination of scores several Examination Boards in Britain have included tasks where the information transmitted verbally is transferred to a non-verbal form, e.g., by labelling a diagram, completing a chart or numbering a sequence of events (see Appendix IV for interesting examples of this in the JMB Test).

Advantages

1. Information transfer techniques are particularly suitable for testing an understanding of process, classification or narrative sequence and are useful for testing a variety of other text types. It avoids possible contamination from students having to write answers out in full.

2. It is a realistic task for various situations and its interest and authenticity gives it a high face validity in these contexts.

Disadvantages

1. A good deal of care needs to be taken that the non-verbal task the students have to complete does not itself complicate the process. In some tasks students may be able to understand the text but not what is expected of them in the transfer phase.

2. There is a danger of cultural and educational bias. Students in certain subject areas may also be disadvantaged, e.g., some students in the social sciences may not be as adept in working in a non-verbal medium as their counterparts in science disciplines.

4.1.8   Conclusion

For testing reading abilities we would recommend the use of short answer questions together with selective deletion gap filling. The C-test is an interesting alternative to the latter and its acceptability to students and validity are worthy of further investigation. If we are to develop the communicative nature of our tests it is perhaps important to focus on performance tasks in reading tests, and the use of information transfer techniques and other restricted response formats is advocated.

4.2   Testing listening comprehension

4.2.1   Testing extensive listening skills

The rationale behind the construction of many of the earlier listening comprehension tests was described by Valette (1967, p. 49): 'The main object of a listening test is to evaluate the student's comprehension. His degree of comprehension will depend on his ability to discriminate phonemes, to recognise stress and intonation patterns, and to retain what he has heard.'

It was thought that, if a learner was tested in phoneme discrimination, stress and intonation, the sum of the 'discrete' sub-tests would be equivalent to his proficiency in listening comprehension. An example of the test of this type is the ELBA test battery constructed by Ingram (1964) which placed the emphasis on 'discrete' listening items such as sound recognition, intonation and stress, using short items rather than continuous passages of discourse or dialogue. As Ryan (1979) pointed out, even the section described as listening comprehension seemed more a test of appropriate-response mechanisms than a test of comprehension of continuous speech in an authentic context.

A noticeable trend in recent years has been the attempt to differentiate between tests of auditory discrimination and contextualised tests of listening comprehension. Templeton (1973) outlined how research began to focus on these integrative tests of listening comprehension in preference to discrete point tests of phoneme discrimination, intonation and word and sentence stress.

Since 1969 the JMB no longer tests individual aural skills in isolation, but instead tests listening comprehension in an integrated context of lecturettes or dialogues (see McEldowney, 1976, and Appendix IV). This paradigm shift can also be observed in the 1977 version of EPTB (see Davies, 1978) which substituted for the earlier analytical, phoneme discrimination, stress and intonation tasks, an overall listening comprehension sub-test containing, for example, an integrated test of listening comprehension based on a lecture with simulated note-taking.

Davies (1978, pp. 146−8) illustrated how similar changes had occurred between the listening tasks described in the first and second editions of Valette's book on testing (cf. Valette, 1967; 1977): 'we can characterise the difference between Valette (1967) and Valette

(1977) as a move from linguistics to sociolinguistics, from structuralism to functionalism, from taxonomy and breaking down into skills, into discrete parts, to integration and building up into wholes.' In the second edition of Valette (1977) Davies noted (p. 147): 'a move from a concentration on sound, the production of speech, the phonology, to meaning and communication.'

A strong argument against auditory discrimination as a test of proficiency in listening comprehension was that the ability to distinguish between phonemes, however important, did not necessarily imply an ability to understand verbal messages. Furthermore, as Ryan (1979) pointed out, occasional confusion over selected pairs of phonemes does not matter too greatly, because in real life situations the listener has contextual clues to facilitate understanding. For Valette (1977, p. 102): 'The key concern of the evaluator is to determine whether the students have received the message that was intended and not whether they made certain sound discriminations or identified specific structural signals.'

J.W. Morrison (1974) after assessing the listening comprehension needs of science students at the University of Newcastle-upon-Tyne, concluded that at the ESP/EST level, performance needs to be considered at a level beyond phonology and grammatical structure, thus taking into account the communicative context of spoken discourse. Chaplen (1970a, p. 19) had earlier concluded that: 'Whatever the contribution of the elements of oral/aural communication — intonation, stress and phonemic discrimination — to a test of oral/aural communication, their importance appears to be minimal at any level of proficiency beyond a very elementary stage.'

Holes (1972) developed test instruments which focused on the ability to handle academic lectures, a communicative task regarded by departments as both crucial and difficult for their overseas students. He approached test design from a 'job-sampling' viewpoint and attempted to assess the more global, less 'pure' ability of students to interpret 'message content' as well as eliciting data on their linguistic competence. He used the Davies Test as part of his concurrent validation procedures and an interim academic success/failure rating for predictive validity purposes. Though the predictive validity correlations of tests versus subject examination results were non-conclusive, Holes concluded (p. 134) that: 'The value of the tests lay rather in what they revealed about the kinds of difficulty which overseas students experience in lectures.'

In line with the paradigm shift described above it is usual to provide ongoing and sequential texts as stimuli in a test battery, though, in terms of the tasks, items and scoring, it might be desirable in certain components of the test to focus on discrete items. As with tests of reading comprehension, a balance of integrative and 'discrete point' is felt to be the most satisfactory approach for maximising reliability and validity in a test.

Multiple-choice questions

In our consideration of the use of this technique in the assessment of reading in Section 4.1.1. above it is clear that the disadvantages of employing the technique far outweigh any advantages it might have. These disadvantages are equally applicable for using this format in the testing of listening.

Because of the problems associated with the serial nature of the listening process there are additional difficulties in employing this technique as a measure of listening ability, for example, the extra burden that is placed on processing by having to keep four options in mind (Heaton, 1975). The format is artificial and is increasingly perceived as an invalid method for assessing comprehension by teachers, materials designers and language testers. The new General Certificate of Secondary Education (GCSE) examinations in the United Kingdom will not be employing multiple-choice format largely because of hostile comment from teachers' organisations on its validity as a teaching and testing technique.

The RSA CUEFL examination, despite conscientious efforts to maximise authenticity in the stimulus texts selected, is heavily dependent on this format and its variants (for example true-false items) and has been criticised for the retreat from realistic discourse processing that this involves (see Appendix III). The use by the RSA of these more objective formats highlights the need for trying to establish realism in both text stimulus and the tasks that are expected of the student, and the sometimes contradictory pulls of reliability and validity.

Short answer questions (SAQs)

Advantages

1. Short Answer Questions can be a realistic activity for testing listening comprehension, for example, if one wishes to simulate real life activities where notes are taken as somebody communicates a spoken message. With sufficient care the responses can be limited and so the danger of the writing process interfering with the measurement of listening is largely avoided (see Appendix I).

2. In contrast to the multiple-choice or the true-false formats employed in some examinations, one can be more certain that correct answers have not been arrived at by chance.

Disadvantages

1. If the candidate has to write an answer at the same time as listening to continuous discourse there are obvious problems. An unnecessary load might be placed on the memory and vital information in the ongoing discourse might be missed while the answer to a previous question is being recorded.

Information transfer techniques

This technique was discussed above in connection with reading and it is worthy of consideration for similar reasons in a listening test (see Appendix IV).

Advantages

1. A particular advantage for using this technique in testing listening is that the student

does not have to process written questions while trying to make sense of the spoken input. It is particularly efficient for testing an understanding of sequence, process, relationships in a text and classification.

Disadvantages

1. It is often very difficult to find spoken texts which lend themselves to a non-verbal format. Whereas in reading a certain amount of editing of texts is feasible and in general a greater variety of texts are more readily available, this is not the case for listening texts taken from authentic sources.

Limitations on the testing of extensive listening

It is important to note that, if one wishes to make test tasks more like those in real life, the serial nature of extended spoken discourse and the greater processing problems associated with understanding spoken English preclude items which focus on the more specifically linguistic skills such as working out the meaning of words from context or recognising the meaning value of specific features of stress or intonation. It is, for example, extremely difficult for students to backtrack and focus on very specific features of discourse while listening to and attempting to understand a non-interactive, uninterrupted monologue. To preserve the integrative nature of the test, therefore, we have to focus questions on the more global processing skills such as inferencing, listening for specifics or identifying the main ideas.

A serious problem in testing extensive listening by use of the tape recorder is that the visual element, the wealth of normal exophoric reference and paralinguistic information, is not available to the candidate and perhaps, therefore, the listening task is made that much more difficult for the candidate. The listener does not normally have to process disembodied sounds from a tape recorder in real life (apart from the obvious exceptions such as listening to the radio).

Until there is greater accessibility to video equipment the artificiality of a straight audio listening task will remain a problem. Even video is likely to have its own practical difficulties though, e.g., the number of screens required so that all viewers are treated equally or the incompatibility of various systems. Whatever the instrumentality, in a test situation the student is in any case denied the natural context provided by the experience of using the language in contiguous situations.

There is a great danger in listening tests that the candidates might be expected to cope with additional difficulties arising from the restricted context available and steps need to be taken to compensate for this or we might seriously underestimate the ability to process spoken language.

4.2.2 *The testing of intensive listening*

Reference was made above to the difficulty of focusing on specific listening points while candidates are exposed to ongoing discourse. Given the need to enhance the reliability of our test batteries it is often advisable to include a more discrete format with the possibility this gives of including a greater number of specific items. A dictation or listening recall test can provide this discreteness as well as being valid in content terms for certain groups of candidates, particularly those involved in academic study through the medium of English.

Dictation

It is important that the candidates should be assessed in situations as close as possible to those in which they will be required to use the language. For dictation, this involves them listening to dictated material which incorporates oral messages typical of those they might encounter in the target situation.

Advantages

1. Given our concern with reliability as well as validity, it is perhaps advisable to improve the overall reliability of a listening battery by including a format which has a proven track record in this respect. A dictation can provide this reliability through the large number of items that can be generated as well as being valid for specific situations where dictation might feature as a target group activity.

2. There is a lot of evidence which shows dictation correlating highly with a great variety of other tests, particularly with other integrative tests such as cloze and it is often employed as a useful measure of general proficiency. There is some evidence that the use of a semantic scoring scheme (see Weir, 1983a) as against an exact word system serves to enhance the correlations with other construct valid tests of listening.

3. Criticisms of dictation in the past stemmed from a viewpoint heavily influenced by structural linguistic that favoured testing the more discrete elements of language skills and wished to avoid the possibility of muddied measurement. Heaton (1975) commented: 'as a testing device it measures too many different language features to be effective in providing a means of assessing any one particular skill'.

4. The proponents of dictation, however, consider its very 'integrative' nature to be an advantage since it reflects more faithfully how people process language in real life contexts.

5. The new interest in dictation reflected the pardigm shift in testing values and objectives referred to above. Whereas in 1967 Valette had observed that foreign language specialists were not in agreement on the effectiveness of dictation as an examination for more advanced students, significantly ten years later she was able to state that dictation was a precise measure of overall proficiency and an excellent method of grouping incoming students according to ability levels.

6. An important factor in the return of dictation to popularity as a testing device was the research carried out by Oller, which formed part of a wider interest in integrative testing. Oller (1971) rejected current criticisms of dictation and argued that it was an adequate test of listening comprehension because it tested a broad range of integrative skills.

7. Oller (1979) claimed that a dynamic process of analysis by synthesis was involved. Dictation draws on the learner's ability to use all the systems of the language in conjunction with knowledge of the world, context, etc., to predict what will be said (synthesis of message) and after the message has been uttered to scrutinise this via the short term memory in order to see if it fits with what had been predicted (analysis).

8. Dictation for Oller tests not only a student's ability to discriminate phonological units but also his ability to make decisions about word boundaries; in this way an examinee discovers sequences of words and phrases that make sense and from these he reconstructs a message. The identification of words from context as well as from perceived sounds is seen by Oller as a positive advantage of dictation in that this ability is crucial in the functioning of language. The success with which the candidate reconstructs the message is said to depend on the degree to which his internalised 'expectancy grammar' replicates that of the native speaker. Fluent native speakers nearly always score 100 per cent on a well-administered dictation while non native learners make errors of omission, insertion, word order, inversion, etc., indicating that their internalised grammars are, to some extent, inaccurate and incomplete; they do not fully understand what they hear and what they reencode is correspondingly different from the original.

9. According to Oller (1979), research showed that dictation test results were powerful predictors of language ability as measured by other kinds of language tests (see Oller, 1971; Valette, 1977).

Disadvantages

1. Alderson (1978a) concludes that the evidence concerning dictation is inconclusive and that it is useful only as part of a battery of listening tests rather than a single solution. He points out (1978a, p. 365) that:

   The reason it correlates more with some sub-tests than with others does not appear to be due to the claimed fact that it is an integrative test, but because it is essentially a test of low level linguistic skills. Hence the dictation correlates best with those cloze tests, texts and scoring methods which themselves best allow the measurement of these skills.

2. Dictation will be trivial unless the short term memory of the students is challenged and the length of the utterances dictated will depend on the listeners' ability up to the limit that native speaker counterparts could handle.

3. Marking may well be problematic if one wishes to take into account seriousness of error or if one wishes to adopt a more communicatively oriented marking scheme where a mark is given if the candidate has understood the substance of the message and redundant features are ignored.

4. If the dictation is not recorded on tape, the test will be less reliable, as there will be differences in, for example, the speed of delivery of the text to different audiences.

5. The exercise can be unrealistic if the texts used have been previously created to be read rather than heard.

Listening recall

In contrast to dictation, very little evidence is available about listening recall tests (see Furneaux, 1982; Henning, 1982; and Beretta, 1983 for a full description of this procedure). The student is given a printed copy of a passage from which certain content words have been omitted (these deletions are checked in advance to ensure that they cannot be repaired by reading). The words deleted are normally content words felt to be important to an understanding of the discourse and the blanks occur at increasingly frequent intervals.

Students are given a short period of time to read over the text, allowing for activation of their expectancy grammars. They have to fill in the blanks, having heard a tape recording of the complete passage twice. They are advised to listen the first time and then attempt to fill in the banks during a short period allowed for writing in the answers. They hear the passage a second time and then are allowed a short period of time to write in any remaining missing words. These limited write-in times draw on their short term memories. The format involves many of the linguistic factors outlined above for dictation and this is reflected in the other names which have been given to the test: spot dictation, listening recall, and combined cloze and dictation.

Advantages

1. Like dictation it can be administered rapidly and scored objectively and it allows the tester to focus on items which are deemed to be important (as in selective deletion gap filling).

2. High correlations have been reported with other more direct tests of listening (Beretta, 1983) and with test totals for listening batteries.

3. It has advantages in large scale testing operations in that it is easy to construct, administer and mark.

Disadvantages

1. The difficulty in this technique lies in stating what it is that is being tested. As only one word is deleted it may not be testing anything more than an ability to match sounds with symbols aided by an ability to read the printed passage containing the gaps.

2. It is an inauthentic task and involves reading ability as well as listening. Careful construction is needed to ensure that the students cannot fill in the blanks simply by reading the passage without having to listen at all.

3. Given the high correlations that have been discovered between listening recall and dictation (see Furneaux, 1982; Beretta, 1983), and roughly equivalent practicality and reliability, the greater potential validity of dictation for certain groups, e.g., for students

studying through the medium of English, might lead to a preference for dictation over listening recall.

4.2.3 Conclusion

Where possible listening tests should include an authentic performance task. An attempt should be make to incorporate information transfer techniques (see Appendix IV) where appropriate. We might usefully include short answer questions and consideration could be given to dictation (see Appendix I).

4.3 Testing writing

Two different approaches for assessing writing ability can be adopted. Firstly, writing can be divided into discrete levels, e.g., grammar, vocabulary, spelling and punctuation, and these elements can be tested separately by the use of objective tests. Secondly, more direct extended writing tasks of various types could be constructed. These would have greater construct, content, face and washback validity but would require a more subjective assessment.

4.3.1 Indirect methods for assessing linguistic competence

In Section 4.1 above we examined the formats of cloze, selective deletion gap filling and C-tests, and commented on the value of these techniques for testing the more specifically linguistic, sentence bound reading skills, viz., items focusing on an understanding of vocabulary, structure or cohesion devices.

Both productive and receptive skills can be broken down into levels of grammar and lexis according to a discrete point framework. McEldowney (1974, p. 8) commenting on the syllabus of the JMB Test in English (Overseas) stated:

> To be able to operate these four skills (listening, reading, speaking and writing) in the various function areas it is necessary to be able to manipulate items from three levels of language. That is, to communicate, it is necessary to have an adequate vocabulary, to know basic items of English grammar and to be able to handle English sounds, stress and intonation.

The JMB Test in English (Overseas), as well as including tasks testing written production, also has tasks which test knowledge of 'basic productive vocabulary' and 'minimum grammatical items' (see Appendix IV). The problems which face the constructors of vocabulary tests are manifold. Chaplen (1970a) who constructed the sub-tests for the vocabulary sections of the early JMB tests noted two main problem areas:

1. The selection of lexical items for testing.
2. Methods used to test the lexical items.

If the examinees are studying a variety of different subjects, as is the case in an EAP context, then there is a serious problem of selection. The more generalised the subject matter, the more difficult it is to select for testing purposes. In specialised courses, where there is an identifiable, agreed register, selection is easier but still exacting.

An additional problem occurs in the relative weighting that should be given to items selected from future reading materials as against the items that are likely to be employed in extended writing tasks. Do we test active or passive vocabulary? Furthermore, how do we establish the frequency and importance levels of the lexical items intended for use in the test?

Given the constraints on testing these items discretely it is by no means clear whether the results of such tests should form part of a profile of reading or of writing ability. They do not fit comfortably into either.

Similar problems occur in the selection of grammatical items for inclusion in an indirect test of linguistic competence. A quantitative survey of the occurrence of structural items in the receptive and productive written materials a test population will have to cope with in future target situations is obviously beyond the scope of most test constructors. A more pragmatic, subjective method of taking decisions on which items to be included is needed. It would seem sensible to examine the content of existing tests and coursebooks at an equivalent level to determine what experts in the field have regarded as suitable items for inclusion for similar populations.

There also seems to be a problem in reporting on what is being tested in these discrete point grammar tests. Should the performance on an indirect test of grammatical knowledge be reported on under the profile for reading or writing? Additionally indirect techniques are restricted in terms of their perceived validity for test takers and the users of test results. An interesting attempt to retain the objectivity and coverage of the discrete point approach whilst enhancing validity can be found in the editing task in Paper Two of the TEEP test (see Weir, 1983a and Appendix I).

Editing task

In the editing task the student is given a text containing a number of errors of grammar, spelling and punctuation of the type noted as common by remedial teachers of students in the target group and is asked to rewrite the passage making all the necessary corrections.

Advantages

1. As well as being a more objective measurement of competence, this task may have a good washback effect in that students may be taught and encouraged to edit their written work more carefully.

2. It is certainly more face valid than other indirect techniques as it equals part of the writing process.

Disadvantages

1. If the student rewrites the passage in his own words instead of just correcting the errors, the problems of marking are considerable. There is also some doubt as to whether the ability to correct somebody else's errors equates with an ability to correct one's own.

2. Marking can be problematic also if a candidate alters something which is already correct; a sin of commission rather than omission.

4.3.2 The direct testing of writing

With a more integrative and direct approach to the testing of writing, we can incorporate items which test a candidate's ability to perform certain of the functional tasks required in the performance of duties in the target situation. For doctors in a hospital this might involve writing a letter to a local GP about a patient on the basis of a set of printed case notes. For a student in an EAP context it might involve search reading of an academic text to extract specified information for use in a written summary (see Appendix I).

Essay tests

This is a traditional method for getting students to produce a sample of connected writing. The stimulus is normally written and can vary in length from a limited number of words to several sentences. The topics are often very general and rely heavily on the candidate providing the content out of his or her head. The candidates are not usually guided in any way as to how they are expected to answer the question.

Advantages

1. The essay has traditionally been accorded high prestige as a testing technique which may explain a widespread reluctance to discard it despite the problems in marking that have been encountered (see Coffman, 1971; Gipps and Ewen, 1974).

2. The topics are extremely easy to set and it is a familiar testing technique to both the candidates and the users of test results. It thus has a superficial face validity in particular for the lay person.

3. It is a suitable vehicle for testing skills, such as the ability to develop an extended argument in a logical manner, which cannot be tested in other ways.

4. The big advantage it shares with other tests of extended writing is that a sample of writing is produced which can provide a tangible point of reference for comparison in the future.

Disadvantages

1. Free, open-ended writing is problematic. An ability to write on general open-ended topics may depend on the candidate's background or cultural knowledge, imagination or creativity. These may not be factors we wish to assess.

2. The candidate may not have any interest in the topic he is given and if a selection of topics is provided it is very difficult to compare performances especially if the production of different text types is involved.

3. Candidates tend to approach an open ended question in different ways and examiners have to assess the relative merits of these different approaches. This increases the difficulty of marking the essays in a precise and reliable manner.

4. Time pressure is often an unrealistic constraint for extended writing and writing timed essays is not normally done outside of academic life. For most people the writing process is lengthier and may involve several drafts before a finished version is produced.

5. The inclusion of an extended writing component in an examination is time consuming in terms of the total amount of test time that is available for testing all the skills.

Controlled writing tasks

There is obviously a very strong case for including a test of writing on the grounds of the perceived content validity of 'job sample' tasks. It tests important skills which no other form of assessment can sample adequately. To omit a writing task in situations where writing tasks are an important feature of the student's real life needs might severely lower the validity of a testing programme.

Wall (1982) carried out an illuminating investigation of the kinds of writing task engineering students were required to perform as part of their coursework and compared these with the types of essay they were set in the Michigan Battery used for assessing students' language proficiency on entry to the university. She (p. 166) summarised the differences as follows:

> The main difference seems to be that in the engineering tasks there is much prior input and the task itself is explicitly outlined, whereas in the composition the writer has only a suggestion to respond to and must not only create the content of the writing but a context, audience and purpose as well. The criteria for marking would also seem different.

The conclusion to the investigation was disturbing. The research produced: 'a correlation study between the Michigan Battery total and part scores and the student's first term GPA, in which no significant relationship between tests and the criterion for academic success could be found.' In other words no relationship at all could be found between writing performance in the test and subsequent indicators of performance in the course of study.

Free, uncontrolled writing would seem to be an invalid test of the writing ability required by most students. It is easier to extrapolate from writing tests when care is taken in specifying for each task: the media, the audience, the purpose and the situation in line with target level performance activities (see Wall, 1982). When the task is determined more precisely in this manner it is also easier to compare performances of different students and to obtain a greater degree of reliability in scoring. If the writing task is uncontrolled examinees may also be able to cover up weaknesses by avoiding problems.

There are various types of stimuli that can be used in controlled writing tasks. Stimuli can be written, spoken or most effectively non-verbal, e.g., a graph, plan or drawing which the student is asked to interpret in writing (see Appendix IV; Dunlop, 1969; McEldowney, 1974, 1976, 1982; Weir, 1983a, and Appendix I for examples of these).

Advantages

1. The advantage of non-verbal stimuli is that if they present information in a clear and precise way the candidate does not have to spend a long period of time decoding a written text. The task is most effective when the candidate is asked to comment on particular trends shown in a graph, or to compare and contrast one set of figures with another. Different stimuli can be used to elicit written performance of a number of different language functions such as argumentation, description of a process, comparison and contrast or writing a set of instructions.

Disadvantages

1. Problems have arisen when, through a desire to favour no particular groups of candidates, a test has resorted to extremely specialised areas such as bookbinding or mediaeval helmets for its visual stimuli. Often candidates are unable to cope with the mental challenge of taking this sort of test and give up rather than jump through the intellectual hoops necessary to get into the writing task.

   Problems are always likely to occur when the complexity of the stimulus obstructs the desired result, i.e., one needs to understand a very complex set of instructions and/or visual stimuli to produce a relatively straightforward description of a process or a classification of data.

2. The difficulties generated by these information transfer type tasks may arise through educational or cultural differences in ability to interpret graphs or tables or line drawings.

Summary

Advantages

1. Summary can be a valid test in certain domains, for example, it is very suitable for testing a student's writing ability in terms of the tasks he has to cope with in an academic situation. The writing of reports and essays requires the ability to select relevant facts from a mass of data and to re-combine these in an acceptable form. Summary of the main points of a text in this fashion involves the ability to write a controlled composition containing the essential ideas of a piece of writing and omitting non-essentials.

Disadvantages

1. The problem of the specificity of the text candidates are expected to produce arises in summary tasks as in other controlled writing tasks. There is often a difficulty in selecting appropriate stimulus texts because their subject specificity would create too many problems for non-specialists in the subject and the test might therefore be invalid. One alternative is to choose deliberately obscure texts which in theory favour nobody, to get at underlying abilities. This might bring into play features we do not want to test such as imagination.

If, however, students in the fields of science and engineering have to read 'general' or 'neutral' texts and then summarise using a wide range of non-scientific vocabulary and demonstrating qualities of literary style and imagination there might be serious validity problems for these students. Though a science student may not be able to summarise a piece on why a cat might make a suitable pet for an old lady he might be able to summarise the salient features of a process.

2. The main difficulty with an integrated writing component of this type is making the marking reliable and consistent. To assess students' responses reliably one needs to formulate the main points contained in the extract, construct an adequate mark scheme and standardise markers. Some subjectivity inevitably remains and it is easy to underestimate the difficulty of marking reliably.

The relative merits of impressionistic and analytic approaches to marking for improving the reliability and validity of a writing sub-test are examined below. Little attention is normally accorded to improving the reliability of marking extended writing in the literature and so an attempt has been made to survey the field and bring together what is known about the main approaches to this problem. In terms of the overall structure of this book it occupies a relatively large amount of the discussion on test method but given the crucial importance of this particular skill to students studying through the medium of English the extended treatment is considered worthwhile. The comments made on the marking of writing apply, *mutatis mutandis*, to the assessment of spoken production. In both we have an identifiable product which can be evaluated in terms of previously specified criteria.

4.3.3 Analytical and general impression marking

Comparison of the two approaches

We have discussed how, by controlling the writing tasks in our battery, we might improve their validity and reliability. We concluded that there was a need for 'controlled' writing sub-tests in which the register, context and scope of the writing task were determined for the candidate. This would facilitate marking and allow more reliable comparison across candidates. In this section we examine how the standardised application of impressionistic and analytic approaches to marking might also aid us in our attempt to improve the reliability and validity of our writing sub-tests.

Analytical marking refers to a method whereby each separate criterion in the mark scheme is awarded a separate mark and the final mark is a composite of these individual estimates.

The impression method of marking usually entails two or more markers giving a single mark based on their total impression of the composition as a whole (see Wiseman, 1949; E. Ingram, 1970). Each paper is scored using an agreed scale and an examinee's score is the average of the combined marks. The notion of impression marking specifically excludes any attempt to separate the discrete features of a composition for scoring purposes.

According to Francis (1977), in its purest form, impression marking usually requires each marker to read a sample of scripts, perhaps 10—25 per cent, to establish a standard in his mind and thereafter to read all scripts quickly and allocate each script to a grade or mark range.

Hartog *et al.* (1936) conducted one of the earliest studies into the relative effectiveness of analytical and general impression marking for assessing English composition. They were intent on finding out which method produced the superior results in terms of ability to reduce marker error. Their research found (p. 123) that variation between markers was, to some extent, reduced by the analytic method: 'there are greater discrepancies between marks awarded by impression than between marks awarded by details ... it appears that these discrepancies are entirely due to greater differences in the standards of marking of different examiners when they mark by impression.'

The investigation also demonstrated that a large number of examiners were consistently biased in terms of either leniency or severity in their marking. The evidence they produced of discrepancies in rank order placements was in many ways more serious, since disagreements of this kind are not susceptible to correction in the same way as differences deriving from mark range bias. Both could, however, have been corrected by the provision of a detailed mark scheme and by the efficient standardisation of examiners prior to the marking exercise.

Like Hartog *et al.* (1936), Cast (1939) found the analytical method slightly superior in a single marker system. His criticisms of the impression method were that, though it discriminated more widely among individual candidates, it judged them on more superficial characteristics than the analytic method. However, although the analytical method was considered the more suitable, Cast felt that the results did not provide definitive evidence of the superior reliability of analytical marking and, therefore, refused to advocate the exclusive use of either method.

Cast pointed to important characteristics inherent in the two systems. An important feature of the analytical method to which he drew attention (pp. 263—4) was: 'on averaging their marks for all the questions, the range inevitably shrinks .... This "regression" is the inevitable consequence of all forms of summation of incompletely correlated figures.' In comparison, he noted (p. 263) that impression marking discriminated more widely among individual candidates and that the range of marks awarded by different examiners to the same script tended to be unusually wide.

Cast (p. 264) also noted the tendency of impression marking:

> to seize on a few salient or superficial points — errors of spelling, grammar or fact, perhaps — and weight those out of all proportion to the rest: on the other hand, the analytic methods, by dealing with numerous isolated and possible inessential points, may overlook certain general qualities that characterize the essays as a whole.

Francis (1977) also pointed out that a great danger of impression marking a piece of writing is that impression of the quality as a whole will be influenced by just one or two aspects of the work. He argues that the prejudices and biases of the marker may play a greater part in determining the mark than in the analytical scheme.

Multiple marking

Wiseman (1949) investigated the possibilities of improving assessment by summing the multiple marks of four independent, unstandardised markers, using a rapid impression method. He found that multiple marking by impression method improved reliability and was much quicker than comparable analytic procedures. He (p. 205) estimated that if the average inter-correlation of a group of four impression markers was as low as 0.6 with each other: 'the estimate of the probable correlation of averaged marks with "true" marks is 0.92. This is very much higher than we could expect from *one* analytic marker.'

Wiseman (p. 208) took pains to stress that: 'The efficiency of markers should be judged primarily by their self-consistency.' He pointed out (p. 204) that the consistency coefficient obtained by a pure mark, re-mark correlation (intra-marker reliability), using the same marking method on both occasions: 'is the one single measure which is quite clearly a true consistency, and one which is closest allied to the normal concept of test reliability.' By using a system of multiple marking based on this principle of self consistency he was able to achieve very high levels of reliability.

The work of Coffman and Kurfman (1968) and Wood and Wilson (1974) similarly drew attention to the problem of the instability of examiner marking behaviour. They produced evidence that marking behaviour does not remain stable during the whole marking period, when a large number of scripts are involved (see Edgeworth, 1888). They argued for subjecting each script to more than one judgement, which might help to neutralise the effects of inconsistent marking behaviour over a protracted period of assessment.

Though some doubt has been expressed in the past (see Edgeworth, 1888) about the expediency of having more than one marker, more recently Britton (1963), Britton *et al.* (1966), Head (1966), Lucas (1971) and Wood and Quinn (1976) all found that multiple marking improved the reliability of marking English essays.

Britton *et al.* (1966), in an experiment designed to devise a more reliable marking apparatus for use by examining boards, compared experimental multiple marking with the single marking carried out by a GCE examining board. They found (p. 21): 'The figures clearly indicate that in this case marking by individual examiners with very careful briefing and elaborate arrangements for moderation was in fact significantly less reliable than a multiple mark.' When the official marking and multiple marking were correlated with external criteria of coursework produced by candidates throughout the year, multiple marking was found to correspond more closely.

Head (1966) conducted an experiment to discover whether the added impression marks of two examiners would be more reliable than individual examiners. He found (p. 71): 'The raising of the coefficient from 0.64 for single mark correlations to 0.84 for paired mark correlations shows clearly that the added marks were more reliable.'

Lucas (1971) found that despite using somewhat inconsistent markers (mean mark/remark correlation only 0.65) multiple marking by impression increased the reliability of the mark awarded significantly. The greatest increase in reliability occurred in the change from one to two markers.

Wood and Quinn (1976) using 'O' level English Language essay and summary questions found that impression marking by pairs of markers was more reliable than a single marking. They suggested, however, that there is no more to be gained in reliability from a single analytic marking than from a single impression marking. The real improvement is in double marking.

As regards the advantages of impression as against analytic marking though, there is evidence which indicates that multiple impression marking is not necessarily superior to multiple analytic marking. Penfold (1956) compared impression marking with analytic marking and found the latter much more effective in reducing inter-marker variance than the impression scheme. R.B. Morrison (1968) found that using impression marking did not produce more reliable marks than the standard analytical marking procedures employed by the Examining Board at the time. R.B. Morrison's findings (1968) were confirmed by a similar study he conducted a year later (R.B. Morrison, 1969).

In many of the studies we have examined there often seems to be an undisputed belief that work marked independently by two different markers, with their marks being averaged, is a more reliable estimate than if it were marked by a single marker. This general viewpoint needs qualifying though, for as was noted by Coffman and Kurfman (1968), Wiseman (1949) and Wood and Wilson (1974) in the discussion above, it is dependent on the markers being equally consistent in their own individual assessments for the duration of the marking period. If this is not the case the reliability of the more consistent marker on his own might in fact be superior to the combined reliability estimate for two markers who exhibit unequal consistencies.

These provisos must be borne in mind in considering the potential value of a double marking system. With an adequate marking scheme and sufficient standardisation of examiners, however, a high standard of inter-marker and intra-marker reliability should be feasible and the advantages of a double as against a single marker system would obtain.

Logistical considerations (time, money, computing, personnel) affecting multiple marking have, however, led to a widespread reluctance especially among examining boards to adopt it in large scale marking operations (see Penfold, 1956). A serious problem with multiple marking is that examiners sometimes find it difficult to avoid annotating a script to help them form their impression. If this script is to be remarked then either the second examiner approaches it in a dissimilar state to the first, the marks have to be tediously removed, or multiple copies of the script need to be made. In addition, practical difficulties in getting results out in a reasonable period after the conduct of an examination and the cost effectiveness of the procedure have led examining boards to employ single markers for all their examinations and this situation is not likely to change easily.

Holistic scoring

Jacobs *et al*. (1981) offer a different perspective on the various approaches to composition evaluation. They made a primary distinction between holistic scoring and frequency-count marking as against the rather overlapping division into impression and analytic marking used by the body of researchers referred to above. It was based on a classification by Cooper (1977). Jacobs *et al*. (p. 29) described the division as follows: ' "Holistic" in Cooper's terms means "any procedure which stops short of *enumerating* linguistic, rhetorical, or informational features of a piece of writing".'

In holistic evaluations, markers base their judgements on their impression of the whole composition: in frequency-count marking (see Steel and Talman, 1936), markers total or enumerate certain elements in the composition such as: cohesive devices, misspelled words, misplaced commas, or sentence errors. Jacobs *et al.* argue that the latter method is highly objective and, therefore, also highly reliable. Not so certain is its validity because a composition evaluated by a frequency-count method has been judged not for its communicative effect, but for its number or kinds of elements.

Holistic evaluation would appear to be more subjective as it depends on the impressions formed by the markers. Jacobs *et al.* (p. 29) point out though:

> In spite of (or perhaps because of) this subjectivity, holistic evaluation has been shown capable of producing highly reliable assessments. Most of the studies cited ... were, in fact, based on holistic evaluation of one type or another and all of those studies obtained reader reliabilities in the mid-to-high eighties or nineties. Intuitively it would seem that composition scores based on holistic responses from readers who attend to the writer's message must be more valid than those based on frequency-count methods, which at best pay only lip service to the writer's meaning and ideas. As Cooper (1977) puts it, 'holistic evaluation by a human respondent gets us closer to what is essential in communication than frequency-counts do'.

Holistic evaluation is obviously to be preferred where the primary concern is with evaluating the communicative effectiveness of candidates' writing. This was the case in the TEEP project (see Weir, 1983a and Appendix I) where the preference was for an analytic, holistic marking scheme over an impressionistic one, favouring an explicit rather than implicit list of features or qualities to guide judgements.

It was felt strongly that too little attention had been paid in the past to the actual criteria to be applied, implicitly or explicitly, to samples of written production. Even in the analytic schemes referred to in the studies above, there is too much room for idiosyncratic interpretation of what constitutes the criterion that is being applied to a script. The application of clear, appropriate criteria was felt to be important.

Chaplen (1970a) had suggested that more reliable results might be obtained from the impression method of marking if the scale employed was one in which each grade was equated with a distinct level of achievement which was closely described. This was the approach initially adopted by the British Council in the ELTS testing system. It may be described as an impression based banding system. An example of such a banded mark scheme can be found in B.J. Carroll (1980b, p. 136).

Carroll's approach is fine in conception as it allows a more detailed description to be presented to institutions. The problem is that, as with Chaplen's (1970a) band system, it fails in practice because it does not cater for learners whose performance levels vary in terms of different criteria. A candidate may be a band 7 in terms of 'fluency', but a band 5 in terms of 'accuracy'. This leaves aside other trenchant criticisms we might have, such as the vagueness of such descriptions as 'authoritative writing', 'good style', 'fluency', etc.

This problem of collapsing criteria is avoided by a more 'analytic' mark scheme, whereby a level is recorded in respect of each criterion and to a certain extent one of the most integrative of measures is brought back somewhat to a discrete point position. This method had the added advantage in that it would lend itself more readily to full profile reporting and could perform a certain diagnostic role in delineating students' strengths and weaknesses in written production.

Additionally an analytic mark scheme is seen as a far more useful tool for the training and standardisation of new examiners. Francis (1977) pointed out that, by employing an analytic scheme, examining bodies can better train and standardise new markers to the criteria of assessment. A measure of agreement about what each criterion means can be established and subsequently markers can be standardised to what constitutes a different level within each of these criteria. Analytic schemes have been found to be particularly useful with markers who are relatively inexperienced. The data reported by Adams (1981) and Murphy (1982) are consistent with this view.

Analytic mark schemes are devised in an attempt to make the assessment more objective, insofar as they encourage examiners to be more explicit about their impressions. Although one of these criteria may take account of the relevance and adequacy of the actual content of the essays, they are normally concerned with describing the qualities which an essay is expected to exhibit. Brooks (1980) pointed out that the qualities assessed by analytical mark schemes in the past were often extremely elusive. She cited as examples the qualities 'gusto' and 'shapeliness of rhythm' outlined in the *Schools Council Working Paper — Monitoring Grade Standards in English*, as being particularly nebulous and inaccessible to assessment. Thus, although analytic schemes may facilitate agreement amongst examiners as to the precise range of qualities that are to be evaluated in any essay, the actual amount of subjectivity involved in the assessment in many schemes may be reduced very little because of lack of explicitness with regard to the applicable criteria, or through the use of vague criteria.

Establishing appropriate criteria for assessing written production: the test in English for educational purposes (TEEP) experience

The failings of analytic mark schemes in the past have been in the choice and delineation of appropriate criteria for a given situation. In the design work for the TEEP test (see Weir, 1983a and Appendix I) it was felt that the assessment of samples of written performance should be based on appropriate, behaviourally described, analytic criteria, graded according to different levels of performance. The criteria needed to be comprehensive and based on empirical job sample evidence.

The data informing the selection of criteria of assessment came from a survey carried out on language teachers in ARELS schools, and more particularly from the returns to that part of a national questionnaire to academic staff in the United Kingdom which had requested an estimation of the relative importance of the different criteria they employed in assessing the written work of their students. Empirical evidence was gathered from 560 lecturers to help decide upon those criteria which could be used for assessing the types of written information transfer exercises that occur in an academic context.

As a result of the investigation the criteria of relevance and adequacy, compositional organisation, cohesion, referential adequacy, grammatical accuracy, spelling and punctuation were seen as the most suitable for assessing writing tasks. From the returns to the staff questionnaire it appeared there was a need for evaluation procedures that would assess students, particularly in relation to their communicative effectiveness and in such a way that a profile containing a coarse diagnosis of candidates' strengths and weaknesses could be made available.

To apply these 'valid' criteria reliably an attempt was made to construct an analytic marking scheme in which each of the criteria is sub-divided into four behavioural levels on a scale of 0−3 (see Table below). A level 3 corresponds to a base line of minimal competence. At this level it was felt that a student was likely to have very few problems in coping with the writing tasks demanded of him by his course in respect of this criterion. At a level 2 a limited number of problems arise in relation to the criterion and remedial help would be advisable. A level 1 would indicate that a lot of help is necessary with respect to this particular criterion. A level 0 indicates almost total incompetence in respect of the criterion in question.

TEEP Attribute Writing Scales

A. *Relevance and adequacy of content*

0. The answer bears almost no relation to the task set. Totally inadequate answer.

1. Answer of limited relevance to the task set. Possibly major gaps in treatment of topic and/or pointless repetition.

2. For the most part answers the tasks set, though there may be some gaps or redundant information.

3. Relevant and adequate answer to the task set.

B. *Compositional Organisation*

0. No apparent organisation of content.

1. Very little organisation of content. Underlying structure not sufficiently apparent.

2. Some organisational skills in evidence, but not adequately controlled.

3. Overall shape and internal pattern clear. Organisational skills adequately controlled.

C. *Cohesion*

0. Cohesion almost totally absent. Writing so fragmentary that comprehension of the intended communication is virtually impossible.

1. Unsatisfactory cohesion may cause difficulty in comprehension of most of the intended communication.

2. For the most part satisfactory cohesion though occasional deficiencies may mean that certain parts of the communication are not always effective.

3. Satisfactory use of cohesion resulting in effective communication.

D. *Adequacy of vocabulary for purpose*

0. Vocabulary inadequate even for the most basic parts of the intended communication.

1. Frequent inadequacies in vocabulary for the task. Perhaps frequent lexical inappropriacies and/or repetition.

2. Some inadequacies in vocabulary for the task. Perhaps some lexical inappropriacies and/or circumlocution.

3. Almost no inadequacies in vocabulary for the task. Only rare inappropriacies and/or circumlocution.

E. *Grammar*

0. Almost all grammatical patterns inaccurate.

1. Frequent grammatical inaccuracies.

2. Some grammatical inaccuracies.

3. Almost no grammatical inaccuracies.

F. *Mechanical accuracy I (punctuation)*

0. Ignorance of conventions of punctuation.

1. Low standard of accuracy in punctuation.

2. Some inaccuracies in punctuation.

3. Almost no inaccuracies in punctuation.

G. *Mechanical accuracy II (spelling)*

0. Almost all spelling inaccurate.

1. Low standard of accuracy in spelling.

2. Some inaccuracies in spelling.

3. Almost no inaccuracies in spelling.

The set of criteria developed for TEEP and the behavioural descriptions of the levels within each of them are not seen as irrevocable, but they represent the outcome of a long process of practical trialling and revision. In all, the behavioural descriptions of the levels within the criteria went through five major revisions.

The nature of the problems encountered in the evolution of the criteria provide useful background for the development of similar schemes. The first problem in earlier versions of these assessment criteria was that in some of the criteria an attempt was made to assess two things, namely communicative effectiveness and degrees of accuracy. As a result great difficulty was encountered in attempting to apply the criteria reliably. It was necessary to refine the criteria so that the first four related to communicative effectiveness and the latter three to accuracy. It may well be that the latter three criteria contribute to communicative effectiveness or lack of it, but attempts to incorporate some indication of this into these criteria proved unworkable.

Secondly distinctions between each of the four levels were only gradually achieved and it was also necessary to try and establish roughly equivalent level distinctions across the criteria. Great problems were experienced in the trial assessments in gaining agreement as to what was meant by certain of the descriptions of levels within the criteria. Most sources of confusion were gradually eliminated and this seemed inevitably to result in a much simplified scale for these descriptions of level particularly in the accuracy criteria E–G.

4.3.4 Further considerations in designing writing tasks for inclusion in a test battery

Number of writing tasks

In the discussion of writing so far the concern has been with how marker reliability might be achieved. There are, however, other factors contributing to the reliability of a test which merit attention. Firstly, the number of samples of a student's work that are taken can help control the variation in performance that might occur from task to task.

Both reliability and validity have been found to be increased by sampling more than one composition from each candidate. Finlayson (1951, p. 132) found that: 'the performance of a child in one essay is not representative of his ability to write essays in general.' The research of Vernon and Milligan (1954, p. 69) also threw: 'very grave doubt on the common practice . . . of trying to assess English ability in general from a single essay marked by a single examiner.'

Ebel (1972) showed that the more samples there were of a student's writing in a test, the more reliable the result. Ebel outlined how a test score comprised two elements: the true score and the error measurement. He showed (pp. 250–1) that: 'the contribution (i.e. variability) of the true component in the total score is proportional to the number of elements (items) comprising it . . . increasing test length increases the true score variance more rapidly than it increases the error variance.' In other words, reliability of a test score tends to increase as the number of items in the test is increased (see Willmott and Nuttal, 1975).

Murphy (1978) also found that an important factor in determining the varying reliability of the eight GCE examinations under review was:

> the number of marks for individual parts contributing to the final examination marks. This effect of increasing reliability, by having more parts of an examination is well demonstrated by the case of English 'A' level. This observation is consistent with the established principle that combinations of unreliable measurements are more reliable than the individual measurements themselves.

Jacobs *et al.* (1981, p. 15) recommended that:

> In general, it is advisable to obtain at least two, if not more, compositions from each student.

This helps ensure that the test provides a representative sampling of a writer's ability, by reducing to some extent the effects of variation in an individual's performance from topic to topic or from one test period to another . . . . Our experience and that of others suggests that two carefully formulated writing tasks are probably sufficient for most testing situations.

Obviously the more samples of students' writing that are taken the better this will be for reliability and validity purposes, provided each sample gives a reasonable estimate of the ability.

Question choice

As regards selection of topic(s) it is necessary to ensure that students are able to write something on the topic(s) they are presented with. Whether this means allowing a choice of topics is an important decision that has to be made, for it too could affect the reliability of the test.

Jacobs *et al.* (1981, p. 1) advised:

> For large-scale evaluations, it is generally advisable for all students to write on the same topics because allowing a choice of topics introduces too much uncontrolled variance into the test — i.e., are *observed* differences in scores due to *real* differences in writing proficiency or to the different topics? There is no completely reliable basis for comparison of scores on a test unless all of the students have performed the same writing task(s); moreover, reader consistency or reliability in evaluating the test may be reduced if all of the papers read at a single scoring session are not on the same topic.

Heaton (1975) suggested that offering a choice means, in addition, that some students may waste time trying to select a topic from several given alternatives. Where tests are to be conducted under timed conditions, forcing all students to write on the same topic might also be an advantage for indecisive candidates. Jacobs *et al.* (1981, p. 17) concluded:

> In view of the problems associated with offering a choice of topics, the best alternative, unless skill in choosing a topic is among the test objectives, would seem to be to require all students to write on the same topic, but to provide them more than one opportunity to write.

By basing writing tasks on written and/or spoken text supplied to the candidates or on non-verbal stimuli, it is possible to ensure that in terms of subject knowledge all start equally, at least in terms of the information available to them. All are required to write on the same topic, but they would write on a variety of topics.

Amount of time allowed for each writing task: the ramifications of time limits

Jacobs *et al.* (1981, p. 17) pointed to a need to give due consideration to the purpose of the writing test:

> Is the test a direct outgrowth of certain learning activities, including perhaps, advance preparation for the test composition (reading certain books or conducting research on an assigned topic, practising with a similar topic or the same mode in class and so forth), or is it an impromptu test, which focuses almost entirely on the composing *product*, rather than the composing *process*?

About the only real life parallel of the closely-timed test is that students may encounter examination essays in their academic courses. If we were to replicate reality more closely the test tasks would not be timed at all and students would be allowed maximum opportunity and access to resources for demonstrating their abilities with regard to this construct. Considerations such as time constraints, reliability and test security requirements make longer, process-oriented tests impractical for most testing of this kind.

Jacobs *et al.* (1981, p. 17) pointed to some of the ramifications of this distinction:

> a closely-timed impromptu test can hardly begin to tap the writer's resources in the whole composing process, other than to require that all of the process skills be compressed into a speeded time frame, with the result resembling only vaguely what writers usually do in processing written discourse. It is important to remember this serious limitation of a timed, impromptu test.

As regards an appropriate time for completion of product-oriented writing tasks in an actual examination setting, Jacobs *et al.* (1981, p. 18) argued:

> A composition test given in conjunction with a battery of other measures must of necessity be limited in time if the total test time is to be practical and not introduce too much variance due to fatigue in the examinees .... . We have used this thirty-minute time limit for composition tests given as part of the Michigan Test and believe this time allowance probably provides most students enough time to produce an adequate sample of their writing ability.

They found in their research (p. 19) that: 'with a thirty-minute composition test ... students at all but the most basic level of proficiency can generally write about a page or more.'

4.3.5 *Conclusion*

The writing component of any test should concentrate on controlled writing tasks where features of audience, medium, setting and purpose can be more clearly specified. Attention needs to be paid to the development of adequate and appropriate scoring criteria and examiners trained and standardised in the use of these.

4.4 Testing speaking

Testing speaking ability offers plenty of scope for meeting the criteria for communicative testing, namely that: tasks developed within this paradigm should be purposive, interesting and motivating, with a positive washback effect on teaching that precedes the test; interaction should be a key feature; there should be a degree of intersubjectivity among participants; the output should be to a certain extent unpredictable; a realistic context should be provided and processing should be done in real time. Perhaps more than in any other skill there is the possibility of building into a test a number of the dynamic characteristics of actual communication (see Section 3.1 above).

Set against this are the enormous practical constraints on the large-scale testing of spoken language proficiency, e.g., the administrative costs and difficulties, and the resources necessary for standardising and paying a large number of examiners. Most GCE Examining Boards in England were said to lose money on every candidate who sits an 'O' level language examination in which there is an oral component.

The problems of assessing speech reliably are even greater than those for assessing writing because the interaction, unless captured on tape or video, is fleeting and cannot be checked later. The essential task for the test designer is to establish clearly what activities the candidate is expected to perform, how far the dynamic communicative characteristics associated with these activities can be incorporated into the test, and what the task dimensions will be in terms of the complexity, size, referential and functional range of the discourse to be processed or produced.

Having established what it is that needs to be tested there is available a range of formats of varying degrees of directness. It embraces more direct types such as the face to face interview and the more indirect multiple choice, pencil and paper tests of speaking ability which can be scored by computer. What follows is a brief review of some of the more useful and potentially valid formats for testing speaking ability.

4.4.1 *Verbal essay*

The candidate is asked to speak (sometimes directly into a tape recorder) for three minutes on either one or more specified general topics.

Advantages

1. The candidate has to speak at length which enables a wide range of criteria including fluency to be applied to the output. More discrete short questions or posited situations to which the student has to respond often severely limit the range of criteria that are applicable.

Disadvantages

1. The problems associated with the free uncontrolled writing task above apply equally to this type of oral task. The topic specified may not be of interest to the candidate and it is not something we are normally asked to do extempore in real life. At the very least a period is normally given for preparation. Where there is a choice of topic it is difficult to compare performances.

2. The more open-ended the topic, the more successful performance in it might be dependent on background or cultural knowledge and draw upon factors such as imagination or creativity. The greater the deviation of responses from what is expected in terms of content, the more difficult it might be to maintain reliability in assessment.

3. The use of tape recorders for the conduct of this task might be stressful to some candidates. It is not possible to set the candidates at their ease as easily as it is in, say, an interview.

4.4.2 Oral presentation

The candidate is expected to give a short talk on a topic which he has either been asked to prepare beforehand or has been informed of shortly before the test. This is different from the 'Spoken Essay' described above in so far as the candidate is allowed to prepare for the task.

Advantages

1. It is often very effective to get the candidate to talk about himself. In the TEEP Test (an oral test carried out on tape in a language laboratory) this was intended as a warm up exercise, but it was found that the one minute given to the candidate to talk about *specified* features of his personal life provided a good overall indicator of his spoken language proficiency in terms of the criteria used in assessing all the other tasks. What is important in assessing spoken production is eliciting a sufficient sample of a candidate's speech for sensible assessments to be made. This is one technique which permits of this.

2. By integrating the activity with previously heard or previously read texts the oral task can be made to equate realistically with real life tasks that the candidate might have to perform in the target situation.

Disadvantages

1. If the candidate knows the topic well in advance there is a danger that he can learn it by heart. If little time is given for preparation then one faces the problem that what is being tested may be knowledge rather than linguistic ability. If the task is integrated say with a prior reading passage to ensure that all candidates have a common set of information available to them then one is faced with the problem of reading possibly interfering with the measurement.

2. The multiplicity of interpretations of broad topics may create problems in assessment.

4.4.3 The free interview

In this type of interview the conversation unfolds in an unstructured fashion and no set of procedures is laid down in advance.

Advantages

1. Because of its face and content validity in particular, the interview is a popular means of testing the oral skills of candidates.

2. Free interviews are like extended conversations and the direction is allowed to unfold as the interview takes place. The discourse might seem to approximate more closely to the normal pattern of informal social interaction in real life where no carefully formulated agenda is apparent.

Disadvantages

1. As there are no set procedures for eliciting language the performances are likely to vary from event to event not least because different topics may be broached and differences may occur in the way the interview is conducted.

2. The procedure is time consuming and difficult to administer if there are large numbers of candidates.

4.4.4   The controlled interview

In this procedure there are normally a set of procedures determined in advance for eliciting performance. The FSI interview is close to this model (see Adams and Frith, 1979 and Wilds, 1975).

Advantages

1. There is a greater possiblity in this approach of candidates being asked the same questions and thus it is easier to make comparisons across performances.

2. The procedure has a higher degree of content and face validity than most other techniques apart from the role play and information gap exercises in the UCLES/RSA Certificates in Communicative Skills in English (see Appendix III).

3. It has been shown elsewhere that with sufficient training and standardisation of examiners to the procedures and scales employed, reasonable reliability figures can be reached with this technique. Clark and Swinton (1979) report average intra-rater reliabilities of 0.867 and inter-rater reliability at 0.75 for FSI type interviews.

4. A particularly effective oral interview can occur when the candidate is interviewed and assessed by both a language and a subject specialist who have been standardised to agreed criteria. The procedures followed in the General Medical Council's PLAB oral interview which assesses both medical knowledge and spoken English merit consideration in this respect.

Disadvantages

1. One of the drawbacks of the interview is that it cannot cover the range of situations candidates might find themselves in even where the target level performance is circumscribed as in the case of the FSI. In interviews it is difficult to replicate all the features of real life communication such as motivation, purpose and role appropriacy.

2. Even when the procedures for eliciting performance are specified in advance there is still no guarantee that candidates will be asked the same questions in the same manner, even by the same examiner.

4.4.5 Information transfer: description of a picture sequence

The candidate sees a panel of pictures depicting a chronologically ordered sequence of events and has to tell the story in the past tense. Time is allowed at the beginning for the candidate to study the pictures.

Advantages

1. The task required of the candidates is clear. It does not require them to read or listen and thereby avoids the criticism of contamination of measurement provided the pictures are not culturally or educationally biased.

2. It can be an efficient procedure and one of the few available to get the candidate to provide an extended sample of connected speech which allows the application of a wide range of criteria in assessment. It is also useful for eliciting the candidate's ability to use particular grammatical forms such as the past tense for reporting.

3. Because all candidates are constrained by common information provided by pictures or drawings it allows a comparison of candidates which is relatively untainted by background or cultural knowledge given that the drawings themselves are culture free.

4. The value of the technique is dependent on the pictures being clear and unambiguous and free from cultural or educational bias. The technique is straightforward and much favoured by school examination boards in Britain. In the study of suitable formats for a spoken component for TOEFL (Clark and Swinton, 1979) this proved to be one of the most effective formats in the experimental tests.

Disadvantages

1. The authenticity of this task is limited though it could be said to represent the situation of having to describe something which has happened. This may well be an important function in some occupations.

2. It tells us very little, however, about the candidate's ability to interact orally.

3. If the quality of the pictures is in any way deficient then the candidate may not have the opportunity of demonstrating his best performance. Differences in interpretation might also introduce unreliability into the marking.

4.4.6 Information transfer: questions on a single picture

The examiner asks the candidate a number of questions about the content of a picture which he has had time to study. The questions may be extended to embrace the thoughts and attitudes of people in the picture and to discuss future developments arising out of what is depicted.

Advantages

1. There may be considerable benefit in investigating this technique, which already performs a valuable role in the oral component of the PLAB English test for overseas doctors. In PLAB candidates are shown slides, X-rays, pictures of medical conditions, ECG printouts, etc., and are asked to comment on them as well as answering specific questions relating to them. The task could be useful for testing other groups where relevant pictorial material could be developed.

Disadvantages

1. The candidate is cast in the sole role of respondent and is denied the opportunity to ask questions.

2. The pictures need to be clear and unequivocal for the reasons stated above in discussion of a sequence of pictures. If a large number of candidates are to be examined over several days then the question of test security arises if the same pictures are to be employed. If different pictures are to be used the issue of comparability must be faced.

4.4.7 Interaction tasks

Information gap student–student

In these tasks students normally work in pairs and each is given only part of the information necesary for completion of the task. They have to complete the task by getting missing information from each other. Candidates have to communicate to fill in an information gap in a meaningful situation.

The UCLES/RSA Certificates in Communicative Skills in English have particularly realistic examples of this (see Appendix III). As a development from this interaction an interlocutor appears after the discussion and the candidates might, for example, have to report on decisions taken and explain and justify their decisions.

Advantages

1. There can be few test tasks which represent the act of communication better than this as it fulfils most of the criteria laid down by Morrow (1979) for what makes a test communicative, e.g., it should be purposeful, contextualised and interactive. The candidates should be free to choose their partners so that they are interacting with somebody they know and feel happy communicating with.

2. As a normal feature of the interaction they can use question forms, elicit information, make requests, ask for clarification and paraphrase in order to succeed in the task.

3. The task is highly interactive and as such comes much closer than most other tasks in this section to representing real communication. It recognises the unpredictability of communicative situations and demands an ability to generate original sentences and not simply an ability to repeat rehearsed phrases.

Disadvantages

1. There is a problem if one of the participants dominates the interaction as the other candidate may have a more limited opportunity to demonstrate communicative potential.

2. Similarly if there is a large difference in proficiency between the two this may influence performance and the judgements made on it.

3. There is also a problem if one of the candidates is more interested in the topic or the task as the interaction may become one sided as a result.

4. Candidates are being assessed on their performance in a single situation and extrapolations are made about their ability to perform in other situations from this.

5. There are also practical constraints such as the time available, the difficulties of administration and the maintenance of test security.

Information gap student−examiner

To avoid the possibility of an imbalance in candidates' contributions to the interaction some boards have the examiner as one of the participants or employ a common interlocutor, e.g., a teacher with whom candidates would feel comfortable.

To examine candidates separately they can be given a diagram, a set of notes, etc., from which information is missing and their task is to request the missing information from the examiner.

Advantages

1. The main advantage is that there is a stronger chance that the interlocutor will react in a similar manner with all candidates allowing a more equitable comparison of their performance.

Disadvantages

1. Interacting with a teacher, let alone an examiner, is often a more daunting task for the candidate than interacting with his peers.

2. There is some evidence that where the examiner is a participant in the interaction, he is sometimes inadvertently assessing his own performance in addition to that of the candidate (Fisher 1979).

4.4.8 *Role play*

A number of examining boards, for example the AEB and UCLES/RSA, include role play situations where the candidate is expected to play one of the roles in an interaction which might be reasonably expected of him in the real world. The interaction can take place between two students or, as in the GCE mould, the examiner normally plays one of the parts. The disadvantage of the latter is that it is difficult to make an assessment at the same time as taking part in the interaction. (The same is of course true for all face to face tests.) As in the information gap exercise involving teacher as interlocutor and examiner there is a danger that the mark awarded will reflect the latter's view of his own performance as well as of the student's.

Advantages

1. The technique can be valid in both face and content terms for a wide variety of situations and the UCLES/RSA experience suggests that it is a practical and potentially a highly valid and reliable means of assessing a candidate's ability to participate effectively in oral interaction.

Disadvantages

1. There is a danger that the histrionic abilities of some candidates may weigh in their favour at the expense of the more introverted. There is also the danger in all oral interactions that a candidate cannot think what to say. The question of role familiarity arises in this technique in the sense that some candidates may not know what it is normal to do in certain situations. Another problem is that candidates often use the language of reporting and say what they would say rather than directly assuming the role.

2. Practical constraints operate here as well, especially in large scale testing operations. If it is necessary to use different role plays then great care needs to be taken to ensure that they are placing equal demands on candidates.

4.4.9   *The training and standardisation of oral examiners*

The relationship between a task and the criteria that can be applied to the product it results in is an essential factor in taking decisions on what to include in a test of spoken or written production. Tasks can not be considered separately from the criteria that might be applied to the performances they result in. Having established suitable tasks and appropriate assessment criteria to accompany them, consideration needs to be given as to how best to apply the criteria to the elicited samples of performance.

In Section 4.3.3 the advantages of analytical as against impressionistic approaches to assessment of written production were examined. The comments made there in relation to the need to establish clear criteria for assessment and to standardise examiners to these criteria apply *mutatis mutandis* to the assessment of oral ability.

The assessment of spoken language is potentially more problematic, though, given that no recording of the performance is usually made. Whereas in writing the script can be reconsidered as often as is necessary, assessments have to be made in oral tests either while the performance is being elicited or shortly afterwards. If the examiner is also an interlocutor then the problems are further compounded.

In oral testing, as in the assessment of written production, there is a need for explicit, comprehensive marking schemes, close moderation of test tasks and mark schemes, and rigorous training and standardisation of markers in order to boost test reliability. These aspects of examining will be briefly discussed below. Though made in the context of oral testing, they apply equally to the testing of the other skills.

Marking schemes

Murphy (1979, p. 19) outlined the nature of the marking scheme demanded by the Associated Examining Board: 'A marking scheme is a comprehensive document indicating the explicit criteria against which candidates' answers will be judged: it enables the examiner to relate particular marks to answers of specified quality.'

In assessing the productive skills it is necessary to provide comprehensive descriptions of levels of performance to aid the examiners in making necessarily subjective judgements about the work of candidates' answers (see Appendix II for an example of such performance descriptors). Murphy (1979, p. 14) described the purpose of the marking scheme as follows:

1. To assist the Chief Examiner and those who will moderate the paper to check the content validity of the tasks which are being set.

2. To help the moderators to check that the demands made in the examination are appropriate and in accordance with stated aims and objectives.

3. To ensure that, where there is more than one examiner, each examiner marks in exactly the same way, awarding equal marks for equal levels of performance.

4. To ensure that each examiner marks consistently throughout the marking period.

The moderation of question papers and mark schemes

In assessing both speaking and writing it is essential that tasks and marking schemes are subjected to a rigorous process of moderation before they become operations. Again using Murphy as the informing source, examples of questions which might be asked of the tasks candidates are expected to perform are listed below:

1. Are the tasks set at an appropriate level of difficulty?

2. Will the paper discriminate adequately between the performance of candidates at different levels of attainment?

3. Does the test assess the full range of appropriate skills and abilities, as defined by the objectives of the examination?

4. Are the tasks unambiguous, giving a clear indication of what the examiner is asking, so that no candidate may take the task to mean something different?

5. Is there an excessive overlap in enabling skills or communicative tasks being assessed in different parts of the test?

6. Can the tasks be satisfactorily answered in the time allowed?

In addition the moderating panel might consider the format and the layout of the question papers. This is important because a badly laid out question paper could be the cause of considerable problems for both candidates and examiners. Instructions to candidates need to be as clear and as concise as possible.

At the same time as the tasks are moderated the panel should consider the appropriateness of the marking scheme. Murphy (1979) again is a valuable informing source for drawing up a list of questions which might be asked of the marking scheme by a moderating panel. The following are examples of the types of questions moderators might address themselves to:

1. Does the mark scheme anticipate responses of a kind that candidates are likely to make?

2. Are the marks allocated to each task commensurate with the demands that task makes on the candidate?

3. Does the mark scheme indicate clearly the marks to be awarded for different parts of a question or the relative weighting of criteria that might be applicable?

4. Does the mark scheme allow for possible alternative answers?

5. Has the mark scheme reduced to the minimum possible, the amount of computational work which the examiner has to undertake to finalise a mark for a candidate's performance?

6. Does the marking scheme, by specifying performance criteria (see Appendix II), reduce as far as possible the element of subjective judgement that the examiner has to exercise in evaluating candidates' answers?

7. Are the abilities being rewarded those which the tasks are designed to assess?

8. Can the marking schemes be easily interpreted by a number of different examiners in a way which will ensure that all mark to the same standard?

The standardisation of marking

Even if examiners are provided with an ideal marking scheme, there might always be some who do not mark in exactly the way required. The purpose of standardisation procedures is to bring examiners into line, so that candidates' marks are affected as little as possible by the particular examiner who assesses them.

Examiners are normally requested to attend a standardisation meeting prior to commencing marking proper. Here the marking criteria are discussed to ensure the examiners understand the criteria that are to be applied. The marking scheme is examined closely and any difficulties in interpretation are ironed out. At this meeting the examiners have to conduct a number of assessments. In respect of an oral test this might involve listening to and/or watching audio tape or video tape recordings of candidates' performances on the test, at a number of different levels.

The examiners are asked to assess these performances and afterwards these are compared to see if they are applying the same marking standards. The aim is to identify any factors which might lead to unreliability in marking and to try and resolve these at the meeting.

In the case of new examiners there might also be extensive discussion with the chief examiner and his deputies about how to conduct an examination, how to make the candidate feel at ease, how to phrase questions, what questions to ask in an interview situation and how to react to candidates.

After the standardisation procedure examiners are allowed to assess candidates. In tests of writing it is possible to ask for sample scripts to be sent in to be re-marked by the chief examiner so that the process of ensuring reliability can be continued. In oral tests the chief examiner may sometimes sit in unannounced on a number of oral tests, observe how they are conducted and discuss the allocation of marks with the examiner subsequently. They might discuss how improvements could be made either in technique or marking.

Profiling ability in the productive and receptive skills

In terms of the criteria for assessing the productive modes of speaking and writing it seems that we are able to be far more explicit than is possible in the receptive skills. We can develop criteria of assessment, write behavioural descriptions of levels within each of the criteria and then apply these to samples of students' speech and writing. Because of the private, internalised nature of the reading and listening processes it does not seem possible to devise such explicit criteria by which candidates' proficiency in the receptive skills can be judged. Whereas we are able to assess candidates' productive ability directly, we can only take indirect measurements of what we label as listening or reading ability. We also have to make the assumption that the sum of the listening or reading skills being measured is equivalent to the whole of what might be described as proficiency in listening or reading.

Though an attempt can be made to specify what each item is testing in these receptive areas, the candidates' responses can only be judged right or wrong. It does not seem possible to establish levels of attainment on individual receptive skills items, however explicit we can be about what an individual item is testing. Whereas in writing or speaking tests we are presented with something more tangible to make qualitative judgements about, it is more difficult to see at what stage the process might have broken down in items testing the receptive skills or to employ anything other than a dichotomous rating scale. We cannot normally say how near a candidate came to getting an item right in assessment of receptive skills and the more discrete the item the more this must be the case.

Where the intention is to present a profile of proficiency in the macro-skills of reading, listening, speaking and writing, the differences in the way we are able to assess these will obviously affect the manner in which we are able to decide how overall grades are to be awarded in each macro-skill (see Angoff, 1971; Cresswell, 1983; Houston, 1983; Weir, 1983a; and Zieky and Livingston, 1977). The process is likely to be that much easier for the productive skills where explicit criteria can be applied directly to a concrete, integrated product.

4.5 Integrated tests

Relatively little is known about integrated tests, and even less is reported in the literature, with the exceptions of preliminary work in this area by Weir (1983a), Emmings (1986) and Low (1986). Low describes a variety of possible tests along a continuum of directness. At one end there are tests such as TEEP where there is an attempt to include tasks which involve an integration of different macro skills. Weir (1983a) describes the integrated activity in TEEP, where listening and/or reading texts, as well as providing a stimulus for more discrete testing of skills, are also employed as the stimulus material for a writing test (see Appendix I). At the other end of the continuum there are attempts to develop a 'story line' through the whole of the test so that not only are the components of the test related thematically through the content but there is also a development in the content itself throughout the test (see Low, 1986).

These tests are able to tap performance ability more directly by the provision of realistic contexts which simulate target situations more closely. It is argued (see Emmings, 1986) that they offer a better means of assessing the traits underlying language proficiency than is possible if the skills are tested in relative isolation from each other. Low (1986) points to the context effects in real life where the ability to perform for example in conversation 'depends in large measure on the skill with which one picks up information from past discussions and uses it as an aid to formulating new strategy.'

Emmings (1986) investigated the incorporation of contextual developments through integrated testing procedures and compared the reliability and validity of these with more discrete proficiency measures taken from an RSA CUEFL test. While recognising the importance of context for the development of an interaction, he sought to establish whether the enhanced validity of a story line development through sub-tests is negated by the dangers of 'muddied measurement' adversely affecting candidate profiling in an integrated test of this type. He found that:

> in principle, the adoption of clear content criteria can produce a clear reflection of the aims of the test items in the factorial structures and that therefore some indications of testees' abilities to process text can be provided by integrated tests.

He advises caution in employing a purely integrated approach but argues that the findings with regard to validity and reliability were encouraging.

Low (1986) offers a detailed rationale for the use of an integrated approach and makes a number of suggestions for the use of story lines and other developing contexts in tests. He also draws attention to a number of problems involved in the design of integrated tests, such as lower reliability, the possibility of content bias, greater difficulty in design and implementation, and their radical nature as compared to the curricula in operation in certain countries.

Advantages

1. On the grounds of authenticity, or approximations to it, integrated tasks demand consideration. If tests are to simulate reality, as closely as is possible, recognition of the integrated nature of activities in certain contexts is necessary. In academic life, for example, students have to read a variety of texts and process spoken discourse in lectures and seminars in preparation for writing tasks, and work is often discussed with others before a final version is presented for assessment.

2. Increasingly the importance of context in language use is recognised and with it there has been a demand that test tasks should be improved in this respect (see Stansfield, 1986). Low's (1986) advocacy of employing a developing context through the use of a story line across tasks is an attempt to provide for this desire for increased validity.

Disadvantages

1. The question arises as to how integrated a test can ever be; how close can it mirror reality? If Low's (1986) examples of integrated tests are examined carefully, even the most direct of these evidence a good deal of idealisation. The chimera of full authenticity is just that.

2. The dangers of 'muddied measurement' are often referred to in the literature. This relates to a concern about the local independence of items or of tasks within a test battery. The feeling is that performance on one item should not interfere with performance on a subsequent item. In terms of tasks, it is felt, for example, that performance on a writing task should not be dependent on successful performance in coping with prior reading and listening tasks. The profiling of abilities may be problematic if there is difficulty in determining where the process has broken down. If there is a need for separate skills profiling, more discrete test tasks may be required.

3. What is clear is that communicative tests will be more difficult to construct than traditional measures. As well as the need for greater explicitness about what it is that one is trying to test there are serious problems in successfully realising communicative specifications in a test form and in devising suitable assessment procedures. As with all new departures integrated communicative tests are at present difficult to construct, complex to take, difficult to mark and difficult to report results on.

4. Too little is known at present as to whether the advantage of enhanced validity gained by using an integrated format is outweighed by the possible contaminating influence on test scores. It may well be that the latter can be avoided through careful design but at present any claims for integrated tests being the panacea for testing within a communicative paradigm must be tentative. In the customary fashion we can only point to the need for future research to shed light on this.

Chapter Five

Conclusion

For testing within a communicative paradigm there is a need for a priori validation of test tasks at the design stage as well as for a posteriori validation of test results. The concern should be with the construct, content, face and washback validities of tests as well as with their statistical attributes and prognostic value. It is contended that a posteriori validation is a necessary but not a sufficient criterion for testing within this paradigm. A priori validation of test tasks, especially in terms of a concern for content validity, is seen as equally essential if an adequate degree of context is to be built into a test.

In addition it is important that due regard is paid to test efficiency and reliability as both may be more difficult to achieve with communicative tests as compared to the more discrete point tests conceived within earlier paradigms.

Current research suggests that test format may have an undue effect on the measurement of trait. It seems sensible, therefore, to safeguard against possible format effect by including a variety of appropriate testing methods in assessing competence in the various skills.

In the current communicative climate, however, it is axiomatic that the operations performed in test tasks should reflect realistic discourse processing and they should take place under the conditions that might normally prevail in real life in terms of, for example, number of interlocutors, their status and familiarity, a realistic purpose for the task, an appropriate setting, and operation under normal time constraints. The tasks should cover as wide a range as possible of the operations that candidates might be expected to cope with. Efforts should be made to include tasks in each skill area which directly attempt to simulate appropriate real life operations, with contextually appropriate conditions and which can be assessed by relevant target situation criteria.

Performance tasks, such as controlled writing tasks, listening to lectures and note-taking, and face-to-face spoken interaction tasks, are receiving increased attention in the testing literature and, where relevant, they should be developed for inclusion in future tests.

The use of integrated tasks is of considerable interest, and future research needs to look closely at their potential to determine if there is any quantifiable increase or decrease in validity, reliability or efficiency with these tests as against more traditional, indirect, discrete measures of the same constructs.

Considerable attention should also be paid to the development of relevant and adequate scoring criteria and examiners must be trained and standardised in the use of these.

Bibliography

Adams, M.L. and J.R. Frith, (eds.), 1979, *Testing kit in French and Spanish*, Foreign Service Institute, US State Department.

Adams, R., 1981, *The reliability of marking of five June 1980 examinations*, mimeo, Associated Examining Board, Guildford.

Aitken, K., 1979, 'Techniques for assessing listening comprehension in second languages', *Audio-Visual Language Journal* **17/3:** 175–81.

Alderson, J.C., 1978a, *A study of the cloze procedure with native and non-native speakers of English*, PhD thesis, University of Edinburgh.

Alderson, J.C., 1978b, *The effect of certain methodological variables on cloze test performance and its implication for the use of the cloze procedure in EFL testing*, mimeo, Fifth International Congress of Applied Linguistics, Montreal.

Alderson, J.C., 1981a, 'Reaction to the Morrow paper (3)', in Alderson, J.C. and A. Hughes (eds.), 1981: 45–54

Alderson, J.C., 1981b, 'Report of the discussion on communicative language testing', in Alderson, J.C. and A. Hughes (eds.), 1981: 55–65.

Alderson, J.C., 1981c, 'Report of the discussion on testing English for specific purposes', in Alderson, J.C. and A. Hughes (eds.), 1981: 123–34.

Alderson, J.C., 1983, 'The cloze procedure and proficiency in English as a Foreign Language', in Oller, J.W. (ed.), 1983: 205–17.

Alderson, J.C., (ed.), 1985, *Evaluation*, Lancaster practical papers in English language education, vol. 6, London: Pergamon.

Alderson, J.C., 1986a, 'Recent developments in language testing', mimeo, paper delivered at the sixth national symposium on English teaching in Egypt: Testing and Evaluation.

Alderson, J.C., 1986b, 'Innovations in language testing?' in Portal, M. (ed.), (1986): 93–105.

Alderson, J.C., 1988, 'Testing English for specific purposes: How specific can we get?', in Hughes, A. (ed.), 1988.

Alderson, J.C. and A. Hughes (eds.), 1981, *Issues in language testing*, ELT Documents 111, London: The British Council.

Alderson, J.C., K.J. Krankhe, and C.W. Stansfield, 1987, *Reviews of English language proficiency tests*, Washington DC: TESOL.

Alderson, J.C. and A.H. Urquhart, 1985a, 'The effect of students' academic discipline on their performance on ESP reading tests', *Language testing*, **2/2:** 192–204.

Alderson, J.C. and A.H. Urquhart, 1985b, 'This test is unfair: I'm not an economist', in Hauptman, P.C. *et al.* (eds.), 1985: 25–43.

Alexander, L. and M.H. John, 1985, 'Testing oral skills in a FLES short course', *Foreign Language Annuals*, **18:** 235–9.

Allen, D., 1982, *Oxford placement test*, London: Oxford University Press.

Allen, J.P.B. and A. Davies (eds.), 1977, 'Testing and experimental methods', in *The Edinburgh Course in Applied Linguistics 4*, London: Oxford University Press.

Allison, D. and R. Webber, 1984, 'What place for performative tests?' *ELT Journal*, **38/3**: 199–202.

Amato, R., 1979, 'Testing communicative competence: notes on a battery of English language tests for adult students', *Rassenga Italiana dui Linguistica Applicata*, **11**: 151–77.

American Psychological Association, 1974, *Standards for educational and psychological tests and manuals*, American Psychological Association: Washington, DC.

Anastasi, A., 1982, *Psychological testing*, London: Macmillan.

Angelis, P., K. Perkins and B. Pharis, 1984, 'Performance validation of oral interview tests', paper read at the Brussels AILA Congress.

Angoff, W.H., 1971, 'Scales, norms and equivalent scores', in Thorndike, R.L. (ed.) (1971): ch. 15.

Archer, M. and E. Nolan-Woods, 1976, *Practice tests for proficiency*, Middlesex: Nelson.

Aslanian, Y., 1985, 'Investigating the reading problems of ELS students: an alternative', *ELTJ* **39/1**: 20–7.

Associated Examining Board, 1984, *Test in English for educational purposes*, AEB: Aldershot.

Association of Recognised English Language Schools, 1976, 'ARELS and the ARELS oral examination', *Zielsprache Englisch* **1**: 38–9.

Bachman, L.F., 1986, 'The test of English as a Foreign Language as a measure of communicative competence', in Stansfield, C.W. (ed.), (1976): 69–88.

Bachman, L.F., 1989, *Fundamental considerations in testing*, London: Oxford University Press.

Bachman, L.F. and J.L.D. Clark, 1986, 'The measurement of foreign/second language proficiency', paper prepared for the National Language Resource Centre Advisory Committee, USA, unpublished.

Bachman, L.F. and A.S. Palmer, 1980, 'The construct validation of the constructs communicative competence in speaking and communicative competence in reading: a pilot study'. Unpublished discussion papers for the colloquium on the validation of oral proficiency tests at the San Fransciso TESOL Convention.

Bachman, L.F. and A.S. Palmer, 1981a, 'Basic concerns in test validation', in Read, J.A.S. (ed.), 1981a: 41–57.

Bachman, L.F. and A.S. Palmer, 1981b, 'The construct validation of the FSI oral interview', *Language Learning*, **31/1**: 67–86.

Bachman, L.F. and A.S. Palmer, 1982, 'The construct validation of some components of communicative proficiency', *TESOL Quarterly*, **16**: 449–65.

Bachman, L.F. and S. Savignon, 1986, 'The evaluation of communicative language proficiency: a critique of the ACTFL oral interview and suggestions for its revision and development', *Modern Language Journal*, **70**: 380–90.

Bailey, K.M., 1985, 'If I had known then what I know now: performance testing of foreign teaching assistants', in Hauptman, P.C. *et al.* (eds.), 1985: 153–80.

Baillie, R.F., 1981, *Testing oracy in English as a Foreign Language*, MEd, University of Wales.

Barnes, D., 1980, 'Situated speech strategies: aspects of the monitoring of oracy', *Education Review*, **32**: 123–31.

Barnes, D. and J. Seed, 1981, *Scales of approval: an analysis of English examinations at 16 plus*, University of Leeds, School of Education.

Bartz, W.H., 1979, *Testing oral communication in the foreign language classroom*, Arlington, Va.: Center for Applied Linguistics (Language in Education Theory and Practice 2/17).

Beardsmore, H.B., 1974, 'Testing oral fluency', *IRAL*, **12/4**: 317–26.

Bensoussan, M., 1982, 'Testing the test of advanced EFL reading comprehension: to what extent does the difficulty of a multiple-choice comprehension test reflect the difficulty of the text?' *System*, **10/3**: 285–90.

Beretta, A., 1983, 'A comparison of three tests of listening in the context of English for academic purposes', University of Edinburgh MSc Applied Linguistics Assignment.

Berkoff, N.A., 1982, 'Testing oral proficiency — a suggested new approach', *English Teachers' Journal (Israel)*, **27**: 33–6.

Berkoff, N.A., 1985, 'Testing oral proficiency: a new approach', in Lee, Y.P. *et al.* (eds.), 1985: 93—100.

Best, J. and D. Ilyin, 1976, *Structure tests — English language advanced forms 1 and 2*, Rowley, Mass.: Newbury House.

Boniakowska, M.P., 1986, *Test method effect*, MA Project, University of Lancaster.

Bormuth, J.R., 1962, *Cloze tests as measures of readability and comprehension ability*, PhD thesis, University of Indiana.

Bormuth, J.R., 1970, *On the theory of achievement test items*, University of Chicago Press.

Briggs, S. and C. MacDonald, 1978, 'A practical approach to testing, speaking and listening skills', *Forum*, **16:** 8—15.

Brindley, G., 1986, *The assessment of second language proficiency: issues and approaches*, National Curriculum Resource Centre, Adult Migrant Education Program Australia.

Brindley, G., 1989, *Assessing Achievement in the Learner-Centred Curriculum*, National Centre for English Language Teaching and Research, McQuarie University, Sydney, NSW.

British Council, 1979, *Testing communicative competence*, Report on a workshop held at the British Council Centre, Hong Kong.

Britton, J.N., 1963, 'Experimental marking of English compositions written by fifteen year olds', *Educational Review*, **16/1:** 17—23.

Britton, J.N., N.C. Martin, and H. Rosen, 1966, 'Multiple marking of English compositions: an account of an experiment', *Schools Council Examinations Bulletin*, **12**, HMSO.

Brooks, V., 1980, *Improving the reliability of essay marking. A survey of the literature with particular reference to the English language composition*, University of Leicester.

Brown, G., 1977, *Listening to spoken English*, London: Longman.

Brown G., 1982, 'Teaching and assessing spoken language', *TESL Talk*, **13:** 3—13.

Brown, G., A. Anderson, R. Shillcock and G. Yule, 1984, *Teaching talk strategies for production and assessment*, Cambridge University Press.

Brown, J.D., 1979, 'A correlational study of four methods for scoring cloze tests', paper presented at the 1977 TESOL Convention, Boston.

Brumfit, C.J. and K. Johnson (eds.), 1979, *The communicative approach to language teaching*, Oxford: Oxford University Press.

Brutsch, S.M., 1980, 'Convergent/divergent validation of proficiency in oral and written production of French', paper read at San Francisco TESOL Convention.

Bygate, M., 1987, *Speaking*, Oxford: Oxford University Press.

Campbell, D.T. and D.W. Fiske, 1959, 'Convergent and discriminant validation by the multi-trait/multi-method matrix', *Psychological Bulletin*, **56:** 81—105.

Campbell, R. and R. Wales, 1970, 'The study of language acquisition', in Lyons J. (ed.), 1970, *New horizons in linguistics*, Harmondsworth: Penguin, 242—60.

Canale, M., 1981, 'Communication — how to evaluate it', *Bulletin of the Canadian Association of Applied Linguistics*, **3:** 77—94, revised as 'Testing in a Communicative Approach', in G.A. Jarvis (ed.) *1984 Northeast Conference Report*, Middlebury, Vt.: Northeast Conference (1984) 79—92.

Canale, M., 1983, 'On some dimensions of language proficiency', in Oller, J.W. (ed.) 1983: 333—42.

Canale, M., 1988, 'The measurement of communicative competence', *Annual Review of Applied Linguistics*, **8:** 67—84.

Canale, M. and M. Swain, 1980, 'Theoretical basis of communicative approaches to second language teaching and testing', *Applied Linguistics*, **I:** 1—47.

Candlin, C.N., 1986, 'Explaining communicative competence: limits on testability', in Stansfield, C.W. (ed.) (1986): 38—57.

Carroll, B.J., 1980a, 'Measuring the communicative value of an oral performance', unpublished MS.

Carroll, B.J., 1980b, *Testing communicative performance: an interim study*, Oxford: Pergamon.

Carroll, B.J., 1981a, 'The assessment of group oral communication', unpublished MS Notes.

Carroll, B.J., 1981b, 'Specifications for an English language testing service', in Alderson, J.C. and A. Hughes (eds.) 1981: 66—110.

Carroll, B.J., 1983, 'Issues in the testing of language for specific purposes', in Hughes, A. and D. Porter (eds.) 1983, 109–14.

Carroll, B.J., 1985, 'Second language performance testing for university and professional contexts', in Hauptman, P.C. et al. (eds.), 1985: 73–88.

Carroll, B.J. and P.J. Hall, 1985, Make your own language tests, London: Pergamon Press.

Carroll, J.B., 1961, 'Fundamental considerations in testing for English language proficiency of foreign students', in Allen, H.B. and R.A. Campbell (eds.), 1972, Teaching English as a Foreign Language, New York: McGraw-Hill, 313–20.

Cast, B.M.D., 1939, 'The efficiency of different methods of marking English composition', British Journal of Educational Psychology, 9/1: 257–69.

Cast, B.M.D., 1940, 'The efficiency of different methods of marking English composition', British Journal of Educational Psychology, 10/2: 49–60.

Chaplen, E.F., 1970a, The identification of non-native speakers of English likely to under-achieve in university courses through inadequate command of the language, PhD thesis, University of Manchester.

Chaplen, E.F., 1970b, 'Oral examinations, in Centre for Information on Language Testing and Research', Examining Modern Languages, London: CILT and Committee on Research and Development in Modern Languages (CILT Reports and Papers 4): 38–45.

Chaplen, E.F., 1971, 'The reliability of the essay sub-test in a university entrance test in English for non-native speakers of English', in Perren, G.E. and J.C.M. Trim (eds.), 1971, 167–71.

Chaplen, E.F., 1976, Measuring achievement in adult language learning, Committee for out-of-school education and cultural development, Strasbourg.

Clapham, C.M., 1981, 'Reaction to the Carroll paper (1)', in Alderson, J.C. and A. Hughes (eds.), 1981: 111–6.

Clark, J.L.D., 1972, Foreign language testing: theory and practice, Philadelphia, Pa: Center for Curriculum Development.

Clark, J.L.D., 1975, 'Theoretical and technical considerations in oral proficiency testing', in Jones and Spolsky (eds.), 1975, 10–28.

Clark, J.L.D. (ed.), 1978, Direct testing of speaking proficiency: theory and application, Princeton, NJ Education Testing Service.

Clark, J.L.D., 1986, A study of the comparability of speaking proficiency interview ratings across three Government language training agencies, Washington, D.C.: CAL.

Clark, J.L.D. and A.G. Grognet, 1985, 'Development and validation of a performance-based test of ESL "survival skills"', in Hauptman, P.C. et al., (eds.), 1985: 89–110.

Clark, J.L.D. and S.S. Swinton, 1979, An exploration of speaking proficiency measures in the TOEFL context, Princeton NJ: Educational Testing Services (TOEFL Research Reports 4).

Clark, J.L.D. and S.S. Swinton, 1980, The test of spoken English as a measure of communicative ability in English-medium instructional settings, Princeton, NJ: Educational Testing Service (TOEFL Research Reports 7).

Clifford, R.T., 1977, Reliability and validity of oral proficiency testing, PhD thesis, University of Minnesota.

Clymer, T., 1972, 'What is "reading"?: some current concepts', in Melnik, A. and J. Merritt (eds.), 1972: 48–66.

Coffman, W.E., 1971, 'Essay examinations', in Thorndike, R.L., (ed.), 1971: 271–302.

Coffman, W.E. and D. Kurfman, 1968, 'A comparison of two methods of reading essay examinations', American Educational Research Journal, 5/1: 101–20.

Cohen, A., 1985, 'On taking language tests: what the students report', Language Testing, 1/1: 70–81.

Concannon-O'Brien, M. (ed.), 1973, Testing in second language teaching: new dimensions, ATESOL, Ireland.

Cooper, C.R., 1977, 'Holistic evaluation of writing', in Cooper, C.R. and L. Odell (eds.) 1977: 3–31.

Cooper, C.R. and L. Odell (eds.), 1977, Evaluating writing: describing, measuring, judging, Urbana, Ill.: National Council of Teachers of English.

Cooper, R.L., 1968, 'An elaborated language testing model', in Upshur, J.A. and J. Fata (eds.), 1968: 57−72.

Courchene, R.J. and J.I. de Bagheera, 1981, 'Testing communicative competence problems and perspectives', *Medium*, **6**: 57−69.

Courchene, R.J. and J.I. de Bagheera, 1985, 'A theoretical framework for the development of performance tests', in Hauptman, P.C. *et al.* (eds.), 1985: 45−58.

Cowie, A.P. and J.B. Heaton (eds.), 1977, *English for academic purposes*, University of Reading: BAAL/SELMOUS Publication.

Cresswell, M.J., 1983, *TEAP: setting the grade boundaries*, mimeo, Associated Examining Board.

Crocker, A.C., 1981, *Statistics for the teacher*, Slough: NFER, Nelson.

Cronbach, L.J., 1970, *Essentials of psychological testing*, New York: Harper and Row.

Cronbach, L.J., 1971, 'Test validation', in Thorndike, R.L., (ed.), 1971: 443−507.

Cross, D., 1982, 'The oral test: some practical solutions', *British Journal of Language Teaching*, **20**: 93−5.

Culhane, T., C. Klein-Braley, and D.K. Stevenson, (eds.), 1982, *Practice and problems in language testing*, University of Essex, Department of Language and Linguistics, Occasional Papers 26.

Cummins, J., 1980, 'The cross-lingual dimensions of language proficiency: implications for bi-lingual education and the optimal age issue', *TESOL Quarterly*, **14/2**: 175−88.

Cziko, G.A., 1981, 'Psychometric and edumetric approaches to language testing implications and applications', *Applied Linguistics*, **11/1**: 27−43.

Cziko, G.A., 1982, 'Improving the psychometric, criterion-referenced and practical qualities of integrative language tests', *TESOL Quarterly*, **16**: 367−80.

Darnell, D.K., 1968, *The development of an English language proficiency test of foreign students using a clozentropy procedure*, Boulder Co.: Department of Speech and Drama, University of Colorado.

Davies, A., 1965, *Proficiency in English as a second language*, PhD thesis, University of Birmingham.

Davies, A. (ed.), 1968, *Language testing symposium. A psycholinguistic approach*, London: Oxford University Press.

Davies, A., 1973, 'Language proficiency testing and the syllabus', in Concannon-O'Brien, M. (ed.), 1973: 18−26.

Davies, A., 1977, 'The construction of language tests', in Allen, J.P.B. and A. Davies (eds.), 1977: 38−104.

Davies, A., 1978, 'Language testing. Survey article Parts I and II', *Language Teaching and Linguistics Abstracts*, **II 3/4**: 145−59 and 215−31.

Davies, A., 1981a, 'A review of communicative syllabus design', *TESOL Quarterly*, **15/3**: 332−8.

Davies, A., 1981b, 'Reaction to the Palmer and Bachman and the Vollmer Papers (2)', in Alderson, J.C. and A. Hughes (eds.), 1981: 182−6.

Davies, A., 1982, 'Criteria for evaluation of tests of English as a Foreign Language', in Heaton, J.B. (ed.), 1982: 11−16.

Davies, A., 1983, 'The validity of concurrent validation', in Hughes A. and D. Porter (eds.), 1983: 141−6.

Davies, A., 1984, 'Validating three tests of English language proficiency', *Language Testing*, **1/1**: 50−69.

Davies, A., 1985, 'Follow my leader: is that what language tests do?', in Lee, Y.P. *et al.* (eds.), 1985: 3−14.

Davies, A., 1986, 'Indirect ESP testing: old innovations', in Portal, M. (ed.), 1986: 56−67.

Davison, J.M. and P.M. Geake, 1970, 'An assessment of oral testing methods in modern languages', *Modern Languages*, **51**: 116−23.

Douglas, D., 1986, 'Communicative competence and tests of oral skills', in Stansfield, C.W., 1986: 156−74.

Douglas, D. and C. Pettinari, 1983, 'Grounded ethnography: a method adaptable to the production of communicative ESP materials', paper presented at TESOL Conference.

Douglas, D. and L. Selinker, 1985, 'Principles for language tests within the "discourse domains" theory of interlanguage: research, test construction and interpretation', *Language Testing*, **2/2**: 205–26.

Doye, P., 1986, *Typologie der Testaufgaben für den Englischunterricht*, Munich: Langenscheidt-Longman.

Dunlop, I., 1969, 'Tests of writing ability in EFL', *ELTJ*, **24/1**: 54–8.

Ebel, R.L., 1972, 'Why is a longer test usually a more reliable test?', *Educational and Psychological Measurement*, **32**: 249–53.

Edgeworth, F.Y., 1888, 'The statistics of examinations', *Journal of the Royal Statistical Society*, **LI/III**.

Educational Testing Service, 1982, *Test of spoken English: manual for score users*, Princeton, NJ.

Educational Testing Service, 1986, *Test of spoken English: examinee handbook*, Princeton, NJ.

Educational Testing Service, 1986, *TOEFL test of written English*, Princeton, NJ.

Ellis, R., 1980, 'Oral skills and their identification', *Teaching English*, **14(1)**: 31–4.

Ellis, R., 1981, 'The assessment of oral skills', *Teaching English*, **14(3)**: 19–23.

Ellis, R., 1984, 'Communication strategies and the evaluation of communicative performance', *English Language Teaching Journal*, **38/1**: 39–44.

Ellis, R., 1985, 'Sources of variability in interlanguage', *Applied Linguistics*, **6/2**: 118–31.

Ellis, R., (ed.), Forthcoming, *Contextual variability and second language acquisition*, Collins.

Emmings, B., 1986, *Integrated testing: a preliminary investigation*, MA thesis, University of Lancaster.

Engelskirchen, A., E. Cottrell and J.W. Oller, 1981, 'A study of the reliability and validity of the Ilyin oral interview', in Palmer, A.S. *et al.* (eds.), 1981: 83–93.

Engineer, W.D., 1977, *An investigation of a reading model for English as a second language*, PhD thesis, University of Edinburgh.

English Language Testing Service, 1987, *An introduction*, University of Cambridge Local Examinations Syndicate/The British Council.

Farhady, H., 1983, 'The disjunctive fallacy between discrete-point and integrative tests', in Oller, J.W. (ed.), 1983: 311–22.

Farhady, H., 1983, 'New directions for ESL proficiency testing', in Oller, J.W. (ed.), 1983: 253–64.

Finlayson, D.L., 1951, 'The reliability of the marking of essays', *British Journal of Educational Psychology*, **21/2**: 126–34.

Fisher, M.S.S., 1979, *The reliability of RSA, FCE and ARELS oral examinations*, BPhil thesis, University of Birmingham.

Fisher, M.S.S., 1981, 'To pass or not to pass — an investigation into oral examination procedures', *Spoken English*, **14**: 109–11.

Fok, A., R. Lord, G. Low, and B.K. T'Sou (eds.), 1981, *Language testing. Working papers in linguistics and language teaching 4*, Language Centre of University of Hong Kong.

Fowler, W.S. and N. Coe, 1978, *Nelson English language tests*, Middlesex: Nelson.

Francis, J.C., 1977, 'Impression and analytic marking methods', mimeo, MS Aldershot: Associated Examining Board.

Francis, J.C., 1978, 'An investigation into the reliability of impression and analytic marking methods in the oral test in Italian at Ordinary Level', MS, Aldershot: Associated Examing Board (Ref. RAC/72).

Francis, J.C., 1981, 'The reliability of two methods of marking oral tests in modern language examinations', *British Journal of Language Teaching*, **19**: 15–21.

Fried, L., 1985, 'On the validity of second language tests', in Hyltenstam, K. and M. Pienemann (eds.), 1985: 349–72.

Furneaux, C., 1982, *Comparing listening recall and dictation as possible sub-tests for inclusion in the AEB's test in English for academic purposes*, MA thesis, University of Reading.

Gardiner, C.P., 1972, *Assessment of oral proficiency in English as a Foreign Language*, MEd thesis, University of Manchester.

Gipps, C. and Ewen, E., 1974, 'Scoring written work in English as a Second Language: the use of the T-unit', *Educational Research*, **16/2**: 121−5.

Girard, C. and R. Sheen, 1981, 'The oral interview: is it really worth the trouble?' *SPEAQ Journal*, **5**: 77−93.

Godshalk, F.I., F. Swineford and W.E. Coffman, 1966, *The measurement of writing ability. ETS research monograph 6*, Princeton: College Entrance Examination Board.

Guerra, E.L., D.A. Abramson and M. Newmark, 1964, 'The New York City foreign language oral ability rating scale', *Modern Language Journal*, **48**: 486−9.

Guilford, J.P., 1965, *Fundamental statistics in psychology and education*, fourth edition, McGraw-Hill.

Haarman di Federico, L. (ed.), 1982, *Testing English for academic purposes*, Bergamo, Istituto de Studi Linguistici dell'Universita degli Studi di Camerino.

Harrison, A., 1979, *Techniques for evaluating learners' ability to apply threshold level proficiency to everyday communication*, Strasbourg Council of Europe (Ref. DECS/EES(79)77).

Harrison, A., 1983, 'Communicative testing: jam tomorrow', in Hughes, A. and D. Porter (eds.), 1983: 77−86.

Hartog, P.J., E.C. Rhodes and C. Burt, 1936, *The marks of examiners*, London: Macmillan.

Hauptman, P.C., R. Le Blanc and M.B. Wesche (eds.), 1985, *Second language performance testing*, Ottawa: Unviersity of Ottawa Press.

Hawkey, R., 1982, *An investigation of inter-relationships between cognitive/affective and social factors and language learning. A longitudinal study of 27 overseas students using English in connection with their training in the United Kingdom*, PhD thesis, University of London.

Hayward, T., A. Michiels and J. Noel, 1982, 'Report on the experiment in activated group achievement testing for advanced students of spoken English', in Culhane, T. *et al.* (eds.), 1982: 48−57.

Head, J.J., 1966, 'Multiple marking of an essay item in experimental "O" level Nuffield biology examinations', *Educational Review*, **19/1**: 65−71.

Heaton, J.B., 1975, *Writing English language tests*, London: Longman.

Heaton, J.B. (ed.), 1982, *Language testing*, Oxford: Modern English Publications.

Hendricks, D.G., R. Scholz, R. Spurling, M. Johnson and L. Vandenburg, 1980, 'Oral proficiency testing in an intensive English language program', in J.W. Oller and K. Perkins (eds.), 1980: 77−91.

Henning, G., 1982, 'Growth referenced evaluation and the critical intervention index', paper presented at the 1982 TESOL convention, Hawaii.

Hieke, A.E., 1985, 'A componential approach to oral fluency evaluation', *Modern Language Journal*, **69**: 135−42.

Hill, G., 1982, 'Oral assessment: a scheme for the assessment of the oral English of trainee teachers', *World Language English*, **I**: 124−6.

Hinofotis, F.B., K.M. Bailey and S.L. Stern, 1981, 'Assessing the oral proficiency of foreign teaching assistants: instrument development', in Palmer, A.S. *et al.* (eds.), 1981: 106−25.

Hiple, D.V., 1982, *Provisional proficiency guidelines*, Hasting-on-Hudson, NY: American Council on the Teaching of Foreign Languages.

Holden, S. (ed.), 1977, *English for specific purposes*, Oxford: Modern English Publications.

Holes, C.D., 1972, *An investigation into some aspects of the English language problems of two groups of overseas postgraduate students at Birmingham University*, MA thesis, University of Birmingham.

Houston, J.G., 1983, 'Norm and criterion referencing of performance levels in tests of educational attainment', mimeo, AEB Research Advisory Committee.

Howard, F., 1980, 'Testing communicative proficiency in French as a Second Language: a search for procedures', *Canadian Modern Language Review*, **36**: 272−89.

Hughes, A., 1981a, 'Reaction to the Palmer and Bachman and the Vollmer Papers (1)', in Alderson, J.C. and A. Hughes (eds.), 1981: 176−81.

Hughes, A., 1981b, 'Conversational cloze as a measure of oral ability', *ELTJ*, **XXXV/2**: 161−8.

Hughes, A., 1986, 'A pragmatic approach to criterion-referenced foreign language testing', in Portal, M. (ed.), 1986: 31−41.

Hughes, A. (ed.), 1988, *Testing English for university study*, ELT Document 127, Oxford: Modern English Publications.

Hughes, A., 1989, *Testing for language teachers*, Cambridge: Cambridge University Press.

Hughes, A. and D. Porter (eds.), 1983, *Current developments in language testing*, London: Academic Press.

Hulstijn, H.H., 1985, 'Testing second language proficiency with direct procedures. A comment on Ingram', in Hyltenstam, K. and M. Pienemann (eds.), 1985: 277−82.

Hutchinson, T. and A. Waters, 1981, 'Performance and competence in English for specific purposes', *Applied Linguistics*, **II/I**: 56−69.

Hyltenstam, K. and M. Pienemann (eds.), 1985, *Modelling and assessing second language acquisition*, Clevedon, Avon: Multilingual Matters Ltd.

Hymes, D.H., 1972, 'On communicative competence', in Pride, J.B.J. and Holmes (eds.) 1972: 269−93.

Ilyin, D., 1976, 'Assessing oral communication in adult program English second language classes', MS, Revision of a paper read at the New Orleans 1971 Annual Meeting of TESOL.

Ingram, D.E., 1981, 'The Australian Second Language Proficiency Ratings: their nature, development and trialling', in Read, J.A.S. (ed.), 1981a: 108−36.

Ingram, D.E., 1982, 'Report on the formal trialling of the Australian Second Language Proficiency Ratings (ASLPR)', unpublished MS, Brisbane Mount Gravatt College of Advanced Education.

Ingram, D.E., 1984a, *Australian Second Language Proficiency Ratings*, Canberra: Department of Immigration and Ethnic Affairs.

Ingram, D.E., 1984b, *Report on the formal trialling of the Australian Second Language Proficiency Ratings (ASLPR)*, Studies in Adult Migrant Education, Canberra: Australian Government Publishing Service.

Ingram, D.E., 1985, 'Assessing proficiency: an overview on some aspects of testing', in Hyltenstam, K. and M. Pienemann (eds.), 1985: 245−76.

Ingram, D.E. and E. Wylie, 1981, *Australian Second Language Proficiency Ratings*, Brisbane: Queensland Education Department.

Ingram, E., 1964, *English Language Battery (ELBA)*, University of Edinburgh, Department of Linguistics.

Ingram, E., 1970, 'Report on the marking of English compositions', mimeo, University of Edinburgh, Department of Linguistics.

Ingram, E., 1977, 'Basic concepts in testing', in Allen, J.P.B. and A. Davies (eds.), 1977: 11−37.

Irvine, P., P. Atai and J.W. Oller, 1974, 'Cloze, dictation and the test of English as a Foreign Language', *Language Learning*, **24/2**: 245−52.

Jacobs, H.L., S.A. Zinkgraf, D.R. Wormuth, V. Faye Hartfiel and J.B. Hughey, 1981, *English composition program. Testing ESL composition: a practical approach*, Rowley, Mass.. Newbury House.

Jakobovits, L.A., 1970, *Foreign language learning: a psycholinguistic analysis of the issues*, Rowley, Mass.: Newbury House.

James, G.C., 1984, 'Development of an oral proficiency component in a test in English for academic purposes', paper read at the Brussels AILA Congress.

James, G.C., 1985, 'A comparison of three techniques in oral communication testing', paper read at the Edinburgh BAAL meeting.

James, G.C., 1986, 'Twenty-five years of oral testing, and the next twenty-five', paper presented at the ACROLT LT + 25 Meeting, Qiriyat Anavim, Israel.

Johnson, K. and D. Porter, 1983, *Perspectives in communicative language teaching*, London: Academic Press.

Jones, R.L., 1978, 'The FSI oral interview', in Spolsky, B. (ed.), 1979: 104−225.

Jones, R.L., 1980, *An international survey of research in language testing*, Duisburg: Interuniversitaere Sprachtestgruppe (Workpapers).

Jones, R.L., 1981, 'Scoring procedures in oral language proficiency tests', in Read, J.A.S. (ed.), 1981a: 100−7.

Jones, R.L., 1985a, 'Second language performance testing: an overview', in Hauptman, P.C. *et al.* (eds.), 1985: 15−24.

Jones, R.L., 1985b, 'Some basic considerations in testing oral proficiency', in Lee, Y.P. *et al.*, (eds.), 1985: 77−84.

Jones, R.L. and B. Spolsky (eds.), 1985, *Testing language proficiency*, Arlington Va.: Center for Applied Linguistics.

Jones, S. and K. Friedl, 1986, 'Examinee strategies for answering grammar items', paper given at the TESOL Convention.

Kelly, R., 1978, *On the construct validation of comprehension tests: an exercise in applied linguistics*, PhD thesis, University of Queensland.

Kelly, R., 1981, 'Aspects of communicative performance', *Applied Linguistics*, **II/2:** 169−79.

Kennedy, G.D., 1978, *The testing of listening comprehension*, SEAMEO Regional Language Centre, Singapore University Press.

Kennedy, G.D., 1981, 'Performance variability and listening proficiency', in Read, J.A.S. (ed.), 1981b: 20−9.

Kinsella, V. (ed.), 1978, *Language teaching and linguistics: surveys*, Cambridge: Cambridge University Press.

Klein-Braley, C., 1981, *Empirical investigations of cloze tests*, PhD thesis, Universität Duisburg.

Klein-Braley, C., 1985, 'A cloze-up on the C-test: a study in the construct validation of authentic tests', *Language Testing*, **2/1:** 76−104.

Klein-Braley, C., and U. Raatz, 1984, 'A survey of research on the C-test', *Language Testing*, **1/2:** 134−46.

Klein-Braley, C. and D.K. Stevenson (eds.), 1979, *Practice and problems in language testing I.*, Duisburg: Verlag Peter D. Lang.

Klein-Braley, C. and D.K. Stevenson (eds.), 1981, *Practical problems in language testing*, Duisburg: Peter Lang (Orbis Linguisticus 1).

Krowitz, M.J., 1982, 'Evaluation procedures for proficiency in oral communication', paper read at the Honolulu TESOL Convention.

Lado, R., 1961, *Language testing: the construction and use of foreign language tests*, London: Longman.

Lange, D.L. and R.T. Clifford, 1980, *Testing in foreign languages, ESL and bilingual education, 1966−1979: a select ammotated ERIC bibliography*, Arlington, Va.: Center for Applied Linguistics, ERIC Clearinghouse on Languages and Linguistics.

Lapkin, S., 1985, 'Pedagogical implications of direct second language testing: a Canadian example', in Hyltenstam, K. and M. Pienemann (eds.), 1985: 333−48.

Lee, Y.P., 1981a, 'Evaluation and measurement of communicative competence: the case for direct language tests', in Read, J.A.S. (ed.), 1981b: 86−98.

Lee, Y.P., 1981b, 'Some notes on internal consistency reliability estimation for tests of language use', in Fok, A., *et al*, (eds.), 1981: 19−27.

Lee, Y.P., 1985, 'Investigating the validity of the cloze score', in Lee, Y.P. *et al.* (eds.), 1985: 137−48.

Lee, Y.P., A.C.Y.Y. Fok, R. Lord and G. Low (eds.), 1985, *New directions in language testing*, Oxford: Pergamon.

Lewis, C.J., 1981, 'Testing communicative competence', *MALS Journal*, **6:** 19−62.

Lewkodwicz, J. and J. Moon, 1985, 'Evaluation: a way of involving the learner', in Alderson, J.C. (ed.), 1985: 45−80.

Liskin-Gasparro, J.E., 1984, 'The ACTFL Proficiency Guidelines: gateway to testing and curriculum', *Foreign Language Annals*, **17:** 475−89.

Lombardo, L., 1984, 'Oral testing, getting a sample of real language', *Forum*, **22:** 2–6.

Low, G.D., 1982, 'The direct testing of academic writing in a second language', *System*, **10/3:** 247–57.

Low, G.D., 1985, 'Validity and the problem of direct language proficiency tests', in Alderson, J.C. (ed.), 1985: 151–68.

Low, G.D., 1986, 'Storylines and other developing contexts in use-of-language test design', *Indian Journal of Applied Linguistics* (Special Issue on Language Testing).

Low, G.D. and Y.P. Lee, 1985, 'How shall a test be referenced?', in Lee, Y.P. *et al.* (eds.), 1985: 119–26.

Lowe, P., 1975, 'The oral interview — a criterion-referenced test?', paper read at a Washington, DC Meeting of the American Council on Teaching Foreign Languages.

Lowe, P., 1981, 'Structure of the oral interview and content validity', paper read at the Colloquium on the Validation of Oral Proficiency Tests at the Boston TESOL Convention, in Palmer, A.J., *et al.* (eds.), 1981: 71–80.

Lowe, P. and R.T. Clifford, 1980, 'Developing an indirect measure of overall oral proficiency (ROPE)', in Frith (ed.), 1980, *Measuring Spoken Language Proficiency*, Georgetown University Press: 31–9.

Lucas, A.M., 1971, 'Multiple marking of a matriculation biology essay question', *British Journal of Educational Psychology*, **41/1:** 78–84.

Lunzer, E. and K. Gardner (eds.), 1979, *The effective use of reading*, Heinemann Educational Books Ltd. for Schools Council.

Lutjeharms, M. and T. Culhane (eds.), 1982, *Practice and problems in language testing*, Studiereeks van het Tijdschrift van de Vrije Universiteit Brussel (Nieuwe Serie Nr 10).

McCall, D.K., 1979, *The development of an oral test designed to assess foreign learners' ability to communicate and interact with a native speaker in English*, MPhil thesis, University of York.

McEldowney, P.L., 1974, 'Notes for the guidance of teachers offering candidates for the university entrance test in English (overseas)', JMB, Manchester.

McEldowney, P.L., 1976, *Test in English (Overseas), the position after ten years*, Occasional Paper 36, Manchester: JMB.

McEldowney, P.L., 1982, 'A place for visuals in language testing', in Heaton, J.B. (ed.), 1982: 86–91.

Madsen, H.S., 1981, 'Selecting appropriate elicitation techniques for oral proficiency tests', in Read, J.A.S. (ed.), 1981a: 87–99.

Madsen, H.S., 1983, *Techniques in testing*, New York: Oxford University Press.

Madsen, H.S. and R.L. Jones, 1981, 'Classification of oral proficiency tests', in Palmer, A.S. *et al.* (eds.), 1981: 15–30.

Mead, R., 1981, 'Review of J. Munby "Communicative Syllabus Design"', *Applied Linguistics*, **III/1:** 71–8.

Melnik, A. and J. Merlu (eds.), 1972, *Reading: today and tomorrow*, London: University of London Press.

Meloche, A.L., 1972, 'A balanced approach to oral testing', *Canadian Modern Language Review*, **28:** 23–5.

Mets, J., 1982, 'Testing oral proficiency in life-like settings: rating scales and reliability', in Culhane, T. *et al.* (eds.), 1982: 95–103.

Mitchell, R., 1985, 'The use of role play tasks in assessing foreign language communicative performance', *British Journal of Language Teaching*, **23/3:** 169–72.

Moller, A.D., 1977, 'A case for a crude test overseas', in Cowie, A.P. and J.B. Heaton (eds.), 1977: 25–33.

Moller, A.D., 1981a, 'Assessing proficiency in English for use in further study', in Read, J.A.S. (ed.), 1981a: 58–71.

Moller, A.D., 1981b, 'Reaction to the Morrow paper (2)', in Alderson, J.C. and A. Hughes (eds.), 1981: 38–44.

Moller, A.D., 1982a, 'Criteria for assessing oral competence', in Haarman di Federico, L. (ed.), 1982: 33–44.

Moller, A.D., 1982b, *A study in the validation of proficiency tests of English as a Foreign Language*, PhD thesis, University of Edinburgh.

Morrison, D.M. and N. Lee, 1985, 'Simulating an academic tutorial: a test validation study', in Lee, Y.P. *et al.* (eds.), 1985: 85–92.

Morrison, J.W., 1974, *An investigation of problems in listening comprehension encountered by overseas students in the first year of postgraduate studies in sciences in the University of Newcastle-upon-Tyne and the implications for teaching*, MEd thesis, University of Newcastle upon Tyne.

Morrison, R.B., 1968, *English language 'O' Level — June 1967 marking experiment*, mimeo, Guildford: AEB.

Morrison, R.B., 1969, *English language 'O' Level — June 1968 marking experiment*, mimeo, Guildford: AEB.

Morrison, R.B., 1970, *English language 'O' Level — June 1969 marking experiment*, mimeo, Guildford: AEB.

Morrison, R.L. and P.E. Vernon, 1941, 'A new method of marking English compositions', *British Journal of Educational Psychology*, **11/2**: 109–19.

Morrow, K.E., 1977, *Techniques of evaluation for a notional syllabus*, London: Royal Society of Arts.

Morrow, K.E., 1979, 'Communicative langue testing: revolution or evolution', in Brumfit, C.J. and K. Johnson (eds.), 1979: 143–58.

Morrow, K.E. 1986, 'The evaluation of tests of communicative performance', in Portal, M. (ed.), 1986: 1–13.

Mullen, K.A., 1978, 'Direct evaluation of second-language proficiency: the effect of rater and scale in oral interviews', in Redden, J.E. (ed.), *Proceedings of the Second International Conference on Frontiers in Language Proficiency and Dominance Testing*, Carbondale, Illinois: Southern Illinois University (Occasional Papers on Linguistics 3) 240–50, reprinted in *Language Learning*, **28**: 301–8.

Munby, J.L., 1977, *Designing a processing model for specifying communicative competence in a foreign language: a study of the relationship between communication needs and the English required for specific purposes*, PhD thesis, University of Essex.

Munby, J.L., 1978, *Communicative syllabus design*, Cambridge: Cambridge University Press.

Murphy, R.J.L., 1978, 'Sex differences in objective test performance', mimeo, Associated Examining Board Research Report RAC/56.

Murphy, R.J.L., 1979, *Mode 1 examining for the General Certificate of Education. A general guide to some principles and practices*, mimeo, Guildford: AEB.

Murphy, R.J.L., 1980, 'Sex differences in GCE examination entry statistics and success rates', *Educational Studies*, **6/2**: 169–78.

Murphy, R.J.L., 1982, 'A further report of investigations into the reliability of marking of GCE examinations', *British Journal of Education Psychology*, **52/1**: 58–63.

Nakle, P.L. (ed.), 1974, 'Interaction: research and practice for college-adult reading', *Twenty-third Yearbook of the National Reading Conference*.

Norager, P. and M. Warburg, 1984a, 'Foreign language testing — how to make it communicative', unpublished MS, University of Aarhus.

Norager, P. and M. Warburg, 1984b, 'The testing of foreign language communicative competence', paper read at the Brussels AILA Congress.

Oller, J.W., 1971, 'Dictation as a device for testing foreign language proficiency', *English Language Teaching*, **25/3**: 254–9.

Oller, J.W., 1972, 'Assessing competence in ESL reading', *TESOL Quarterly*, **6**: 313–25.

Oller, J.W., 1973, 'Pragmatic language testing', *Language Sciences*, **28**: 7–12.

Oller, J.W., 1976, 'Evidence for a general language proficiency factor: an expectancy grammar', *Die Neueren Sprachen*, **75**: 165–74.

Oller, J.W., 1979, *Language tests at schools*, London: Longman.

Oller, J.W., 1980, 'A comment on specific variance versus global variance in certain EFL tests', *TESOL Quarterly,* **14/4**: 527–30.

Oller, J.W., 1983, 'A consensus for the eighties?', in Oller, J.W. (ed.), 1983: 351–6.

Oller, J.W. (ed.), 1983, *Issues in language testing research,* Rowley, Mass.: Newbury House.

Oller, J.W., 1986, 'Communication theory and testing: what and how', in Stansfield, C.W., (ed.), 1986: 104–55.

Oller, J.W. and K. Perkins (eds.), 1978, *Language in education: testing the tests,* Rowley, Mass.: Newbury House.

Oller, J.W. and K. Perkins (eds.), 1980, *Research in language testing,* Rowley, Mass.: Newbury House.

Olshtain, E. and S. Blum-Kulka, 1985, 'Crosscultural pragmatics and the testing of communicative competence', *Language Testing,* **2/1**: 16–30.

Oskarsson, M., 1981, 'Subjective and objective assessment of foreign language performance', in Read, J.A.S. (ed.), 1981a: 225–39.

Palmer, A.S., 1981, 'Measurements of reliability and validity of two picture-description tests of oral communication', in Palmer, A.S. *et al.* (eds.), 1981: 127–39.

Palmer, A.S., and L.F. Bachman, 1981, 'Basic concerns in test validation', in Alderson, J.C. and A. Hughes (eds.), 1981: 135–51.

Palmer, A.S., P.J.M. Groot, and G.A. Trosper (eds.), 1981, *The construct validation of tests of communicative competence,* TESOL: Washington D.C.

Pattison, B., 1986, 'Professional and linguistic assessments board test for doctors qualified overseas and seeking limited registration for medical practice in the UK', *Language Testing Update,* **2**: 6–8.

Penfold, E.D.M., 1956, 'Essay marking experiments: shorter and longer essays', *British Journal of Educational Psychology,* **26/2**: 129.

Perkins, K., 1980, 'Using objective methods of attained writing proficiency to discriminate among holistic evaluations', *TESOL Quarterly,* **14/1**: 61–9.

Perren, G.E. and J.L.M. Trim (eds.), 1971, *Applications of Linguistics,* selected papers of the Second International Congress of Applied Linguistics, Cambridge.

Pilliner, A.E.G., 1969, 'Multiple marking: Wiseman or Cox?' *British Journal of Educational Psychology,* **39**: 313–5.

Popham, W.J., 1978, *Criterion referenced measurement,* Englewood Cliffs, NJ: Prentice Hall.

Popham, W.J. and T.R. Husek, 1969, 'Implications of criterion-referenced measurement,' *Journal of Educational Measurement,* **6/1**: 1–9.

Portal, M. (ed.), 1986, *Innovations in language testing,* NFER-Nelson.

Porter, D., 1983, 'Assessing communicative proficiency: the search for validity', in Johnson, K. and D. Porter (eds.), 1983: 189–203.

Porter, D., A. Hughes and C. Weir (eds.), 1988, *Validating the ELTS test: a critical review,* Cambridge: British Council and UCLES.

Pride, J.B. and J. Holmes (eds.), 1972, *Sociolinguistics,* Harmondsworth: Penguin.

Raatz, U., 1981a, 'Are oral tests tests?', in Klein-Braley, C. and D.K. Stevenson (eds.), 1981: 197–212.

Raatz, U., 1981b, 'The C-test. A modification of the cloze procedure', paper delivered at the Fourth International Language Testing Symposium of the IUS, Colchester, England.

Rea, P.M., 1978, 'Assessing Language as Communication', *MALS Journal,* New Series No. 3, University of Birmingham.

Rea, P.M., 1985, 'Language testing and the communicative language teaching curriculum', in Lee, Y.P. *et al.* (eds.), 1985: 15–32.

Read, J.A.S. (ed.), 1981a, 'Directions in language testing', *SEAMEO Regional Language Centre,* Anthology Series 9.

Read, J.A.S. (ed.), 1981b, 'Papers on language testing', *SEAMEO Regional Language Centre,* Occasional Papers No. 18.

Read, J.A.S., 1982, 'An indirect approach to the testing of oral proficiency', paper read at the Honolulu TESOL Convention.

Reves, T., 1980, 'The group-oral Bagrut examination: an experiment', *English Teachers Journal* (Israel), **24:** 19−21.

Ricciardi, J.S., 1980, 'Some thoughts on the use of interviews for assessing second-language proficiency', *Medium*, **5:** 11−22.

Royal Society of Arts (RSA), 1980, *Examinations in the communicative use of English as a Foreign Language. Specifications and specimen papers*, London: Royal Society of Arts.

Royal Society of Arts Examinations Board, 1985, *The communicative use of English as a Foreign Language*, London: Royal Society of Arts.

Ryan, M., 1978, 'How do we judge a speaker's competence?', *Studies in Second Language Acquisition*, **5:** 148−59.

Ryan, M., 1979, *'English for academic purposes'*, MA thesis, UWIST.

Savignon, S.J., 1972, 'Teaching for communicative competence: a research report', *Audio Visual Language Journal*, **10/3:** 153−62.

Savignon, S.J., 1985, 'Evaluation of communicative competence: the ACTFL proficiency guidelines', *Modern Language Journal*, **69:** 129−33.

Savignon, S.J., 1986, 'The meaning of communicative competence in relation to the TOEFL program', in Stansfield, C.W. (ed.), 1986: 17−30.

Schulz, R.A., 1977, 'Discrete-point versus simulated communication testing in foreign languages', *Modern Language Journal*, **62/3:** 94−101.

Seaton, I., 1981, 'Background to the specifications for an English language testing service', in Alderson, J.C. and A. Hughes (eds.), 1981: 121−2.

Seaton, I., 1985, 'Issues in the validation of the ELTS 1976−1983', in Hauptman, P.C. *et al.* (eds.), 1985: 111−29.

Selinker, L. and D. Douglas, 1985, 'Wrestling with context in interlanguage theory', *Applied Linguistics*, **6/2:** 190−204.

Shohamy, E., 1980, 'Further examination of the validity of the oral interview', paper read at the Colloquium on the Validation of Oral Proficiency Tests at the San Francisco TESOL Convention.

Shohamy, E., 1981, 'Inter-rater and intra-rater reliability of the oral interview and concurrent validity with cloze procedure', in Palmer, A.S. *et al.* (eds.), 1981: 94−105.

Shohamy, E., 1982, 'Predicting speaking proficiency from cloze tests: theoretical and practical considerations for test substitution', *Applied Linguistics*, **3:** 161−71.

Shohamy, E., 1984, 'Does the testing method make a difference? The case of reading comprehension', *Language Testing*, **1/2:** 147−70.

Shohamy, E. and T. Reves, 1985a, 'Authentic language tests: where from and where to?', *Language Testing*, **2/1:** 48−59.

Shohamy, E., T. Reves and Y. Bejerano, 1985, 'Testing overall oral proficiency towards a new oral Bagrut test', *English Teachers Journal* (Israel), **31:** 17−26.

Skehan, P., 1984, 'Issues in the testing of English for specific purposes', *Language Testing*, **1/2:** 202−20.

Skehan, P., 1987, 'Variability and language testing', in R. Ellis (ed.), 1987, *Second language acquisition in context*, Englewood Cliffs, NJ: Prentice Hall.

Skehan, P., 1988, 1989, 'State of the art article. Language testing Parts I and II', *Language Teaching*, **Vol 21/4** and **Vol 22/1**, Cambridge: Cambridge University Press.

Smith, M., 1984, 'Assessment of speaking for the assessment of performance unit', *British Journal of Language Teaching*, **22:** 9−14.

Smith, V. and C. Klein-Braley, 1981, 'Practical approaches to the teaching and testing of oral skills for university students in Germany', in Klein-Braley, C. and D.K. Stevenson (eds.), 1981: 161−72.

Spolsky, B., 1968, 'Language testing: the problem of validation', *TESOL Quarterly*, **2:** 88−94.

Spolsky, B., 1976, 'Language testing: art or science', paper read at the Fourth International Congress of Applied Linguistics, Stuttgart: HochSchulVerlag, Germany.

Spolsky, B. (ed.), 1978, *Approaches in language testing*, Advances in Language Testing, Series: 2, Arlington, Va.: Center for Applied Linguistics.

Spolsky, B. (ed.), 1979, *Some major tests*, Advances in Language Testing, Series: 1, Arlington,

Va.: Center for Applied Linguistics.

Spolsky, B., 1985a, 'The limits of authenticity in language testing', *Language Testing*, 2/1: 31–41.

Spolsky, B., 1985b, 'What does it mean to know how to use a language? An essay on the theoretical basis of language testing', *Language Testing*, 2/2: 180–91.

Spolsky, B., P. Murphy, W. Holm and A. Ferrel, 1972, 'Three functional tests of oral proficiency', *TESOL Quarterly*, 6: 221–35. Reprinted in Palmer, L. and B. Spolsky (eds.), 1975, *Papers on Language Testing, 1967–1974*, Washington, DC TESOL: 76–90.

Stansfield, C.W. (ed.), 1986, *Towards communicative competence testing: proceedings of the second TOEFL Invitational Conference*, TOEFL Research Report 21, Princeton, NJ: Educational Testing Service.

Steel, J.H. and J. Talman, 1936, *The marking of English compositions*, Nisbet.

Stevenson, D.K., 1974, *A preliminary investigation of construct validity and the test of English as a Foreign Language*, PhD thesis, University of New Mexico, Albuquerque.

Stevenson, D.K., 1981, 'Beyond faith and face validity: the Multitrait Multimethod Matrix and the convergent and discriminant validity of oral proficiency tests', paper read at the Colloquium on the Validation of Oral Proficiency Tests at the Boston TESOL Convention, in Palmer, A.S. *et al.* (eds.), 1981: 37–61.

Stevenson, D.K., 1985a, 'Authenticity, validity and a tea party', *Language Testing*, 2/1: 41–7.

Stevenson, D.K., 1985b, 'Pop validity and performance testing', in Lee, Y.P. *et al.* (eds.), 1985: 111–18.

Swain, M., 1985, 'Large-scale communicative language testing: a case study', in Lee, Y.P. *et al.* (eds.), 1985: 35–146.

Swain, M., G. Dumas and N. Naiman, 1974, 'Alternatives to spontaneous speech elicited translation and imitation as indicators of second language competence', *Working Papers on Bilingualism* (Ontario Institute for Studies in Education) 3: 68–79.

Tarone, E., 1983, 'On the variability of interlanguage systems', *Applied Linguistics*, 4/2: 143–63.

Taylor, C., 1979, *An assessment of the University of Cambridge Certificate of Proficiency in English*, MA thesis, University of London.

Taylor, W.L., 1953, 'Cloze procedure: a new tool for measuring readability', *Journalism Quarterly*, 30: 415–33.

Templeton, H.R., 1973, *Cloze procedure in aural proficiency tests for foreign students studying in English*, MEd thesis, University of Manchester.

Thorndike, R.L. (ed.), 1971, *Educational measurement (second edition)*, Washington, DC: American Council on Education.

Toney, T., 1986, 'Validation of the mini-platform parallel version', in *Language Testing Up-Date*, 2: 49–54.

Underhill, N., 1980, 'The great reliability/validity trade-off: problems in assessing the productive skills', unpublished MS, London: International Language Centres.

Underhill, N., 1981, 'Objectivity in oral testing — can we have it and do we want it anyway?', *Spoken English*, 14: 102–5.

Upshur, J.A. and J. Fata (ed.), 1968, 'Problems in foreign language testing', *Language Learning Special*, 3.

Ur, P., 1981, 'A new system for the Bagrut oral test', *English Teachers' Journal* (Israel), 25: 36–40.

Valdmand, A. and M. Moody, 1979, 'Testing communicative ability', *French Review*, 52: 552–61.

Valette, R.M., 1967, *Modern language testing — a handbook, (first edition)*, New York: Harcourt, Brace and World.

Valette, R.M., 1977, *Modern language testing (second edition)*, New York: Harcourt, Brace Jovanovich.

Van Weeren, J., 1981, 'Testing oral proficiency in everyday situations', in Klein-Braley, C. and D.K. Stevenson (eds.), 1981: 54–66.

Vernon, P.E. and Milligan, G.D., 1954, 'A further study of the reliability of English essays', *British Journal of Statistical Psychology*, 7/2: 65–74.

Vollmer, H.J., 1979, 'Why aren't we interested in general language proficiency?', in Klein-Braley, C. and D.K. Stevenson (eds.), 1979: 96–123.

Vollmer, H.J., 1981, 'Why aren't we interested in general language proficiency?', in Alderson, J.C. and A. Hughes (eds.), 1981: 152–74.

Vollmer, H.J., 1983, 'The structure of foreign language competence', in Hughes, A. and D. Porter (eds.), 1983: 3–30.

Walker, C.A., 1981, *Reliability and validity of global versus analytic mark schemes in oral proficiency testing*, MA thesis, University of York.

Wall, D., 1982, 'A study of the predictive validity of the Michigan Battery, with special reference to the composition component', in Culhane, T. *et al.* (eds.), 1982: 156–69.

Weir, C.J., 1983a, *Identifying the language needs of overseas students in tertiary education in the United Kingdom*, unpublished PhD thesis, University of London.

Weir, C.J., 1983b, 'The Associated Examining Board's Test in English for Academic Purposes: an exercise in content validation', in Hughes, A. and D. Porter (eds.), 1983: 147–53.

Weir, C.J., 1988, 'The specification, realization and validation of an English language proficiency test', in Hughes, A. (ed.), 1988.

Weir, C.J. and J. Ormiston, 1978, 'A comparison of the rankings of students on a cloze test as against a composition test', MSc Applied Linguistics Assignment, University of Edinburgh.

Wesche, M.B., 1979, 'Oral proficiency test', MS, University of Ottawa.

Wesche, M.B., 1981, 'Communicative testing in a second language', *Canadian Modern Language Review*, **37/3**: 551–71.

Wesche, M.B., 1985, 'Introduction', in Hauptman, P.C. *et al.* (eds.), 1985.

Widdowson, H.G., 1978, *Teaching language as communication*, Oxford: Oxford University Press.

Widdowson, H.G., 1983, *Learning purpose and language use*, Oxford: Oxford University Press.

Wilds, C.P., 1975, 'The oral interview test', in Jones, R.L. and B. Spolsky (eds.), 1985: 29–44.

Wilkins, D.A., 1980, 'Review of "Communicative Syllabus Design" by J. Munby', *British Journal of Educational Studies*, **28**.

Wilmott, A.S. and D.L. Nuttal, 1975, *The reliability of examinations at 16+*, London: Macmillan.

Wiseman, S., 1949, 'The marking of English composition in grammar school selection', *British Journal of Education Psychology*, **19/3**: 200–9.

Wood, R. and B. Quinn, 1976, 'Double impression marking of English language essay and summary questions', *Educational Review*, **28/3**: 229–45.

Wood, R. and D. Wilson, 1974, 'Evidence for differential marking discrimination among examiners of English', *The Irish Journal of Education*, **8/1**: 37 *et seq*.

Woods, A., P. Fletcher and A. Hughes, 1986, *Statistics in Language Studies*, Cambridge: Cambridge University Press.

Yamagoshita, K., J. Macfarlane and R.D. Inouye, 1982, 'Mass oral grading criteria', paper read at the Honolulu TESOL Convention.

Yorozuya, R. and J.W. Oller, 1980, 'Oral proficiency scales: construct validity and the halo effect', *Language Learning*, **30**: 135–53.

Yule, G., 1982, 'The objective assessment of aspects of spoken English', *World Language English*, **1**: 193–9.

Zieky, M.J. and S.A. Livingston, 1977, *Manual for setting standards on the basic skills assessment tests*, Princeton, NJ: Educational Testing Service.

Appendix I

The Associated Examining Board
Test in English for Educational Purposes
(TEEP)

Examination Specifications

The Associated Examining Board (A.E.B.)

The A.E.B. is one of the largest of the G.C.E. boards operating in England, Wales and Northern Ireland. Its first examinations were taken in 1955 but in 1982 it had grown to the extent that over 160 totally external examinations were offered in 4,174 centres in the United Kingdom and 198 centres overseas. The total number of candidates entering these and other, special, examinations was 471,717 (17,116 of them overseas) and the total number of subject entries was 916,013 (37,250 of them overseas).

Towards an English Examination for Educational Purposes

G.C.E. examinations (among others) enable students to obtain qualifications for entry to Higher Education in the United Kingdom. Increasingly, Universities and Polytechnics have found that numbers of non-native speakers of English, whether resident in the United Kingdom or overseas, are not able adequately to cope with the English they encounter, or need to use, in lectures, seminars and their general academic environment. There seemed to be a need for a more suitable test for these students from overseas and groups in the United Kingdom. Also, during the period 1976–8, the A.E.B. was approached by a number of its centres and asked to make available an examination which would provide receiving institutions in tertiary education with a comprehensive picture of the English Language proficiency of students for whom English was not the mother tongue.

The A.E.B., therefore, decided in 1978 to undertake research into this field of examining English as a foreign language and subsequently developing an examination which would assess performance of students in English for Academic Purposes. It later became called the Test in English for Educational Purposes (T.E.E.P.), for students who have to study through the medium of English.

Description of Research and Development of the Test

The Research and Development have been carefully and deliberately staged. The first three stages were concerned with:

1. establishing the levels, discipline areas and institutions where overseas students enrol in further and higher education sectors

2. ascertaining the language demands made on students in the disciplines most commonly studied by overseas students (i.e. arts/business/administrative/social studies and science/engineering studies) by

   a) a series of observational visits to a variety of educational institutions

   b) circulation of a national questionnaire (based on the observation schedule) to staff and students in a similar wide variety of educational institutions. (Completed questionnaires were returned by 940 overseas students, 530 British students and 559 staff)

3. constructing a test battery to assess a student's ability in performing language tasks relevant to the academic context in which he has to operate, based on information obtained through stages 1, 2a) and 2b). The pre-test battery incorporated a variety of test formats to establish the best methods for assessing a student's performance on those tasks and under those constraints that the research indicated as important to overseas students following English-medium courses.

In the pre-test version of the test battery, there were two components. The first component was to be taken by all candidates. Spoken and written texts, which the Project Working Party thought would be accessible to candidates from all disciplines, were selected. Two versions of the second component, Paper II, were also prepared. Paper IIA was intended for students in the fields of Arts, Social, Business and Administrative Studies. Paper IIB was intended for students in the fields of Engineering and Science. The texts in both versions were selected from written and spoken sources in the appropriate discipline areas. The test tasks in Papers IIA and IIB were parallel.

In Paper I and both versions of Paper II, candidates are required to demonstrate their proficiency in reading, listening and writing. A variety of test formats are used in Paper I and Paper II to test a candidate's proficiency in the range of enabling skills required to operate successfully in the various study modes. In addition to testing specifically the constituent enabling skills underlying abilities in reading, listening and writing, we also include a more integrated task in each of the Papers, in which reading and/or listening activities lead into a writing task.

Pre-tests of Paper I and both versions of Paper II were carried out on groups of G.C.E. Advanced Level, first year undergraduate and one year post-graduate native and non-native students in the academic disciplines mentioned above.

A third Paper, testing ability in spoken English, was prepared in collaboration with the ARELS Examinations Trust with whom the test will be jointly administered. This Paper was pre-tested with a number of overseas students in various educational establishments, most of them ARELS schools.

The pre-tests of all Papers and a number of other checks enabled the Board to carry out a great deal of internal and external validation of the tests. This in turn enabled the determination of the final format of the examination.

Purposes of the test

On the basis of candidates' performance in the test, the A.E.B. will be able to provide a profile of each candidate's proficiency in reading, listening, writing and speaking.

The profile will be intended a) to show receiving institutions how well or badly students might be expected, on the basis of their performance in the test, to cope with the language demands made on them in an educational environment and b) to show those responsible for English language teaching those areas in which a student might need help.

The Test

The **Aim** of the test is:

> To provide, by means of individual profiles, information on students' understanding and use of written and spoken English in academic situations.

Objectives of the test

In the examination, students will be assessed on their ability:

> A. to produce adequate written English for formal academic writing tasks;
>
> B. to understand spoken English for listening to lectures and discussion;
>
> C. to understand written English for reading textbooks and other sources of information both intensively and extensively;
>
> D. to produce adequate spoken English for taking part in academic discussions and presenting papers.

These objectives are further elaborated below. It is candidates' performances on A-D above which will be reported in the profile of results.

OBJECTIVE A

Candidates will have to demonstrate their ability to produce adequate written English for formal academic writing tasks.

Candidates may be expected to demonstrate proficiency in planning and organising information in:

(1) narrative
(2) description of phenomena and ideas
(3) description of process and change of state
(4) argument

Candidates' written work will be assessed according to the following criteria:

(1) relevance and adequacy of content
(2) compositional organisation
(3) cohesion
(4) adequacy of vocabulary for purpose
(5) grammar
(6) punctuation
(7) spelling

OBJECTIVE B

Candidates will have to demonstrate their ability to understand lectures and discussion. Candidates may be expected to demonstrate proficiency in the following enabling skills:

1. understanding conceptual meaning, e.g. comparison, degree, cause, result, purpose;

2   distinguishing the main idea from supporting detail, differentiating the whole from its parts, fact from opinion, statement from example, a proposition from its argument;

3. skimming
    (a) listening to obtain the gist
    (b) listening for specifics;

4. skills concerned with understanding and meaning, especially the ability to recognise the speaker's attitude towards the listener and topic of utterance, as conveyed mainly by intonation;

5. understanding ideas and information in the text not explicitly stated, e.g. through making inferences;

6. (a) extracting salient points to summarise the whole text, a specific idea or topic, the underlying idea or point

    (b) selective extraction of relevant key points from a text especially involving the co-ordination of related information

    (c) reducing text through rejecting redundant or irrelevant information.

OBJECTIVE C

Candidates will have to demonstrate their ability to understand written English for reading textbooks and other sources of information both intensively and extensively. Candidates may be expected to demonstrate proficiency in the following enabling skills:

1. deducing the meaning and use of unfamilar lexical items through understanding word formation and contextual clues;

2. understanding relations within the sentence;

3. understanding relations between parts of text through cohesion devices especially grammatical cohesion, e.g. pronoun reference;

4. understanding relations between parts of text by recognising indicators in discourse especially for introducing, development, transition and conclusion of ideas;

5. understanding the communicative function/value of sentences with and without explicit indicators, e.g. definition, example;

6. understanding conceptual meaning, e.g. comparison, means, cause, result, purpose;

7. separating the essential from the non-essential in text: distinguishing the main idea from supporting detail, differentiating the whole from its parts, fact from opinion, statement from example, a proposition from its argument;

8. skimming
    (a) surveying to obtain the gist
    (b) scanning for specifics;

9. understanding ideas and information in a text not explicitly stated;
10. notemaking
    (a) extracting salient points for summary of specific ideas/topics in the text
    (b) selective extraction of relevant points from a text for summary especially involving the co-ordination of related information;
11. critical evaluation (social science).

OBJECTIVE D

Candidates will have to demonstrate their ability to produce adequate spoken English for taking part in academic discussions and presenting papers. Candidates may be expected to demonstrate proficiency in:

1. free connected speech
2. oral summary of material presented graphically
3. asking and answering questions
4. responding to remarks and situations both academic and social
5. responding to and expressing opinions.

Candidates' oral work will be assessed according to the following criteria:

1. relevance and adequacy of content
2. intelligibility
3. appropriacy
4. adequacy of vocabulary for purpose
5. grammar
6. fluency.

What the Test Contains

There are three Papers described on this and the following two pages:

PAPER I

Part One

is a test of candidates' ability to read in English and to write in English about what they have read. They have *2 tasks* to do in 75 minutes.

> *Task One* — they have to write a summary of parts of a passage. To help them to do this, they should make brief notes while reading the passage.

> *Task Two* — they have to write short answers to a number of questions on the same passage.

Part Two

is a test of candidates' ability to understand spoken English. They have *one task* to do in approximately 10 minutes.

They hear a short tape recording once only. During pauses in the recording, they have to write down, in the space provided in the answer booklet, what the speaker has said.

Part Three

is another test of candidates' ability to understand spoken English. They have to make notes and use them to answer a number of questions. They have *2 tasks* to do in approximately 50 minutes.

> *Task One* — they hear a tape recording of a short lecture once only. A written outline of the main points of the lecture is printed in the answer booklet to help them to follow what the speaker is saying. This lecture outline consists of important statements from the passage, each followed by questions. While listening to the lecture they have to make notes in the spaces provided as, after the lecture, they have time to go through these notes and use them to write answers.

> *Task Two* — they have to write a summary of parts of the lecture, using the lecture outline and their notes and answers.

PAPER II
(A and B)*

Part One

is a test of candidates' ability to read in English. There are 2 different reading passages. They have *2 tasks* to do in 50 minutes.

Task One — establishing where words are missing from a passage and writing these words in spaces provided.

Task Two — writing short answers to a number of questions on a second passage.

Part Two

is a test of candidates' ability to understand spoken English by making notes and using them to answer questions. They have *one task* to do in 30 minutes.

They hear a tape recording of a short interview once only. A written outline of the interview is printed in the answer booklet to help them to follow what the speakers are saying. The outline consists of a number of questions. They have to make notes in the spaces provided while they are listening to the interview. After this interview, they have time to go through the notes they have made and use them to write answers.

Part Three

is a test of the candidates' ability to write in English, in complete sentences, and organise their work so that what they write is clear and answers the questions they are asked. They have *2 tasks* to do in 65 minutes.

Task One — writing a summary using:
a) notes made on the second reading passage in Part One;
b) relevant information from Part Two.

Task Two — rewriting a short passage which contains a number of errors, making all the necessary corrections.

*Note: Papers IIA and IIB are identical in format and test types. They differ in the nature of the source material used. Paper IIA has material more suitable for arts/social/administrative/business studies students and is illustrated in the specimen paper (see pp. SBIIA 1—2 and TBIIA 1—14) included in this booklet. Paper IIB (not illustrated in this booklet) has material more suitable for science/engineering studies. A specimen paper IIB is in preparation.

PAPER III*

This is a test of candidates' ability to speak in English.
The test is in five parts.

Part One

Candidates have to speak about themselves for one minute.

Part Two

Candidates have to respond to a number of remarks that might be made to them, or to situations they might find themselves in when they are in Britain.

Part Three

Candidates have to imagine they are in a small discussion group. They listen to a discussion and at certain points they have to answer questions or give their opinions.

Part Four

Candidates have a specific task to complete, which involves asking questions relating to non-verbal information, e.g. charts, diagrams, graphs, etc.

Part Five

Candidates are given verbal and numerical tables to study. They have five minutes in which to prepare an answer to a question set on this material. They then have two minutes to present their answer to the question.

---

*Note: Paper III is optional. That is to say, candidates may enter for Papers I and II (examination number 951) only, or for Paper III (examination number 950) as well as Paper I and II. Paper III cannot be entered for by itself.

PROFILE OF RESULTS

As mentioned earlier, candidates' results will be reported in the form of a profile for each of the skills: listening, reading, writing and, if it is also taken, speaking. In each of the skills candidates' performances will be reported in terms of the five grades listed below.

4   Proficiency in the study mode approaching that of native speaker tertiary level contemporaries; a limited number of weaknesses may be evident, but not sufficient to hamper academic progress seriously.

3   Moderate proficiency; some weaknesses which could affect performance in the study mode; some remedial language tuition would be helpful.

2   Limited proficiency; considerable weaknesses affecting performance in the study mode; some remedial language tuition is necessary.

1   Elementary language level; a large number of weaknesses are evident in performance in the study mode; these could seriously hamper academic progress; considerable remedial language tuition would probably be needed.

0   Beginner language level; almost no proficiency; cannot cope at all in the study mode; needs long-term language tuition before starting an academic course of study.

There will be *no* overall result, since it is felt that different subjects and departments vary as far as requirements for the various skills are concerned. The information given in the profiles should be interpreted by the person(s) responsible for admission on individual courses, in the light of the skills required by those courses.

More about the Test

The Test has been designed for speakers of English as a foreign or second language who wish to study through the medium of English at a University, Polytechnic or College of Higher or Further Education. At any such receiving institution students will have to understand what they hear in lectures and/or seminars and what they read. Sometimes they will have to select material from what they hear and read in order to perform writing tasks.

Paper I is based on a lecture situation. In the sample questions, as in the examinations, there will be a thematic link. For example, Part One of the sample questions is about "Changes in the position of women", and the two tasks are tests of reading comprehension on the same source material on that subject. Part Two involves dictation of a text about the role of women. Part Three involves listening to a lecture on "Issues in the Women's Liberation Movement" on which candidates have to write answers (Task One) to questions and subsequently (in Task Two) a summary of what the lecture was about.

This Paper is an attempt to simulate the student's situation in which some preliminary reading (as in Part One) leads into a lecture (as in Part Three) which, quite often, includes dictation of some details (as in Part Two). The tasks performed by candidates in the examination are a simulation of what happens in the study situation.

Paper II, which is more suited to arts/social/administrative/business studies in Paper IIA or to science/engineering studies in Paper IIB, is based on a seminar situation. As for Paper I, there is a thematic link. All the source material is based on matters of concern for the two groups and on subject matter with which students in the two groups would be familiar. For example, in the sample Paper IIA (please note there is no sample Paper IIB in this booklet), Part One is about difficulties overseas students face, Task One being about language difficulties of overseas students and Task Two being about employment difficulties of recent graduates. In Part Two, where, as there would be in a seminar, there are two or more speakers, there is a discussion about qualifications and difficulties in finding employment. Part Three involves writing about what they have read in Part One and listened to in Part Two. Finally, in Part Three, there is an editing task still on the subject of employment difficulties.

Paper III, the Oral Test, is conducted using a tape-recording and the candidates record their responses to various stimuli also on tape.

Part One is for the candidates to speak about themselves, their family, country, interests, thoughts on U.K., etc.

Part Two is concerned with social and academic situations. The candidate has to reply appropriately to various things said to him or he may be required to respond to situations described on the tape.

Part Three is a simulation of participation in a small discussion group in which there are a number of speakers talking about a topic on which the candidate will from time to time be asked questions or be required to give opinions.

Part Four requires the candidate to seek information which may be missing from non-verbal information, for example charts, diagrams, printed in the candidates' Source Booklet.

Part Five requires the candidate to summarise, using the appropriate given information, certain elements of verbal and numerical tables printed in the Source Booklet. The summary will be in response to a question also printed in the Source Booklet.

It is important to note that all the tasks in all three Papers are devised as a result of the extensive research into the needs of, and difficulties encountered by, overseas students studying in further and higher education.

It is also important to note that, although Papers IIA and IIB are more suitable for arts / social / administrative / business studies for the former and science / engineering studies for the latter, students on all courses would find Paper I and Paper III readily accessible. A specimen Paper IIB is in preparation.

Test in English for Educational Purposes (TEEP)

Source Booklet

CHANGES IN THE POSITION OF WOMEN

Introduction

Over the past forty years there have been a number of important changes in Britain in the material position of women and the overall political situation that influenced both the renewal of feminism in the late 1960s and the form which that renewal took. The changes have highlighted some of the limits in the gains made by the earlier feminist movement. In particular the notion of sexual equality has come to seem less and less relevant to the problem of overcoming women's specific oppression.

To illustrate this shift in women's material position let us look at the changes that have occurred in patterns of marriage and fertility on the one hand and patterns of education and employment on the other.

Section 1

In looking at the changes that have occurred in patterns of fertility since the 1920s two tendencies stand out. The first is the growth in the proportion of women in the population, until the mid-1960s at least, who have become mothers at some stage of their lives. The second is the compression of fertility for women within their lives as a whole.

The proportion of women having children at some stage in their lives has risen for three reasons. First there has been a growth in the proportion of women marrying, especially amongst the younger age groups. The proportion of women married in the age group 30–44, after which childbirth is unlikely to occur, rose from 72% in 1921 to 89% in 1971. The rise for the youngest age groups was much steeper: from 2%–10% for those aged 16–19 and from 27%–58% for those aged 20–24 (see Table 2).

TABLE 2

Percentage of women married by age group 1921–71 GB

Age	1921	1931	1951	1961	1971
16–19	2.3	2.3	5.1	8.4	10.0
20–24	26.7	25.4	46.5	57.3	58.0
25–29	56.1	57.8	76.1	83.6	84.2
30–44	72.3	73.9	81.9	86.8	88.8
45–59	60.0	60.0	72.6	76.6	80.3
60–74	45.5	47.5	48.0	49.8	53.3
75 and over	16.7	17.2	19.8	18.1	18.2
All ages	37.7	40.7	48.1	49.3	49.3

Source: Social Trends (1972)

Secondly, there has been a decline in childless marriages; whilst 16% of women married between 1920 and 1924 had no children, only 9% of women married between 1955 and 1959 were childless (see Table 3). More recent figures are not yet available but it is possible that, with the decline in the birthrate since the mid-1960s, the proportion of childless marriages may have recently risen again.

TABLE 3

Distribution of family size GB (births occurring to first marriages)

No. of children live-born in marriage	Percentage of women married in period		
	1920–4	1935–9	1955–9
0	16	15	9
1	24	26	18
2	24	29	34
3	14	15	20
4	8	7	(11)*
5 or more	14	8	(8)*
average no. of children	2.38	2.07	2.38

*Part-estimates

Source: Office of Population Censuses and Surveys (1973). *Report of the Population Panel.* Cmnd 5258.

20
The third reason for the rise in the proportion of women having children is the growth in childbirth outside marriage. In England these rose from 5.5 births for every 1,000 unmarried women aged 15–44 in the mid-1930s to 19.1 for every 1,000 in the years 1961–65 (Finer Report, 1974, Vol 1, p. 60).

25

30
Whilst fewer and fewer women had remained either single or childless since the years of the earlier feminist movement, at least until the mid-1960s, the proportion of a woman's life spent in bearing children declined. More than half of all babies are now born within the first five years of marriage and more than three quarters within eight years (Finer Report, 1974, Vol 1, p. 32). The typical mother spends about four years only now in a state of pregnancy and in nursing a child for the first year of life, compared to fifteen years at the turn of the century, or about 7% of her adult life-time (which is also longer) compared to one third around 1900 (Titmuss, 1958, p. 91).

Section 2

In the field of employment the major changes have occurred since World War II. From the 1940s onwards there has been a massive increase in the proportion of women in regular paid employment. The growth in the female labour force is described in more detail in an article by Hilary Land, 'The Myth of the Male
5
Breadwinner'. This article also points out a tendency for the importance of female labour in the total work force to have been undervalued during the whole of this century.

10
The growth in female employment has mostly occurred amongst women in the age groups 35 and over and amongst women whose children are old enough to be at school (see Table 4). However, from the mid-1960s there has also been a rapid rise in employment of women with pre-school children. The female paid-labour force before World War II was predominantly young and single. Now two thirds are married women who normally have major domestic responsibilities. From 1960 onwards nearly all the growth in women's employment has been in part-time work.

TABLE 4

Historical changes in married females' activity rates, by age, 1921–71

Age	1921	1931	1951	1961	1966	1971
20–24	12.5	18.5*	36.5	41.3	43.5	45.7
25–34	9.4	13.2	24.4	29.7	34.3	38.4
35–44	8.9	10.1	25.7	37.1	48.6	54.5
45–54	8.4	8.5	23.7	36.1	49.8	57.0
55–59	—	7.0	15.6	26.4	38.4	45.5
60–64	—	5.6	7.2	12.8	21.3	25.2
65 and over	4.2	2.9	2.7	3.3	5.5	6.5
All	8.7	10.0	21.7	29.7	38.1	42.2

*Aged 21–24

Source: Department of Employment, 'Women and Work: a statistical survey'. *Manpower*, paper 9.

15   The sexual division of labour in paid employment has been reinforced rather than eroded with the expansion of female employment. Most of the growth has occurred in the service sector in occupations that have become established as women's work, e.g. shop work, secretarial, nursing, teaching. In manual work there has been a decline in the proportion of women doing work which is defined as skilled (see Table
20   5).

What implications do these developments have for the re-emergence of a women's movement at the end of the 1960s? On the one hand there had been a rise in the proportion of women who had children at some stage of their lives at a time when maternity had become quantitatively less and less significant in women's lives as a
25   whole. On the other hand there has been a rise in the proportion of married women and mothers in the paid-labour force and with it a rise in the proportion of women with a double workload of housework and paid-work.

TABLE 5

The percentage of female workers in major occupational groups, 1911–66.

Occupational groups	1911	1921	1931	1951	1961	1966
1 Employers and proprietors	18.8	20.5	19.8	20.0	20.4	23.7
2 White-collar workers	29.8	37.6	35.8	42.3	44.5	46.5
(a) Managers, administrators	10.0	17.0	13.0	15.2	15.5	16.7
(b) Higher professionals	6.0	5.1	7.5	8.3	9.7	9.4
(c) Lower professionals, technicians	62.9	59.4	58.8	53.5	50.8	52.1
(d) Foremen, inspectors	4.2	6.5	8.7	13.4	10.3	11.4
(e) Clerks	21.4	44.6	46.0	60.2	65.2	69.3
(f) Salesmen, shop assistants	35.2	43.6	37.2	51.6	54.9	58.7
3 Manual workers	30.5	27.9	28.8	26.1	26.0	29.0
(a) Skilled	24.0	21.0	21.3	15.7	13.8	14.7
(b) Semi-skilled	40.4	40.3	42.9	38.1	39.3	42.6
(c) Unskilled	15.5	16.8	15.0	20.3	22.4	27.5
4 Total occupied population	29.6	29.5	29.8	30.8	32.4	35.6

Source: Department of Employment, 'Women and work: a statistical survey', *Manpower*, paper 9.

Section 3

Such changes highlight the limitations for women in the rights fought for by the earlier liberal feminists and delineated by John Stuart Mill. The right to choose freely between occupation of housewife and mother on the one hand and a career on the other is even less meaningful now than it was then. In mid-Victorian England almost one third of all women aged 20–44 never married because higher male mortality and large-scale emigration created a surplus of women. Many of these women were a driving force in the development of the earlier feminist movement, influencing it towards concentration on equal rights rather than special rights. As far as middle class single women were concerned the battle was partially won by the 1920s, as we have seen, with women's entry into the main professions accompanying the winning of the vote.

The progress of women in the professions did not continue in the intervening period however. The proportion of women relative to men in certain higher professions has actually tended to be lower since 1945 than in the 1920s and 1930s. This is partly because the older professions continued to discriminate and partly due to the demographic changes described below. With the decline in the proportion of single, childless women there are fewer women to benefit from equal rights as such.

Moreover, the strength of sex-stereotyping in the socialization process and the pressures on women to see their sexual identity in conventional feminine terms have not been challenged by equal rights legislation. Thus middle class women, although in a stronger position than working class women, because of greater potential for achieving economic independence and for minimizing the burdens of housework and childcare, have grown increasingly frustrated with their limited progress. For working class women the benefits derived from equal rights have been correspondingly less. In particular the position of the working class woman in part-time employment makes it increasingly obvious that it is not the realization of equal rights which will allow women to break out of their oppression. The limited success of equal pay legislation bears loud testimony to the inadequacy of simple, equal rights campaigning.

Section 4

The changes I have described are amongst the influences contributing to the growth of a modern women's movement in the late sixties in Britain. In what ways does it in fact differ from the earlier feminist movement? What is its relationship to the politics of reform and revolution? What is its social composition and how is its development related to the material changes in women's position that have been outlined?

The women's movement that emerged in Britain in the late sixties has two social and political strands. One is the Women's Liberation Movement and the other is organized pressure for women's rights within the labour movement. Neither has yet been seriously studied and therefore what follows is necessarily a somewhat speculative account.

Test in English for Educational Purposes (TEEP)

Paper I (sample)

GENERAL INTRODUCTION TO PAPER I

Paper I of the test has three parts. You must write all your answers in this booklet. Here is a brief description of the three parts of the test so that you know what to expect. There will be detailed instructions before each part.

PART ONE

This is a test of your ability to read in English and to write in English about what you have read. You have **2 tasks** to do in 75 minutes.

Task One — You have to write a summary of parts of a passage. To help you to do this you should make brief notes while reading the passage.

Task Two — You have to write short answers to a number of questions on the same passage.

PART TWO

This is a test of your ability to understand spoken English. You have **one task** to do in approximately 10 minutes.

You will hear a short tape recording once only. During pauses in the recording, you have to write down, in the space provided in this booklet, what the speaker has said.

PART THREE

This is another test of your ability to understand spoken English. You have to make notes and use them to answer a number of questions. You have **2 tasks** to do in approximately 50 minutes.

Task One — You will hear a tape recording of a short lecture once only. A written outline of the main points of the lecture is printed in this booklet to help you to follow what the speaker is saying. This Lecture Outline consists of important statements from the passage, each followed by questions. While listening to the lecture you have to make notes in the spaces provided. After the lecture you will have time to go through these notes and use them to write answers.

Task Two — You have to write a summary of parts of the lecture using the Lecture Outline and your notes and answers.

PART ONE — READING COMPREHENSION

This is a test of your ability to read in English and to write in English about what you have read. You have **2 tasks** to do in 75 minutes.

TASK ONE

Read the passage "Changes in the Position of Women" in the Source Booklet and then summarise, in your own words as far as possible,

WHAT THE AUTHOR SAYS ABOUT THE EMPLOYMENT OF WOMEN FROM THE 1940's ONWARDS.

Your summary should be about **200 words** in length.

You should use the space below to make notes which will help you to write your summary. These notes will not be marked.

WARNING: some of the sections in the passage are not relevant to this writing task. Remember the topic of the summary is only

THE EMPLOYMENT OF WOMEN FROM THE 1940s ONWARDS.

You should spend only **40 minutes** on this task.

NOTES:

TASK TWO

Look carefully at the questions below to see what information you need to answer them. Read again the passage "Changes in the Position of Women", and answer the questions in the spaces provided. Check your answers carefully.

You should spend only 35 minutes on this task.

1. What influenced the 'renewal of feminism' mentioned in line 3 of the Introduction?

2. What does 'The second', as used in Section 1, line 4, refer to?

3. Write another word or phrase that could replace 'Whilst' in Section 1, line 22.

4. Copy the first three words of a sentence from Section 1 describing a situation which is not known to be a definite fact.

5. Copy the first three words of the sentence from lines 22–30 of Section 1 which best summarises the content of the paragraph.

6. Look at the first paragraph of Section 3. What showed that middle-class single women had partly won the battle for equal rights by the 1920s?

TURN OVER

7. Look at the second paragraph of Section 3. What was partly the result of certain professions continuing to discriminate against women after 1945?

    _____

8. Now look at the third paragraph in Section 3. Why are middle-class women still making only limited progress?

    _____

    _____

9. Below are four headings for sections 1–4 in the text. Against each heading indicate the section of the text for which that heading would be most suitable.

    a) Women in the professions   Section_____

    b) Composition and context of the
       women's movement: some questions   Section_____

    c) Women in the labour force   Section_____

    d) Patterns of fertility   Section_____

10. Give one reference the author uses for information about the employment of women as manual workers.

    _____

    _____

11. What is the major difference between the typical female worker before World War II and the typical female worker now?

    _____

    _____

12. What does Table 3 of the Source Booklet suggest about changes in average family size between 1920 and 1959?

    _____

    _____

    _____

    _____

    _____

13. The final paragraph to the passage is not shown. The following six sentences originally
    formed that final paragraph, but they are not in the correct order. Indicate, by numbering
    1 to 6 in the boxes provided, the order in which you think the sentences originally appeared.

Originally the demands were equal pay, equal job and
educational opportunity, free nurseries available for all,
free contraception and abortion on demand.

Subsequently the demand for legal and financial
independence for women has been added.

Its main strength is at local level in the form of
small women's groups although it does have national
conferences and a set of demands.

However, unlike the earlier feminist movement, the
WLM has placed far greater emphasis on challenging
certain aspects of women's position in society than
on campaigning for a specific issue or issues.

The Women's Liberation Movement (WLM) emerged as a
national movement in 1970 when the first conference
took place in Oxford.

Thus a large part of WLM activity has been concerned
with the spreading of feminist ideas and the development
of feminist theory.

TURN OVER

PART TWO — LISTENING COMPREHENSION

This dictation is a test of your ability to understand spoken English. You have **one task** to do in approximately 10 minutes.

The speaker is going to dictate a text **once** only, with pauses. During the pauses write down what you have heard. You will have **2 minutes** at the end to check and correct what you have written down.

When you hear numbers you can write them down as figures or words.

You will have to work fast. First, we will give you a short piece for practice. We will **not** mark this. Write down what you hear.

_____

_____

_____

_____

_____

_____

The practice session is now finished.

Now write down what you hear on the tape. Remember you will hear it only **once**.

Write here:

_____

_____

_____

_____

_____

_____

_____

_____

_____

_____

PART THREE — LISTENING COMPREHENSION

This is another test of your ability to understand spoken English. You have to make notes and use them to answer a number of questions. You have **2 tasks** to do in approximately **50 minutes**.

TASK ONE

You are going to hear part of a lecture on "Issues in the Women's Liberation Movement".

The recording is about 10 minutes long and it will be played once only.

A Lecture Outline starts on the next page of this booklet and consists of three important statements, in capitals and underlined, each followed by questions. There is a space after each question for notes and below that a space for your answer.

While listening to the lecture, make notes in the space provided (these notes will **not** be marked).

You will be given time after the lecture is finished to use these notes to write your answers.

Use all the information in the lecture outline. It will help you to find exactly what information you need to listen for.

LECTURE OUTLINE

STATEMENT 1. SINCE THE EARLY 1970'S WOMEN'S GROUPS HAVE FORMED REGIONAL AND NATIONAL GROUPINGS, AND HAVE MOUNTED REGIONAL AND NATIONAL CAMPAIGNS.

1.1 These campaigns have concentrated on 4 central demands. What are they?

NOTES: a) _____

b) _____

c) _____

d) _____

ANSWER: a) _____

b) _____

c) _____

d) _____

STATEMENT 2. AN IMPORTANT ISSUE IN THE DEVELOPMENT OF THE WOMEN'S LIBERATION MOVEMENT HAS BEEN THAT OF THE INVOLVEMENT OF MEN IN THE MOVEMENT'S ACTIVITIES.

2.1 What, according to the speaker, did women particularly resent from the beginning?

NOTES: _____

_____

ANSWER: _____

_____

2.2 Why did men dominate the discussion in the early meetings of the movement?

NOTES: _____

_____

ANSWER: _____

_____

2.3 What happened at the Skegness conference in 1971?

NOTES: _____

_____

ANSWER: _____

_____

2.4 What decision was taken with respect to the involvement of men in Movement activities?

NOTES: _____

_____

ANSWER: _____

_____

STATEMENT 3. A SECOND ISSUE WIDELY DISCUSSED IN WOMEN'S GROUPS
IS THE QUESTION OF WAGES FOR HOUSEWORK

3.1 According to the speaker, what is the effect on the woman of the situation in which the
man goes out to work, but the woman stays at home and does the housework?

NOTES: _____

_____

ANSWER: _____

_____

3.2 In what way is the housework done by a woman at home less pleasant than a man's work out of the home?

NOTES: _____

_____

ANSWER: _____

_____

3.3 What is the major difference, according to the speaker, between a woman's work in the home and a man's work outside it?

NOTES: _____

_____

ANSWER: _____

_____

3.4 The suggestion of state wages for housework is rejected by most women for three reasons. What are they?

NOTES: a) _____

         b) _____

         c) _____

ANSWER: a) _____

        b) _____

        c) _____

3.5 What is the attitude of the speaker to regarding the family allowance as a basis for a scheme of state wages for housework?

NOTES: _____

_____

ANSWER: _____

_____

TASK TWO

For this task you should look at the information provided in the Lecture Outline on pages 11–13 of this booklet *and* the information you have written down yourself.

Then, using all this information, summarise, in your own words as far as possible, what the talk was about.

You should write about **200 words**.

You have **20 minutes** to complete this writing task.

Write here:

Test in English for Educational Purposes (TEEP)

Source Booklet
Paper IIA (sample)

The experiences of unemployment among recent science and engineering graduates.

The magazine *New Scientist* invited recent science graduates to describe their experiences of unemployment and hunting for jobs. As the responses showed, the increase in the level of graduate unemployment over the past few years is of growing concern to everyone, not least to the graduates themselves. Enormous sums of money
5 are invested in students to equip them with the knowledge and skills they will need when they eventually enter employment — the irony of simply replacing grant cheques with unemployment-benefit cheques is wasted on none of the graduates in the survey.

It is impossible to put an exact figure on the number of unemployed graduates at
10 any time; even statistics compiled by the Association of Graduate Careers Advisory Services refer to graduates from 15 months before. The Department of Employment does not collect such figures, and while universities and polytechnics often try to gather their own, they are usually inaccurate and incomplete.

As a rough guide, about 85 000 first-degree students have graduated in each of the
15 past three years. Of these just over one-third are science graduates (including engineering and technology but not medical, dental or veterinary graduates). In the past three years the annual rate of unemployment among these graduates averaged 12 per cent.

What is certain, and somewhat surprising, is that in the last two years the biggest
20 rises in unemployment have been among graduates in science and technology. Physical scientists rate with language graduates at 12 per cent; for life scientists and biologists, unemployment is about 15 per cent; for botanists and zoologists the rate is around 20 per cent.

In some ways, however, all unemployment statistics conceal almost as much as they
25 reveal. For example, many graduates these days cannot find work "using their degrees": over 50 per cent of biologists for example, must look outside the discipline for work. And while some may find permanent jobs in other fields, there is also a large body of graduates employed in temporary jobs, community schemes, seasonal work, familial employment (nepotism, apparently, is rife), working or travelling
30 abroad; or, and this is possibly the largest group, working in jobs that make no use of their qualifications and skills.

Thus, all statistics for graduate unemployment are misleading, so *New Scientist* asked readers to write about their experiences. The investigation was not intended to be either exhaustive or scientific but it was hoped that it might give some insight
35 into the problems facing graduates, and reveal any patterns or common experiences.

Reading the 85 or so responses gave a clear idea that many graduates follow a similar pattern in their search for employment and, in nearly all cases, unemployment induces feelings of bitterness, loss of confidence and frustration. Also, although only a very small sample of the respondents represented a fairly wide range of subjects
40 and qualifications, one fifth of them were women. All the main science degree subjects were represented from astronomy to zoology, at various levels of specialisation.

More than one-quarter of those who wrote were in employment when they wrote. Only four of these, however, described their work as permanent jobs. Three more were on community schemes: all the others had jobs that were either temporary or
45 completely irrelevant to what their degree was. They had been unemployed for between two months and over two years. Some of the respondents moved in and out of temporary jobs fairly frequently, so their situations were rarely stagnant. Surprisingly, poor qualifications were not the main reason for unemployment among those who wrote. Over one-quarter had either a PhD or an MSc, while a further
50 eight had a first class or 2.1 bachelor's degree: the biggest group had obtained 2.2s in the BSc courses.

Quality control and analysis, and research and development are traditionally the careers with most openings for science graduates who want to use their specialisations — this applies to bachelor's degree as well as doctorate level. Yet, even before
55   the recession began to bite, only half the physicists, one-third of the chemists and one-tenth of the mathematicians went straight into these professions. Nevertheless, the most popular careers mentioned are still analytical chemist or researcher. Those who responded to the survey must be optimists; or perhaps the extent of job shortages in these areas has not yet filtered through to graduates? Customary fall-backs for
60   those who don't make it into those two options have been posts as technicians in university laboratories and hospitals, and teaching in secondary schools. Now there are fewer opportunities in those areas too.

Some people considered careers that were not obvious progressions from their formal qualifications. Such a decision did not seem to make the searching process any easier.
65   Fish farming was one very popular example, and so was computing. Interestingly, none of the respondents had taken a degree in computer science, yet well over one quarter had this down as a first or second career choice. People who tried for jobs in computing, say after a life sciences degree, met with little success: competing with graduates in computer science for vacancies, they felt at a distinct disadvantage.
70   In short, respondents said that finding a job in a non-relevant area was just as difficult as finding one where they would use what they had studied.

Whether respondents see their degrees as vocational training or not, the pain of not achieving their aspirations is the same, and thoughts turn to where to lay the blame. Many felt that the problem began with poor advice from teachers at secondary
75   schools. Apparently schools still point the most able pupils towards physics, chemistry and mathematics or biology from O-level onwards. But a number of people mentioned that their schools had not encouraged them to think ahead and plan their futures. For many, getting to university was as far as their plans went. Once at university, students seem to opt for a subject they performed well in at school, and at the end
80   of their studies they possess a degree but not much idea of what to do with it. Perhaps strangely, careers advisers at universities and polytechnics came in for little criticism.

Test in English for Educational Purposes (TEEP)

Test Booklet
Paper IIA (sample)

GENERAL INTRODUCTION TO PAPER II

Paper II of the test has three parts. You must write all your answers in this booklet. Here is a brief description of the three parts of the test, so that you know what to expect. There will be detailed instructions before each part.

PART ONE

This is a test of your ability to read in English. There are two different reading passages. You have **2 tasks** to do in 50 minutes.

Task One — Finding words missing from a passage and writing these words in boxes provided.

Task Two — Writing short answers to a number of questions on another passage.

PART TWO

This is a test of your ability to understand spoken English by making notes and using them to answer questions. You will have only **one task** to do in approximately 30 minutes.

You will hear a tape recording of a short interview **once** only. Written questions on the interview are printed in this booklet to help you to follow what the speakers are saying. You have to make notes in the spaces provided while you are listening to the interview. After the interview, you will have time to go through the notes you have made and use them to write answers.

PART THREE

This is a test of your ability to write in English, in complete sentences, and to organise your work so that what you write is clear and answers the questions you are asked. You have **2 tasks** to do in 60 minutes.

Task One — Writing a summary using:
  a) notes made on the reading passage in Part One, Task Two.
  b) relevant information from Part Two.

Task Two — Rewriting a short passage which contains a number of errors, making all the necessary corrections.

Now start PART ONE of the test.

PART ONE — READING COMPREHENSION

This is a test of your ability to read in English. There are 2 different reading passages. You have **2 tasks** to do in 50 minutes.

TASK ONE

In the following passage a tutor describes staff-student relationships.

One word has been omitted from some of the lines. Those lines with a word missing have a number on the left hand side and a box on the right side. On these lines mark the place where you think a word has been omitted and write the missing word in the box provided.

The first four have been done for you.

You have **20 minutes** for this task.

result
was
who
before

A very striking / obtained from the essays and the discussions of my
sample / the mention of the friendliness and informality among the
majority of the British tutors / had obviously been adept at putting students
at their ease / embarking on constructive criticism or discussion.

1 This was appreciated by almost all students right across sample. One
student, however, a middle-aged male of high status from a Far Eastern
2 culture, only failed to refer to this factor but also had such deeply
3 entrenched proxemic attitudes that he refused sit alongside me when
I discussed his written work, insisting on taking up a position on the other
4 side of the desk. Informality, or what he perceived as, in this case,
clearly disoriented (the word is singularly apt) the student. A further
personal observation in respect of formality is also perhaps worth making.
5 This concerns the initial bewilderment and utter disorientation occur
when students from certain backgrounds (the Turks, I have found to be
most prominent in this respect) find humour mixed with higher learning.
It is not just that humour is often culture bound and frequently exigent
6 in the demands makes on language competence; it is simply that for
7 certain cultures humour and higher learning do mix, and so the tone may
be seen as something akin to frivolousness or even blasphemy. Of course,
in time, students learn to appreciate, or perhaps to put up with, such
8 a style, but the earlier stages may be quite.

9 matter of great concern to the overseas students was the question
10 of tutor accessibility and contact time. The majority of interviewed
11 expressed a view in line one mature student who wrote "Being a tutor
or supervisor means not only to want to help but also to have time to do
12 so." Another complained "Most of the supervisors are too and can only
13 give ten to fifteen to their students in a week, which is not
14 nearly to help a student in his or her research." This is an experience
that seems to be limited to overseas students from Departments whose
15 post-graduates are almost entirely British. a Department consists
16 largely of overseas students it would seem that special need for more
17 generous supervision (at least as regards time) is by the staff;
it is certainly appreciated by the student.

1. _____
2. _____
3. _____
4. _____
5. _____
6. _____
7. _____
8. _____
9. _____
10. _____
11. _____
12. _____
13. _____
14. _____
15. _____
16. _____
17. _____

TASK TWO

Look carefully at the questions to see what information you need from the reading passage in the source booklet in order to answer them.

Then read the passage, *The experiences of unemployment among recent science and engineering graduates*, and answer the questions in the spaces provided.

Check your answers carefully.

You have 30 minutes for this task.

Read the questions on this page and the facing page.

1. What does 'their own' in line 13 refer to?

   _____

2. Which particular group of science and technology graduates have experienced the greatest increase in unemployment in the last two years?

   _____

3. If you were a biologist with a job, what might the fact that you were employed conceal?

   _____

   _____

4. Who are 'the others' mentioned in line 44?

   _____

   _____

5. According to the survey, how important was a good qualification in finding a job?

   _____

6. Write another word or phrase that could replace 'yet' in line 54.

   _____

7. Why does the writer say in lines 57–58 that those who responded to the survey must be optimists?

   _____

   _____

   _____

8. Why, according to the text, would there be little point in applying for a job in a subject which you had not specialised in?

_____

_____

9. According to those who replied to the survey, how are the schools most at fault for the unemployment situation?

_____

_____

10. The final paragraph of the reading passage is not shown. The following four sentences originally formed that paragraph, but they are not in the correct order. Indicate, by numbering 1—4 in the boxes, the order in which you think the sentences originally appeared.

It was as though, deep down, the writers still believe that a degree is a passport to a job.

The fault does not lie with the schools alone, however.

Equally apparent from some responses was the stunning naïveté about finding a job.

On the whole, respondents waited until after graduation to contemplate their futures.

PART TWO — LISTENING COMPREHENSION

This is a test of your ability to understand spoken English by making notes and using them to answer questions. You will have **one task** to do in approximately 30 minutes.

You will hear an interviewer speaking to two people who have recently succesfully completed Master's Degree courses in Linguistics at a British university.

The recording is about 10 minutes long and it will be played **once** only.

On the next three pages of this booklet are a number of questions. They occur in the same sequence as the information in the interview. While listening to the interview make notes in the spaces provided under each of the questions. These notes will **not** be marked.

You will be given time after the interview is finished to use these notes to write your answers. Use the questions to follow what the speakers are saying.

Now read through the questions to try to find exactly what information you need to listen for. You have **3 minutes** to do this.

1. Why is Dulcie not concerned about finding a job?

NOTES: _____

_____

ANSWER: _____

_____

2. Jeremy found that qualifications are always insufficient. Why?

NOTES: _____

_____

ANSWER: _____

_____

3. Why could Jeremy not get the job he would really like to have?

NOTES: _____

_____

ANSWER: _____

_____

4. Why is it necessary for Dulcie to get a Ph.D.?

NOTES: _____

_____

ANSWER: _____

_____

5. Dulcie feels that it will be helpful to have a 'second string to her bow' when she eventually looks for a job. What is the second string in her case?

NOTES: _____

_____

ANSWER: _____

_____

6. Jeremy says he has never had any trouble finding jobs. But what — according to him — must you be prepared to do to find one?

NOTES: _____

_____

ANSWER: _____

_____

7. Jeremy feels that — in his field — the appointment of teachers with Ph.D.s may have negative results. Why?

NOTES: _____

_____

ANSWER: _____

_____

8. According to Jeremy, what may people like him, with an M.A., have to accept if they want to work in a particular part of the world?

NOTES: _____

_____

ANSWER: _____

_____

9. Jeremy says that there was an unwritten promise that an M.A. in Applied Linguistics would be the key to greater things. What did he find when he got it?

NOTES: _____

_____

ANSWER: _____

_____

10. What does he feel would be the result for many people if they did not get a higher qualification, but continued to work in their old job?

NOTES: _____

_____

ANSWER: _____

_____

11. Why, according to Dulcie, do people do M.A.s in General Linguistics?

NOTES: _____

_____

ANSWER: _____

_____

12. Jeremy says that some people who finished university with him and who applied for jobs with the British Council in Europe were rejected: why?

NOTES: _____

_____

ANSWER: _____

_____

PART THREE — WRITING

This is a test of your ability to write in English, in complete sentences, and to organise your work so that what you write is clear and answers the questions you are asked. You have **2 tasks** to do in 60 minutes.

TASK ONE

Re-read the passage in the Source Booklet. As you do so, make notes in the space provided over the page. These will help you to summarise what is written about the usefulness of a good university qualification in finding a suitable job.

WARNING: some of the material in the reading passage is **not** relevant to this writing task.

The notes you make will **not** be marked.

To complete the task you should also use relevant information from both the questions on Part Two, pages 7–9, and the information you wrote down yourself.

Then, as far as possible in your own words,

summarise what is said about the usefulness of a good university qualification in finding a suitable job

and

state your own views on this subject.

You should write about **250 words**.

You have **45 minutes** to complete this writing task.

TASK TWO

The following extract contains a number of errors in grammar, spelling and punctuation. Indicate where these are by underlining the errors. Then correct the errors in the space provided under each line, making only the necessary corrections. Do not re-write the passage in your own words.

> Example:
> I am <u>an</u> student of <u>Inglish</u>
>   a   English
> You have 15 minutes for this task.

New Scientist Survey: the Cost of Unemployment

Nearly all the writers were conscious from the cost of unemployment and the waist of expensive training Some of the costs may to be roughly estimated, such as unemployment-benefit payments or the money spended on training these graduates. a whole range of costs, identified in the letters we reseived, are not so easy to quantify. Their are, for example, costs to organisations, which, in several year's time, is likely to discover the disadvantages of not take a steadily flow of graduate into its lower posts (some respondents said employers were all too awear of the dangers). There is also the cost to science and universities, through the lost of knowledge that will have been contribute presumably to the common store. Often, as respondents pointed out, the drift away from science into other fields is unreversible.

Appendix II

The Associated Examining Board Test in English for Educational Purposes
Assessment Criteria for the Oral Test

Criteria of assessment

Appropriateness

0 Unable to function in the spoken language.
1 Able to operate only in a very limited capacity; responses characterised by socio-cultural inappropriateness.
2 Signs of developing attempts at response to role, setting etc. but misunderstandings may occasionally arise through inappropriateness, particularly of socio-cultural convention.
3 Almost no errors in the socio-cultural conventions of language; errors not significant enough to be likely to cause social misunderstanding.

Adequacy of vocabulary for purpose

0 Vocabulary inadequate even for the most basic parts of the intended communication.
1 Vocabulary limited to that necessary to express simple elementary needs; inadequacy of vocabulary restricts topics of interaction to the most basic; perhaps frequent lexical inaccuracies and/or excessive repetition.
2 Some misunderstandings may arise through lexical inadequacy or inaccuracy; hesitation and circumlocution are frequent, though there are signs of a developing active vocabulary.
3 Almost no inadequacies or inaccuracies in vocabulary for the task. Only rare circumlocution.

Grammatical accuracy

0 Unable to function in the spoken language; almost all grammatical patterns inaccurate, except for a few stock phrases.
1 Syntax is fragmented and there are frequent grammatical inaccuracies; some patterns may be mastered but speech may be characterised by a telegraphic style and/or confusion of structural elements.
2 Some grammatical inaccuracies; developing a control of major patterns, but sometimes unable to sustain coherence in longer utterances.
3 Almost no grammatical inaccuracies; occasional imperfect control of a few patterns.

Intelligibility

0 Severe and constant rhythm, intonation and pronunciation problems cause almost complete unintelligibility.
1 Strong interference from L_1 in rhythm, intonation and pronunciation; understanding is difficult, and achieved often only after frequent repetition.
2 Rhythm, intonation and pronunciation require concentrated listening, but only occasional misunderstanding is caused or repetition required.
3 Articulation is reasonably comprehensible to native speakers; there may be a marked 'foreign accent' but almost no misunderstanding is caused and repetition required only infrequently.

Fluency

0 Utterances halting, fragmentary and incoherent.
1 Utterances hesitant and often incomplete except in a few stock remarks and responses. Sentences are, for the most part, disjointed and restricted in length.
2 Signs of developing attempts at using cohesive devices, especially conjunctions. Utterances may still be hesitant, but are gaining in coherence, speed and length.
3 Utterances, whilst occasionally hesitant, are characterised by an evenness and flow hindered, very occasionally, by groping, rephrasing and circumlocutions. Inter-sentential connectors are used effectively as fillers.

Relevance and adequacy of content

0 Response irrelevant to the task set; totally inadequate response.
1 Response of limited relevance to the task set; possibly major gaps and/or pointless repetition.
2 Response for the most part relevant to the task set, though there may be some gaps or redundancy.
3 Relevant and adequate response to the task set.

Appendix III

UCLES/RSA Certificates in Communicative Skills in English

1. Introduction to the Scheme

1.1 Background

This series of examinations has been developed from the CUEFL exams run by the Royal Society of Arts from 1981 until 1988, and administered since then jointly by the RSA and the University of Cambridge Local Examinations Syndicate (UCLES).

In the first part of 1989 a review of the existing CUEFL scheme was conducted with a view to up-dating the examinations and broadening their appeal. The results of the consultations and discussions on which the review of the existing CUEFL scheme was conducted with a view to up-dating the examinations and discussions on which the review was based are incorporated in this new scheme.

(Footnote: Full details of the Review process are set out in a booklet **Findings of the Review and Proposals for Development** available from the Cambridge Syndicate)

The main features of the CCSE scheme are:

* Separate Certificates are awarded in:
  Reading
  Writing
  Listening
  Oral Interaction
* Certificates in each area are awarded at 4 Levels
* Task-based assessment
* Authenticity and relevance of tasks and texts
* Full published specification of the performance necessary to pass at each
  level.

Full details of each of these features are set out below

1.2 Statement of Equal Opportunity

It is the policy of the Cambridge Syndicate that these examinations should be available to all candidates equally and should not favour or prejudice any group or individual on grounds of race, sex or culture. Nonetheless it should be noted that they do require candidates to demonstrate the ability to use language for communication in specific contexts; individuals who, for personal or cultural reasons, find such communication difficult or such contexts inappropriate, should consider their position very carefully before entering the examinations.

Candidates who are sight-impaired should note that, particularly at the higher levels (3 & 4), all the exams may make use of written source material and may call for writing in the completion of the tasks.

Every care will be taken in the construction of the examinations to avoid inadvertent offence to users on grounds of race, sex, or culture.

1.3 Target Audience

The target audience for the examinations is adult (16+) users of English as a non-native language.

Candidates from Overseas

Contexts for the tasks set will normally (but not exclusively) be "in-Britain", but the tests will not require a familiarity with specifically British cultural conventions. Britain merely provides a plausible context for the use of English and one in which tasks can be set without offering an undue advantage to students from any particular language background. The criteria for appropriacy will be based on British usage.

The examination is intended to be accessible to candidates overseas who have never visited Britain and who may have no immediate or long-term plans to do so. The aim is to be able to form judgements about the candidates' ability to perform in and through English communicative tasks of an interactional and transactional nature.

ESL Candidates

These examinations are not intended to provide certification of language skills for long-term or permanent (ESL) residents in the UK. Such candidates may of course enter the examinations, but they may find the tasks and contexts inappropriate for their specific requirements.

1.4 Free-Standing Certificates in Individual Skill Areas

An important feature of this scheme is that each of the skill areas (Reading, Writing, Listening, Oral Interaction) is covered by a separate, free-standing certificate. The intention behind this is to offer candidates the chance to gain certification for what they **can** do, without being penalised by what they **cannot** do.

It is common experience among teachers that some candidates are much better at **receptive** uses of the language (in reading and listening) than **productive** uses (in writing and oral interaction). For others the opposite is the case. Some are better at **oral-based** language (listening and oral interaction) than **writing-based** (reading and writing). And again in some cases, the opposite is true.

This scheme is designed to cater for all these possibilities by allowing candidates to enter only for those Certificates which they need, and to enter each Certificate at a level at which they have a good chance of meeting the specifications.

Different candidates might therefore enter very different combinations of Certificates and levels, e.g.

Candidate 1

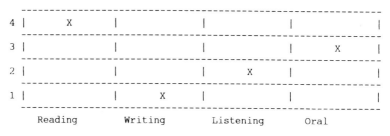

                    Certificates entered

Candidate 2

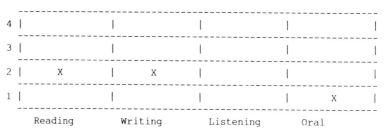

                    Certificates entered

Candidate 3

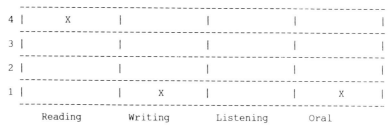

                    Certificates entered

Candidates can choose to enter for 1, 2, 3 or 4 Certificates at any level. However, note that they can enter each Certificate at only one level in each series of exams.
Certificates are awarded only in respect of areas and Levels actually entered, i.e. it is not possible to gain a pass at (say) Level 2 by entering and narrowly failing at level 3.

1.5 Levels

Certificates in all 4 areas, Reading, Writing, Listening and Oral Interaction, are offered at four levels.

It is difficult to give external yardsticks for the levels represented by these Certificates. Hours of study are a notoriously unreliable indication of level of achievement, since so much depends on the individual learner; similarly, it is difficult to compare performance in these Certificates with performance in other tests or examinations, since the content and characteristics of all exams are individual and specific. However, the following approximate equivalencies may be helpful.

<u>Please note that these are NOT proven or exact correspondences. They are offered simply for very general guidance. Information about the level of each of the CCSE Certificates will be found in the detailed specifications set out in this document.</u>

Level 1 is the lowest level, and it is very similar to the **Basic Level** of the old CUEFL scheme. It corresponds **approximately** to the level of the Cambridge Preliminary English Test (PET) and to Band 3 of the English Speaking Union scale.

Level 2 corresponds approximately to the **Intermediate Level** of the old CUEFL scheme. The level is <u>approximately</u> that of a Grade C/D in the Cambridge First Certificate (FCE) and to Band 4/5 of the English Speaking Union scale.

At Level 1 and Level 2 Certificates are awarded on the basis of tasks which, as far as possible, test only the skill area which gives its name to the test, i.e. Reading, Writing, Listening or Oral Interaction.

Level 3 is a new level, aimed between the **Intermediate Level** and the **Advanced Level** of the old CUEFL scheme. The level is <u>approximately</u> that of the new Cambridge Certificate in Advanced English (ACE) and Band 6 of the English Speaking Union scale.

Level 4 is similar to the **Advanced Level** of the old CUEFL scheme. The level is <u>approximately</u> that of Grade B/C in the Cambridge Proficiency (CPE) and Band 7/8 of the English Speaking Union scale.

At Level 3 and Level 4 tasks may be set which involve the integration of skills, e.g. tasks in the Writing test may be based on the reading of a piece of text material; in the Reading test, tasks may involve the production of connected writing. However, the main focus will always be on the skill area which gives its name to the test.

1.6 Approach

In all skill areas, at all levels, the scheme is designed to enable candidates to demonstrate their ability to use English for a variety of specified purposes within a range of specified contexts. The idea of specification is a very important one. By setting out what types of performance are expected from candidates, we can make clear what it means to "pass", and establish clearly the level of each test. Details of the specification for each of the 4 levels within each of the 4 skill areas are set out in the later sections of this booklet. The general framework is the same in all cases.

FRAMEWORK FOR THE SPECIFICATION OF PERFORMANCE

There are three elements:

1.6.1 Tasks

Each test is based upon the performance of a number of tasks. In simple terms, the specification of these tasks defines **what the candidate must do.** At lower levels a limited range of tasks is specified; at higher levels the range increases.

Examples of tasks are:

Reading: **Understanding the gist of a newspaper report**

Writing: **Ordering goods in reply to an advertisement**

Listening: **Identifying and understanding specific information in a news broadcast**

Oral Interaction: **Comparing your home town with that of a friend from another country**

The tasks are all intended to be **authentic.** In other words, they replicate tasks which in the real world, users of a language might actually carry out.

Full details of the tasks at the 4 levels are given in the sections of this booklet dealing with each area, Reading, Writing, Listening and Oral Interaction.

1.6.2 Text Type

An important element of the specification is the type of text which the candidate needs to be able to handle. Clearly tasks involving the production or comprehension of a text will be more or less easy depending upon what sort of text it is.

Examples of text types are:

Reading: **notice**

Writing: **letter**

Listening: **interview**

Oral Interaction: **dialogue**

Texts used as source material for the listening and reading tests are normally **authentic**. In other words, they are taken from real world sources where they have been used for a real purpose. They are not normally simplified or re-written, though they may sometimes be slightly modified to make them suitable for use in a particular task.

Full details of the text types at the 4 levels are given in the sections of this booklet dealing with each area, Reading, Writing, Listening and Oral Interaction.

1.6.3 Degree of Skill

Another way in which the different levels are defined is by specifying different degrees of skill for the performance of tasks. In simple terms, the degree of skill indicates how well a task must be performed in order to meet the criteria for passing the test.

In **Writing** for example, the four levels of performance are described in terms of:

Accuracy: **how formally "correct" the candidate's language needs to be**

Appropriacy: **how appropriate to the specific context the candidate's use of language needs to be**

Range: **how wide a range of language the candidate needs to be able to use**

Complexity: **how complex a text in terms of structure and organisation the candidate needs to be able to produce**

In all cases, the specification at lower levels is relatively "relaxed" compared to that at higher levels. Full details of the specifications for the four levels are given in the sections of this booklet dealing with each area, Reading, Writing, Listening and Oral Interaction.

2. CERTIFICATE IN READING

2.1 Levels

Certificates are awarded at 4 levels. Candidates must enter at the level 1 - 4 in terms of which they wish to be assessed; candidates achieving the specified level of reading performance will be awarded a Certificate at that level.

2.2 Time

At Levels 1 & 2 there is a test of 1 hour; at Levels 3 & 4 the test lasts one hour and a half. In addition, at each level candidates are allowed 10 minutes to look through the question paper and the source material.

2.3 Specification and Content

At every level the test is based on a collection of authentic source material. Candidates must carry out a number of reading tasks based on this material. Source material is selected and tasks are constructed at each level in terms of the criteria which are specified below.

As set out in the introduction, the key elements of this specification are **task** (operation), **text type**, and **degree of skill**.

2.3.1 Task

At Levels 1 & 2, the tasks which the candidates are asked to perform usually involve answering questions of some sort. Further details are given in the section on **formats** below. Wherever possible the questions involve using the text for a purpose for which it might actually be used in "the real world". In other words, the starting point for the examiners setting the tests is not just to find questions which can be set on a given text, but to consider what a "real" user of the language would want to know about the text and then to ask questions which involve the candidates in the same **operations**.

At Levels 3 & 4, the same considerations apply but in addition tasks may involve the production of short pieces of writing (notes, reports etc) based on the texts. Nonetheless, the emphasis, both in the construction of the papers and the marking, will always be on the receptive skill.

N.B. (1) This is not intended to be an exhaustive or prescriptive list. It merely gives an indication of the areas that might be involved.
   (2) The "questions" in the following tables are not intended necessarily to exemplify questions that might be asked in the exam. They are intended simply to clarify what is meant by the descriptions of the operations.

At All Levels

a. Locating and understanding specific information in a text. What time did the President arrive?

b. Understanding the overall message (gist) of a text. What is this passage about?

c. Deciding whether a particular text is relevant (in whole or part) to their needs in completing the task. Which letter contains the information you need?

d. Deciding whether the information given in a text corresponds to information given earlier. Does the train leave the time you were told?

e. Recognising the attitudes and emotions of the writer when these are expressed overtly. Is the writer in favour of the plan?

f. Identifying what type of text is involved (e.g. advertisement; news report etc). What sort of text are you reading?

g. Deciding on an appropriate course of action on the basis of the information in a text. So will you catch the train at 7 o'clock or 8 o'clock?

At Levels 3/4 Only

h. Deciding whether a text is based on e.g. fact, opinion or hearsay. What evidence does the writer draw on?

i. Tracing (and recording) the development of an argument. How does the writer reach this particular conclusion?

j. Recognising the attitudes and emotions of writers as revealed by the text implicitly. Does the writer seem to be in favour of the developments described?

k. Extracting the relevant points to summarise the whole text, a specific idea or the underlying idea. Make notes on ....

l. Appreciating the use made of e.g. typography, layout, images in the communication of a message. How does this advertisement achieve its effect?

2.3.2 **Text Type**

Tasks set may involve candidates in working with following text types.
**N.B. The list below is not exhaustive. Examiners may set tasks based on other
appropriate text types at all levels.**

At All Levels

Leaflet

Advertisement

Letter

Postcard

Form

Set of instructions

Diary entry

Timetable

Map

Plan

Newspaper / magazine article

At Levels 3/4 Only

Newspaper feature

Newspaper editorial

Telex/telegram

Novel (extract)

Poem

Authenticity: where possible the texts used in the examination are genuine
samples of the appropriate text type reproduced in facsimile from the original
publication.

2.3.3 Degree of skill

In constructing the tasks which candidates are asked to carry out, and in assessing candidates' performance, examiners base their expectations of what can be done on the following degree of skill criteria. Note that the performance expected is relatively simple at low levels and progressively more sophisticated at higher levels.

Degree of Skill Specification

CERTIFICATES IN COMMUNICATIVE SKILLS IN ENGLISH: Reading

In order to achieve a pass at a given level, candidates must demonstrate the ability to complete the tasks set. Tasks will be based on the degree of skill in language use specified by these criteria:

	Level 1	Level 2
COMPLEXITY	Does not need to follow the details of the structure of the text.	The structure of a simple text will generally be perceived but tasks should depend only on explicit markers.
RANGE	Needs to handle only the main points. A limited amount of significant detail may be understood.	Can follow most of the significant points of a text including some detail.
SPEED	Likely to be very limited in speed. Reading may be laborious.	Does not need to pore over every word of the text for adequate comprehensions.
FLEXIBILITY	Only a limited ability to match reading style to task is required at this level.	Sequences of different text types, topics or styles may cause initial confusion. Some ability to adapt reading style to task can be expected.
INDEPENDENCE	A great deal of support needs to be offered through the framing of the tasks, the rubrics, and the contexts that are established. May need frequent reference to dictionary for word meanings.	Some support needs to be offered through the framing of the tasks, the rubrics and the contexts that are established. the dictionary may still be needed quite often.

	Level 3	Level 4
COMPLEXITY	The structure of the text will generally be perceived and tasks may require understanding of this.	The structure of the text will be followed even when it is not signalled explicitly.
RANGE	Can follow the significant points of a text including most detail.	Can follow all the points in a text including detail.
SPEED	Can read with considerable facility. Adequate comprehension is hardly affected by reading speed.	Can read with great facility. Adequate comprehension is not affected by reading speed.
FLEXIBILITY	Sequences of different text types, topics cause few problems. Good ability to match reading style to task.	Sequences of different text types, topics and styles cause no problems. Excellent ability to match reading style to task.
INDEPENDENCE	Minimal support needs to be offered through the framing of the tasks, the rubrics and the contexts that are established. Reference to dictionary will only rarely be necessary.	No allowances need to be made framing tasks, rubrics and establishing contexts. Reference to dictionary will be required only exceptionally.

2.4 Formats

For the Reading test, candidates are provided with a pack of source material and a "question" paper, containing the tasks they are to carry out. Normally all the tasks should be completed.

As noted above, at Levels 1 & 2, the tasks which the candidates are asked to perform usually involve answering questions of some sort, while at Levels 3 & 4 they may, in addition, involve the production of short pieces of writing as part of the task.

Usually the same pack of source material will be used at all levels (though not all texts within it will be used at all levels). Because of the nature of the specifications for these examinations, the same text is often used at more than one level; but, except in cases where overlap between levels is deliberately included for technical reasons concerned with monitoring the reliability and validity of the exam, the task set will be different.

At lower levels, rubrics are kept deliberately simple and support is given by numbering pages in the source material and referring candidates to these.

Tasks at Lower levels (1 & 2) normally involve writing in single words/phrases. Where multiple-choice formats are used, they are of a 3-element type.

The formulation DON'T KNOW or IT DOESN'T SAY may be found at all levels to indicate that the information required is not actually given in the text.

e.g. Did the train leave on time?

    a. Yes

    b. No

    c. Don't Know

The choices in multiple-choice items always reflect a choice of **action or outcome**, not merely language variants for expressing the same action or outcome.

Formats including filling in charts/maps etc may be found at all levels, but at lower levels candidates are not to be asked to produce connected writing.

At higher Levels (3 & 4) tasks may involve writing from a single word or phrase, up to notes and brief reports.

2.5 Marking

Marks are awarded to tasks in accordance with a mark-scheme drawn up by the moderating committee. The committee also determines the pass marks for particular tests on the basis of the performance which is deemed to meet the specifications set out above. It should be noted that pass marks are not set in order to ensure that a given proportion of candidates passes (or fails); the basis of passing or failing is the candidate's performance relative to the criteria set out here.
Dictionaries (monolingual or bilingual) may be used freely.

3. CERTIFICATE IN LISTENING

3.1 Levels

Certificates are awarded at 4 levels. Candidates must enter at the level 1-4 in terms of which they wish to be assessed; candidates achieving the specified level of listening performance will be awarded a Certificate at that level.

3.2 Time

At all levels tests last approximately 30 minutes. This includes all pre-recorded gaps and pauses of the tape to allow for reading of the question paper and answering the questions, as well as pre-recorded repetitions of the source material where these are provided.

3.3 Specification and Content

At every level the test is based on recorded source material. Candidates must carry out a number of listening tasks based on this material. Source material is selected and tasks are constructed at each level in terms of the criteria which are specified below.

As set out in the introduction, the key elements of this specification are **task (operation) text type**, and **degree of skill**.

3.3.1 Task

At Levels 1 & 2, the tasks which the candidates are asked to perform usually involve answering questions of some sort. Further details are given in the section on **formats** below. Wherever possible the questions involve using the recorded passage for a purpose for which it might actually be used in the "real world". This "authenticity of purpose" means that many conventional overhearing activities found in course books will <u>not</u> be used in the exams, e.g.

(recording of a customer in a shop)

- What did she buy?
- How much did it cost? etc

The only exceptions to this are where the information overheard is public and likely to be of relevance to the candidate, e.g.

(announcement in railway station)

- What platform is the London train leaving from?

In other words, the starting point for the examiners setting the tests is not just to find questions which can be set on a given recording, but to consider what a "real" user of the language would want to learn from the text and then to ask questions which involve the candidates in the same **operations**.

At Levels 3 & 4, the same considerations apply but in addition tasks may involve the production of short pieces of writing (notes, reports etc) based on the recordings. Nonetheless, the emphasis, both in the construction of the papers and the marking, will always be on the receptive skill.

Tasks set at different levels might require candidates to carry out the following operations.

N.B. (1)   This is not intended to be an exhaustive or prescriptive list. It merely gives an indication of the areas that might be involved.

(2)   The "questions" in the following tables are not intended necessarily to exemplify the questions that might be asked in the exam. They are intended simply to clarify what is meant by the descriptions of the operations.

At All Levels

a. Locating and understanding specific information in a recording. What time did the President arrive?

b. Understanding the overall message (gist) of a recording. What is the speaker trying to say?

c. Deciding whether a particular recording is relevant (in whole or part) to their needs in completing the task. Which recording contains the information you need?

d. Deciding whether the information given in a recording corresponds to information given earlier. Do the two speakers agree about...?

e. Recognising the attitudes and emotions of the speaker when these are expressed overtly. Is the speaker in favour of the plan?

f. Identifying what type of recording is involved (e.g. advertisement; news report etc). What sort of recording are you listening to?

g. Deciding on an appropriate course of action on the basis of the information in a recording. So will you catch the train at 7 o'clock or 8 o'clock?

At Levels 3/4 Only

h. Deciding whether a recording is based on e.g. fact, opinion or hearsay. What evidence does the speaker draw on?

i. Tracing (and recording) the development of an argument. How does the speaker reach this particular conclusion?

j. Recognising the attitudes and emotions of speakers as revealed by the recording implicitly. Does the speaker seem to be in favour of the developments described?

k. Extracting the relevant points to summarise the whole recording, a specific idea or the underlying idea. Make notes on....

l. Recalling specific information, attitudes or emotions revealed by the text. What did the speaker say about...?

3.3.2 **Text Type**

Tasks set may involve candidates in working with following text types.
**N.B. The list below is not exhaustive. Examiners may set tasks based on other
    appropriate text types at all levels.**

<u>At All Levels</u>

Announcements

e.g.

advertisements

weather forecasts

news reports

answerphone messages

road / traffic reports

radio programme announcements.

Interview

Drama

Discussion

Quiz

Commentary

Song

<u>At Levels 3/4 Only</u>

Lecture

Debate

Authenticity: The texts used in the examination are genuine samples of the
appropriate text type recorded e.g. off-air. It may be necessary from time to
time to re-record e.g. an interview, specifically for the examination (perhaps
because of the poor quality of an original recording). In this case every
effort will be made to re-capture the authentic language use of the original.

3.3.3 Degree of Skill

In constructing the tasks which candidates are asked to carry out, and in assessing candidates' performance, examiners base their expectations of what can be done on the following degree of skill criteria. Note that the basis of tasks and the performance expected is relatively simple at low levels and progressively more sophisticated at higher levels.

Degree of Skill

CERTIFICATES OF COMMUNICATIVE SKILLS IN ENGLISH: Listening

In order to achieve a pass at a given level, candidates must demonstrate the ability to complete the tasks set. Tasks will be based on the degree of skill in language use specified by these criteria:

	Level 1	Level 2
COMPLEXITY	Does not need to follow the details of the structure of the text.	The structure of a simple text will generally be perceived but tasks should depend only on explicit markers.
RANGE	Needs to handle only the main points. A limited amount of significant detail may be understood. Most non-standard accents will cause confusion.	Can follow most of the significant points of a text including some detail. Many non-standard accents will still cause confusion.
SPEED	Normal rate of delivery needs to be understood only generally. Slower, more deliberate tempo may lead to more detailed comprehension.	Normal rate of delivery imposes strain after a fairly short time.
FLEXIBILITY	Rapid sequences of different text types, speakers, or topics may cause problems. Background noise of any sort may hamper comprehension.	Sequences of different text types, speakers, topics impose strain after a fairly short time. Background noise influences conderably the ability to understand.
INDEPENDENCE	A great deal of support needs to be offered through the framing of the tasks, the rubrics, and the contexts that are established. Repetition of the text/ input will normally be allowed.	Some support needs to be offered through the framing of the tasks, the rubrics and the contexts that are established. This may involve repetition.

	Level 3	Level 4
COMPLEXITY	The structure of the text will generally be perceived and tasks may require under-standing of this.	The structure of a text will be followed even when it is not signalled explicitly.
RANGE	Can follow the significant points of a text including most detail. Common non-standard accents do not cause confusion.	Can follow all the points in a text including detail. Only extreme non-standard accents cause confusion.
SPEED	Normal rate of delivery imposes strain only after a considerable time.	Normal rate of delivery does not impose strain.
FLEXIBILITY	Sequences of different text types, speakers, topics impose strain only after a considerable time. Only extreme background noise	Sequences of different text types, speakers, topics do not impose strain. Background noise does not significantly hinder comprehension.
INDEPENDENCE	Minimal support needs to be offered through the framing of the tasks, the rubrics and the contexts that are established. Repetition will only rarely be necessary.	No allowances need to be made in framing tasks, rubrics and establishing contexts. Repetition will be required only exceptionally.

3.4 Formats

For the Listening test, candidates are asked to listen to a tape of recorded material and are given a "question" paper, containing the tasks they are to carry out. Normally all the tasks should be completed.

The recorded tape includes all necessary instructions and, where appropriate, pauses and repetitions. Where possible, candidates should be allowed to listen to the recording individually through headphones (e.g. in a language laboratory) but, where these facilities are not available, the recording can be played through a loudspeaker. Clearly though, the performance of candidates may be disadvantaged if acoustic or playback conditions are unsatisfactory.

As noted above, at Levels 1 & 2, the tasks which the candidates are asked to perform usually involve answering questions of some sort, while at Levels 3 & 4 they may, in addition, involve the production of short pieces of writing as part of the task.

Because of the nature of the specifications for these examinations, the same recording is often used at more than one level; but, except in cases where overlap between levels is deliberately included for technical reasons concerned with monitoring the reliability and validity of the exam, the task set will be different.

At lower levels, rubrics are kept deliberately simple and texts are normally played more than once.

Tasks at lower levels (1 & 2) normally involve writing in single words/phrases Where multiple-choice formats are used they are of a 3-element type.

The formulation DON'T KNOW or IT DOESN'T SAY may be found at all levels to indicate that the information required is not actually given in the recording.

e.g. Did the train leave on time?

    a. Yes
    b. No
    c. Don't Know

The choices in multiple-choice items always reflect a **choice of action or outcome,** not merely language variants for expressing the same action or outcome.

Formats including filling in charts/maps etc may be found at all levels, but at lower levels candidates will not be asked to produce connected writing.

At higher Levels (3 & 4) tasks may involve writing from a single word or phrase, up to notes and brief reports or editing a written text on the basis of information provided by the tape. Where appropriate, these will be marked using the criteria from the Writing Test of the level below.

3.5 Marking

Marks are awarded to tasks in accordance with a mark-scheme drawn up by the moderating committee. The committee also determines the pass marks for particular tests on the basis of the performance which is deemed to meet the specifications set out above. It should be noted that pass marks are not set in order to ensure that a given proportion of candidates passes (or fails); the basis of passing or failing is the candidate's performance relative to the criteria set out here.

4. CERTIFICATE IN WRITING

4.1 Levels

Certificates are awarded at 4 levels. Candidates must enter at the level 1-4 in terms of which they wish to be assessed; candidates achieving the specified level of writing performance will be awarded a Certificate at that level.

4.2 Time

The time of the test at each level is as follows:

Level 1: 1 hour
Level 2: 1 hour 30 minutes
Level 3: 2 hours
Level 4: 2 hours 30 minutes

In addition, at each level candidates are allowed 10 minutes to look through the question paper.

4.3 Specification and Content

At every level the test is based on the production of a number of pieces of writing, in accordance with the specifications.

As set out in the introduction, the key elements of these specifications are **tasks** (operation), **text type,** and **degree of skill.**

4.3.1 Tasks

In these examinations, the candidate's task is to produce pieces of writing of the type specified with the degree of skill required for the level. See the section on **Formats** below for further details.

Functions.

Completing the tasks set at different levels in an appropriate way will involve candidates in a range of language **functions.**

e.g.

```
┌─────────────────────────────────────────────────────────────────────┐
│                                                                       │
│  At all Levels                                                        │
│                                                                       │
│  Expressing:  thanks, requirements, opinions, comment, attitude, confirmation,│
│               apology, want/need, information, complaints, reasons,   │
│               justifications                                          │
│                                                                       │
│  Directing:   ordering, instructing, persuading, advising, warning    │
│                                                                       │
│  Describing:  actions, events, objects, people, processes             │
│                                                                       │
│  Eliciting:   information, directions, service, clarification, help,  │
│               permission                                              │
│                                                                       │
│  Narrating:   sequence of events                                      │
│                                                                       │
│  Reporting:   description, comment, decisions                         │
│                                                                       │
│                                                                       │
└─────────────────────────────────────────────────────────────────────┘
```

This is an indication of the areas that might be involved. It is not intended to be an exhaustive or prescriptive list and it makes no distinction in terms of level.

The crucial difference between levels lies in the **degree of skill** with which the functions are expressed and the tasks are performed, and the **text types** which candidates are expected to handle. These are set out below.

4.3.2 Text Types

Tasks set may involve candidates in the production of the following text types:

```
┌─────────────────────────────────────────────────────────────────────┐
│                                                                       │
│  At all Levels                                                        │
│                                                                       │
│  Form                                                                 │
│                                                                       │
│  Letter (personal/business)                                          │
│                                                                       │
│  Message                                                              │
│                                                                       │
│  Note                                                                 │
│                                                                       │
│  Notelet                                                              │
│                                                                       │
│  Notice                                                               │
│                                                                       │
│  Postcard                                                             │
│                                                                       │
│  Recipe                                                               │
│                                                                       │
│  Report                                                               │
│                                                                       │
│  Set of Instructions                                                  │
│                                                                       │
└─────────────────────────────────────────────────────────────────────┘
```

At Levels 3/4 Only

Article

Biography

Curriculum vitae

Memo

Newspaper advertisement

Newspaper report

Notes

Summary

Telex/telegram

4.3.3 Degree of Skill

It will be clear from the specifications above that there is considerable overlap between the levels in terms of the tasks (functions) and text types the candidate may be asked to produce. However, in constructing the tasks which candidates are asked to carry out and, in assessing candidates' performance, examiners base their expectations of what can be done on the following degree of skill criteria. Note that the performance expected is relatively simple at low levels and progressively more sophisticated at higher levels.

Degree of Skill

CERTIFICATES OF COMMUNICATIVE SKILLS IN ENGLISH: Writing

In order to achieve a pass at a given level candidates must demonstrate the ability to complete the tasks set with the degree of skill specified by these criteria:

	Level 1	Level 2
ACCURACY	Grammar, vocabulary, spelling and punctuation may be uncertain but what candidates write is intelligible and unambiguous.	Generally good control of grammar, vocabulary spelling and punctuation though some errors which do not destroy communication are acceptable.
APPROPRIACY	Use of language is broadly appropriate to the task, but no subtlety is expected. The intention of the writer can be perceived without excessive effort. Layout is generally appropriate but may show marked inconsistencies.	Use of language is in most respects appropriate to the task, and some adaptation of style to the particular context is demonstrated. The overall intention of the writer is clear. Layout, including handwriting, is generally appropriate.
RANGE	Severely limited range of expression is acceptable. Candidates may have laboured to fit what they want to say to what they are able to say.	A fair range of language is used. Candidates are able to to express themselves without gross distortion.
COMPLEXITY	Texts may be simple showing little development. Simple sentences with little attempt at cohesion are acceptable.	Texts will display basic organisation with themes and topics linked in a simple way.

	Level 3	Level 4
ACCURACY	Good control of grammar, vocabulary, spelling and punctuation. Any errors must not interface with communication.	Standards of grammar, vocabulary, spelling and punctuation are consistently of a very high level.
APPROPRIACY	Use of language is in almost all respects appropriate to the task. There is clear evidence of the ability to adapt style to the particular context. The intention of the writer, both overall and in detail, is generally clear. Layout, including handwriting, is generally appropriate.	Use of language is consistently appropriate to task, context and intention. Layout is consistent and appropriate. Handwriting does not interfere with communication.
RANGE	An extensive range of language is used. Candidates are able to express themselves clearly and without significant distortion.	Few limitations on the range of language available to candidates are apparent. There is no distortion of communication in order to fit known language.
COMPLEXITY	Texts can be organised with themes and topics appropriately linked and sequenced. There will be a clear structure to the text where appropriate.	There is clear and consistent evidence of the ability, to produce organised coherent and cohesive discourse where appropriate.

4.4 Format & Marking

The tests of writing at all levels consist of tasks which require the production of pieces of writing. These are assessed directly by teams of examiners, by reference to the degree of skill criteria for the particular level. In order to reach a pass level, the piece of writing must meet the specified degree of skill in all respects. In order to pass the exam as a whole, the candidate must meet the specified degree of skill in all the tasks set, though the examiners retain discretion to award a pass to candidates who fail narrowly one task.

It should be noted that pass marks are not set in order to ensure that a given proportion of candidates passes (or fails); the basis of passing or failing is the candidate's performance relative to the criteria set out here.

Because of the nature of the specifications for these examinations, the same task is sometimes used at more than one level. However the degree of skill criteria by which it is assessed will be different.

At lower levels, rubrics are kept deliberately simple and support is offered through the framing of tasks. At higher levels (3 & 4) the input for the tasks may sometimes involve fairly extended pieces of reading.

Dictionaries (monolingual or bilingual) may be used freely.

5. CERTIFICATE IN ORAL INTERACTION

5.1 Levels

Certificates are awarded at 4 levels.   Candidates must enter at the level 1 - 4 in terms of which they wish to be assessed; candidates achieving the specified level of oral performance will be awarded a Certificate at that level.

5.2 Format & Time

At each level the test involves the following personnel:

- **the candidate:**   alone or working in a pair with a fellow candidate.

- **the assessor:**   appointed by the Cambridge Syndicate.   The assessor plays no part in the conduct of the exam but observes each candidate's performance and evaluates it against the degree of skill specifications for the level at which the candidate has entered.

- **the interlocutor:** a teacher from the candidate's school or an external appointment by Cambridge.   The interlocutor is trained to work with the candidate through the tasks that are set, giving her/him the scope to use the language to the best of her/his ability.

- **the usher:**   a member of staff from the candidate's school who helps her/him to prepare for the tasks by explaining any unknown words in the instructions and making sure the candidate knows exactly what to do.

The test is in two sections:

Section I

This consists of a discussion between the candidate and an interlocutor, observed by the assessor (who plays no part in the interaction).   This discussion is based on a task which the candidate has been given, appropriate to the level at which she/he has entered, and lasts approximately 5 minutes.

Section II

Section II is subdivided into two phases, but for the purposes of assessment is considered as a whole.   Both phases are based on a task which is designed to suit the particular level.   Two tasks are prepared for each level and it is the assessor (taking account where appropriate of the views of a representative of the Centre about the suitability of particular tasks for particular candidates) who decides which task should be prepared by particular candidates.

Section II (a): Here the interlocutor initiates an interaction between two candidates based on the task selected.   (The pairing of candidates is the responsibility of the Centre.   Where necessary, a "dummy" candidate can be used to make a pair.)   Immediately the task is under way, the interlocutor withdraws, leaving the candidates to continue with the task.

Section II (b): After 4/5 minutes the interlocutor re-enters the room and at
some natural point re-joins the interaction. The candidates will then be asked
to report briefly on the discussions during the interlocutor's absence and
she/he will lead the interaction into new areas arising from the task. This
will continue for a further 4/5 minutes or until the assessor indicates that
sufficient evidence of each candidate's language use has been produced.

Prior to going into each section of the test, the candidate spends approximately
5 minutes with an usher preparing the task. The usher is not allowed to help
directly with the performance of the task, but is there to ensure that the
candidate understands fully what the task is about.

The overall time of the test at each level is thus approximately 30 minutes per
two candidates, i.e

Section I

Preparation: 5 minutes)
                                    individual candidate
Task: 5 minutes)

Section II

Preparation: 5 minutes)
                                    paired candidates
Task: 10 minutes)

Full guidance is issued to Centres about the administration and logistics of
this test.

Because of the nature of the specifications for these examinations, it may
sometimes happen that the same task or a very similar one is used at more than
one level; but the degree of skill criteria by which it is assessed will be
different.

At lower levels, rubrics are kept deliberately simple and support is offered
through the framing of tasks. At higher levels (3 & 4), the input for the tasks
may sometimes involve fairly extended pieces of reading.

5.3 Specification and Content

At every level the test is based on the candidate's participation in a number of
oral interactions, in accordance with the specifications.

As set out in the introduction, the key elements of these specifications are
task (operation), **text type,** and **degree of skill.**

5.3.1 Tasks

In these examinations, the candidates' task is to take part in oral interactions
of the type specified with the degree of skill required for the level.
Candidates will not be asked to adopt personae or to play fantasy roles.

Functions

Completing the tasks set at different levels in an appropriate way will involve candidates in a range of language **functions**.

e.g.

At all Levels

Expressing: requirements, opinions, comment, attitude, confirmation, apology, want/need, information, complaints, reasons, justifications

Directing: instructing, persuading, advising

Describing: actions, events, objects, people, processes

Eliciting: information, directions, clarification, help, permission

Narrating: sequence of events

Reporting: description, comment, decisions

This is an indication of the areas that might be involved. It is not intended to be an exhaustive or prescriptive list and it makes no distinction in terms of level. It should be noted that certain functions such as ordering or warning are not appropriate to include in the test since it does not involve role play.

5.3.2 Text Types

At all levels candidates will be expected to take part in dialogue with a native-speaker and a non-native speaker, and in multi-participant interaction in a group containing a native-speaker and a non-native speaker.

The native-speakers may be known or not known to the candidates. The interaction with a non-native speaker will normally be with a candidate of a similar level, this person will normally be someone known to the candidate.

5.3.3 Degree of Skill

It will be clear from the specifications above that there is considerable overlap between the levels in terms of the tasks (functions) and text types the candidate may be asked to produce. However, in constructing the tasks which candidates are asked to carry out and, in assessing candidates' performance, examiners base their expectations of what can be done on the following degree of skill criteria. Note that the basis of tasks, and the performance expected is relatively simple at low levels and progressively more sophisticated at higher levels.

Degree of Skill

CERTIFICATES IN COMMUNICATIVE SKILLS IN ENGLISH: Oral Interaction

In order to achieve a pass at a given level, candidates must demonstrate the ability to complete the tasks set with the degree of skill specified by these criteria:

	Level 1	Level 2
ACCURACY	It is acceptable for pronunciation to be heavily influenced by L1 if it is generally intelligible. With support, the candidate must be able to clarify any confusions caused by lexical or grammatical errors.	Pronunciation must be clearly intelligible even if still obviously influenced by L1. Grammatical/lexical accuracy is generally high though some errors which do not destroy communication are acceptable.
APPROPRIACY	Use of the language must be broadly appropriate to to function though it may not correspond to native-speaker expectations. The intention of the speaker can be perceived by a sympathetic listener.	The use of language must be generally appropriate to function. The overall intention of the speaker must be generally clear.
RANGE	It is acceptable for the candidate to have a severely limited range of expression and to have to search often for a way to express the desired meaning.	A fair range of language must available to the candidate. Only in complex utterances is there a need to search for words.
FLEXIBILITY	The candidate is not expected to take the initiative in conversation, or to respond immediately to a change in topic. The interlocutor may have to make considerable allowances and often adopt a supportive role.	There must be some evidence of the ability to initiate and concede a conversation and to adapt to new topics or changes of direction.
SIZE	Contributions limited to one or two simple utterances are acceptable	Must be capable of responding with more than short-form answers where appropriate. Should be able to expand simple utterances with occasional prompting from the interlocutor.

	Level 3	Level 4
ACCURACY	Pronunciation must be clearly intelligible even if some influences from L1 remain. Grammatical/lexical accuracy is high though occasional errors which do not impede communication are acceptable.	Pronunciation must be easily intelligible though some residual accent is acceptable. Grammatical/lexical accuracy must be consistently high.
APPROPRIACY	The use of language must be generally appropriate to function and to context. The intention of the speaker must be clear and unambiguous.	The use of language must be entirely appropriate to context, function and intention. There is nothing to cause confusion.
RANGE	A wide range of language must be available to the candidate. Any specific items which cause difficulties can be smoothly substituted or avoided.	There must be only occasional obvious limitations on the range of language. Few allowances have to be made for the fact that the candidate is not a native-speaker,
FLEXIBILITY	There must be consistent evidence of the ability to "turn-take" in a conversation and to adapt to new topics or changes of direction.	The candidate must be able to "turn-take" and "direct" an interaction appropriately and keep it flowing.
SIZE	Must be capable of making lengthy contributions where appropriate. Should be able to expand and develop ideas with minimal help from the interlocutor.	Must be capable of making lengthy and complex contributions as appropriate. The interlocutor does not need to support the candidate.

5.4 Marking

The tests at all levels consist of tasks which require the productions of pieces of oral interaction. These are assessed directly by the examiner, by reference to the degree of skill criteria for the particular level at which the candidate has entered. In order to reach a pass level, the candidate's production must meet the specified degree of skill in all respects. In order to pass the exam as a whole, the candidate must meet the specified degree of skill in both sections of the exam.

It should be noted that pass marks are not set in order to ensure that a given proportion of candidates passes (or fails); the basis of passing or failing is the candidate's performance relative to the criteria set out here.

Appendix IV

The Joint Matriculation Board
Test in English (Overseas)

Joint Matriculation Board

Test in English (Overseas)
Written English Question Paper

Answer Question 1A in the answer book for Question 1A.
Answer Question 1B in the answer book for Question 1B.

Question 1A (10 marks)

Write a set of instructions to accompany the diagrams below showing how to change a car tyre.

Write between ten and fifteen sentences.

Start with the sentence, "Open the boot."

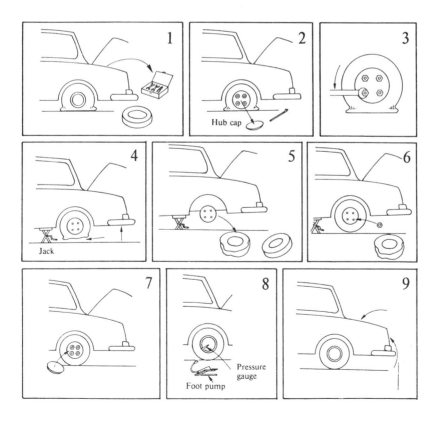

Answer Question 1B in the answer book for Question 1B.

Question 1B (10 marks)

All woven fabrics are produced by the interlacing of yarns. *Warp* (length-wise) yarns are first stretched onto a loom, and arranged so that they can be alternatively raised and lowered by harnesses (movable frames). *Weft* (filling or crosswise) yarns are then inserted at right-angles to the warp, by shuttles. Weave structures can be varied by rearranging the pattern in which warp and weft intersect.

There are three basic weaves, *plain, twill,* which is designed for strength, and *satin,* which is designed for surface appearance. Most other weaves are variations on these three.

By reference to the diagrams below discuss why these three are considered to be basic and different from each other, and how the other weaves relate to these basic weaves.

Write about fifteen sentences.

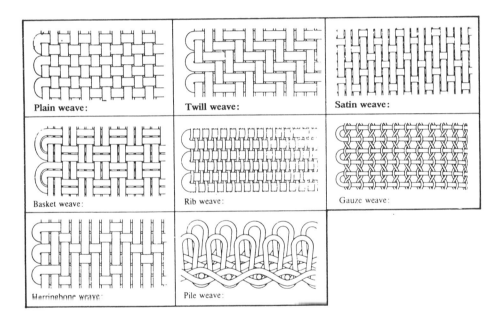

Plain weave: Twill weave: Satin weave:

Basket weave: Rib weave: Gauze weave:

Herringbone weave: Pile weave:

Answer Questions 2, 3, 4 and 5 in the answer book for Questions 2, 3, 4 and 5.

Question 2 (30 marks)

This question is in the answer book.

Question 3A (10 marks)

This question is in the answer book.

Question 3B (10 marks)

Read the passage *The Developing English Language* and answer Question 3B in the answer book.

The Developing English Language

The conquest of England by the Norman invaders brought about an influx of French words which went on increasing in volume for more than three centuries. At first it was little more than a trickle. For a long time the Norman conquerors did not have much to do socially with their Saxon subjects. There are plenty of indications of this, for the languages, too, moved forward in parallel channels. The custom of having one name for a live beast grazing in the field and another for the same beast when it is slaughtered and prepared for the table, is often supposed to be due to our English squeamishness and hypocrisy. Whether or not the survival of this custom through ten centuries is due to the national characteristics just mentioned it would be hard to say, but they certainly have nothing to do with how the custom first arose. That is a much more blameless affair. For the Saxon peasant who had spent hard days and nights to produce the oxen, sheep, calves and swine[1] probably was never allowed to sample the beef, mutton, veal and pork[2] which were consumed by his Norman masters.

Notes

1. Oxen, sheep, calves and swine are all words of Saxon origin for living animals.

2. Beef, mutton, veal and pork are all words of French origin describing the meat that comes from these animals.

Question 4 (22 marks)

Read the passage *Paper Making* and answer Question 4 in the answer book.

Paper Making

Paper-making today is a vast industrial undertaking, but fundamentally the process is the same as that employed hundreds of years ago. Until approximately 1860, the paper mills of Britain depended heavily on adequate supplies of rags, which were collected from all over a region. The sorting of rags was undertaken by women and children; they were seated on benches in a large room full of old linen before a chest or box which was divided into six cases to receive as many different sorts of rags. Each woman had a piece of pasteboard, hung from her girdle and extended on her knees, upon which, with a long, sharp knife, she undid seams and stitches and scraped off all filth. Occasionally such substances as nettle stalks, straw, hay, spent hops and thistle-down were added to rags for special types of paper.

Sometimes the rags, after sorting, were soaked in water, pressed into balls and placed in a damp cellar to ferment for two months or more. During this process they became straw-coloured, but lost nearly one quarter of their weight, and became fragile, making much easier the subsequent processes of macerating and cleaning.

The evil-smelling rags were cut into fragments with chopping knives hinged to wooden blocks and worked up and down by hand. They were then washed in running water and rubbed by hand in an effort to remove the yellow tinge, the presence of which was responsible for the pleasant creamy tinge of old paper. Rag-cutting was considered unhealthy work, for not only were the rags dusty, but they could also carry infectious diseases. Rag-cutters were paid three shillings a week and both boys and girls were engaged in this task.

The next process was the pulping of rags under the pounding of battery hammers. The rags were thrown into a solid oak or stone trough lined with lead and subjected to pounding for three days. Each battery of stamping machines consisted of from three to eight heavy hammers. The stamps used for the first beating were tipped with spikes to tear the rags apart, and the troughs in which they were pounded were fed constantly by a stream of running water to wash away impurities. Woven horsehair mats prevented the escape of any fragments of rag. On the following day, the rags were transferred into a second set of water troughs and beaten with a lightly shod set of stamps. Lastly the pulp was pounded by all-wooden stamps in a tank of static water. No running water at all was used during the third stamping for fear of washing the pulp itself away. For printing paper, size, usually consisting of a mixture of powdered alum and oil, was added at the beating stage so as to provide a smooth surface in the finished paper. The engine boy or engineer, who supervised this stage in the process, was paid an average of two shillings a week.

The pulp vats, where the pulp was then taken, had to be kept warm. Charcoal was often used for fuelling the fire. The contents of the vat also had to be agitated constantly, by a pole with a perforated disc at its tip or by a mechanised paddle called a hog. Overseeing these preparations and the ensuing process was one of the most important craftsmen in a paper mill—the vatman—who was responsible for the actual moulding of the paper.

The equipment required by a vatman consisted of a mould and deckle. The mould was a square mahogany frame with its top covered by a fine wire mesh. This rested loosely within another frame called the deckle, and was essential to ensure straight edges to the sheet of paper. Grasping the mould and deckle, the vatman plunged them into the warm, liquid pulp, turned them horizontally and lifted, sieving out a layer of pulp and letting water drain back into the vat. With almost the same motion he gave his mould two shakes—from right to left and from front to back. This matted the fibres both ways and gave the sheet equal tension strength.

The mould containing the pulp was passed along a bench, called a "bridge" to another craftsman called a coucher, who removed the deckle and turned the mould over on to a piece of woollen felt. Felt and paper were laid in alternate layers to a height of two feet or more, ready for pressing. The paper and felt were then carefully separated and the paper pressed again. After drying, and glazing, the paper was ready for cutting into smaller sheets, ready for despatch from the mill.

Question 5 (15 marks)

Read the passage *Art Work* and answer Questions 5.1 to 5.6 in the answer book.

Art Work

Let us consider the requirements for sketching and painting. The items which you will need every time you paint or draw include a structure to support your work. Ideally you will need to buy or make a support which will accommodate pictures of all sizes and at a variety of heights, and which will enable you to vary the angle of the tilt to avoid awkward light reflections. Make sure, whatever type of easel you use, that it is rigid, and that it will hold hardboard panels, drawing boards, and canvases. Finally, you should bear in mind whether you intend to work indoors or outdoors, or both; for outdoor work you obviously need an easel that is portable.

There are five main types of easel, A—E. All are made of hard woods, except the light folding type, which is metal. The first two types are strong stable structures and are correspondingly expensive. If their cost is prohibitive the home-constructed type C can be a good compromise, but it is too unwieldy to be portable.

A three-legged folding structure made up of lightweight alloy sections, type D is extremely portable. It nevertheless affords some variability in the angle and height of the work panel. In this respect, type C has a drawback: whereas two of the other three indoor types have great flexibility of vertical adjustment, the homemade model only has one height setting. It resembles a pair of stepladders or a nursery blackboard, with the front and back sections hinged together at the top. These open to give a variety of angles to the work, and when opened fully out the four feet of this easel make it quite firm enough to work with. For their vertical adjustment the two factory-made indoor types have a central wooden column with sliding blocks to clamp the top and bottom of the work at a variety of heights. Of these, type B is more versatile than type A, in that it has a bracket at the bottom of the central column, allowing it to be tilted forwards or backwards. The structure of the other's H-shaped base does not permit this.

The best is the last of the floor-standing types. Its three foldable legs give it great rigidity. It folds up into a compact, easily carried form, the legs being swung up to the sides of the box whose lid doubles as a work panel when upright. It has an integral palette and the box contains your materials. The fact that the device has retractable legs means that, when standing, the whole thing may be raised or lowered.

Some artists' suppliers market a table easel (type E). This can be very useful when space indoors is tight. It is simply a square wooden frame with a fixed bottom block and a sliding top block on a central column and a reclining back support. It is not very sturdy, though it does constitute an economical support for indoor work. The box easel, with its legs folded away, also serves perfectly as a table easel. As described above, it is not only highly satisfactory for outdoor work but also for the indoor studio where it serves perfectly as a rigid easel which can be left in position or folded away. It can be purchased at about the same price as type B, but you could hardly take the latter, with its three radial legs and high central column, when sketching out of doors.

Joint Matriculation Board

Office Use	
Question	Mark
2A	
2B	
3A	
3B	
4	
5	
Total	

Test in English (Overseas)
Written English

ANSWER BOOK FOR QUESTIONS 2, 3, 4 AND 5

Wednesday 26 June 1985 9-30–12-15

Surname.. *Other name(s)*..

Centre Number.. *School or College*..

Answer Questions 2, 3, 4 and 5 only in this answer book.

Answer Question 1A in the answer book for Question 1A.

Answer Question 1B in the answer book for Question 1B.

Question 2

In the following passages one necessary word has been omitted from each line. Mark the place where you think such a word has been omitted, ⋏ , and in the space provided write the word that has been omitted.

Passage A (15 marks)

In 1972, the Government accepted the first application by cable

....

television company mount local community television experiments.

....

Greenwich Cablevision Limited, served some 15,000 homes in the

....

Woolwich area South London, began transmissions in July 1972.

....

Four other cable companies their applications accepted three months

....

later. The licences, authorising the services provided broadcast

....

relay organisations covered period to July 1976,

....

but order to allow the Committee of Inquiry to complete

....

its report, licences were extended for another three years. The

....

aim of the experiments to provide a totally local television

....

service extra charge, and, in so doing, discover if the planned

....

programmes could meet community needs and yet still financially

....

viable. The topics, all of were to be transmitted in the

....

early evening, would include only national current affairs

....

and they affected the subscribers, but also news of local events.

....

Passage B (15 marks)

Education is based on the safe assumption that only has to go on

....

collecting more and information for it to sort itself into useful

....

ideas. We have developed tools handling the information; mathematics

....

for extending it, logic for refining it. While culture concerned

....

with establishing ideas, education has the role of passing those

....

established ideas. Both are involved improving ideas by bringing

....

them to date. Now the only available method for changing ideas

....

is conflict which works in two ways. In the first way is a head-on

....

confrontation between opposing ideas. One other of the ideas

....

achieves a practical dominance the other idea which is suppressed

....

but not changed. In the way the new information conflicts

....

with the old idea. As result of this conflict the old idea is

....

supposed to be changed. This is the method science, which is always

....

seeking to generate new information to upset the old ideas bring

....

about new ones. Indeed it is more than this—it is method of

....

human knowledge.

Question 3A (10 marks)

The following terms are used to describe parts of a schooner. Read the definitions and choose the most suitable words from the list below to label each part. Write the number of the chosen word for each part in the appropriate circle on the diagram on page 5. Write X if there is no suitable definition.

1	bowsprit	a large spar projecting forward from the bow of a schooner.
2	flying jib	a sail outside the jib on an extension of the bowsprit.
3	foresail	the lower sail set behind a schooner's foremast.
4	forestaysail	the triangular headsail of a schooner.
5	gaff	the spar upon which the head of a fore and aft sail is extended.
6	jib	a triangular sail set on a stay extending from the head of the foremast to the bowsprit.
7	luff	the forward edge of a fore and aft sail.
8	maingafftopsail	a triangular topsail with its foot extended upon the gaff and its luff upon the maintopmast.
9	mainmast	a sailing ship's principal mast, usually second from the bow.
10	maintopmast	the mast next above the mainmast.
11	ratlines	one of the small transverse ropes attached to the shrouds.
12	shroud	one of the ropes leading usually in pairs from a ship's mastheads to give lateral support to the masts.
13	stay	a large strong rope usually of wire used to support a mast.
14	stay sail	a fore and aft sail hoisted on a stay.

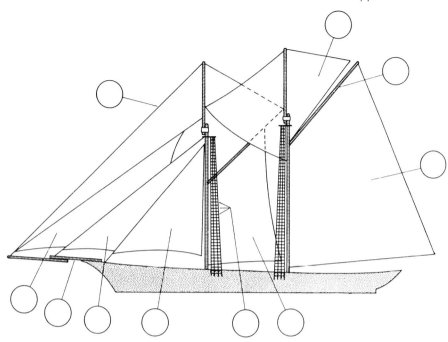

Question 3B (10 marks)

The following words and phrases can be used to replace words and phrases in the passage *The Developing English Language* without any change in the meaning. Write the *exact* words and phrases from the passage in the spaces provided.

caused	....
grew	....
mix	....
separately	....
cooked	....
attributed	....
its origin	....
innocent	....
laboured	....
taste	....

Question 4 (22 marks)

Read the passage *Paper Making* on page 7 of the Question Paper and answer Questions **4.1, 4.2, 4.3** and **4.4** below.

4.1 *Steps in the Process:*

From the following list of steps, select the **ten** that make up the process of paper-making as described in the passage. Put the ten you have selected in the order in which they occur. Indicate your selection and order by putting the letter of each of your chosen items in its correct place in **Column I** (Steps in Order) of the table on the opposite page.

A.   The pulp was shaped

B.   The paper was woven into a matting

C.   Other organic material was introduced

D.   The rags were washed

E.   The paper was compressed

F.   A special fluid was introduced

G.   The rags were diseased

H.   The rags were ground in running water

I.   The rags were saturated and fermented

J.   The rags were divided into types

K.   The pulp was filtered through horsehair

L.   The rags were chopped up

M.   The pulp was heated

4.2 *Non-Essential Steps*

Indicate in **Column II** of the table (Optional Steps) those steps in the process that were optional by placing ticks where appropriate.

4.3 *The Purpose of Each Step*

The following purposes are each associated with a particular step in paper-making.

Write the underlined word or phrase in the correct place in **Column III** of the table (Purpose of Steps).

To <u>ensure finish</u> for printed paper

To <u>produce</u> special paper

To <u>remove</u> colour impurity

To <u>classify</u> material

4.4 *The Personnel Involved*

Using the abbreviations given below, indicate in **Column IV** of the table (Personnel Involved) which stages were the direct responsibility of the named persons.

Vatman —V

Coucher —C

Engineer —E

	I	*II*	*III*	*IV*
	Steps in Order	*Optional Steps*	*Purpose of Steps*	*Personnel Involved*
1.				
2.				
3.				
4.				
5.				
6.				
7.				
8.				
9.				
10.				

Question 5 (15 marks)

Read the passage *Art Work* on page 8 of the Question Paper and answer the questions below. You are advised to answer them in the order given.

5.1 In the first column put **M** if the easel is manufactured, and **DIY** if it is homemade.

5.2 In the second column put **E** if the easel is expensive to buy or make, and **C** if it is cheap.

5.3 In the third column, put **I** if the easel is for use indoors, and **O** if it is for use outdoors. If it can be used either outdoors or indoors put **IO**.

5.4 In the fourth column put **A** if the height of the easel is adjustable, and **NA** if it is not.

5.5 In the fifth column put **T** if the easel's angle of tilt can be varied, **NT** if it cannot.

5.6. On the opposite page there are six illustrations. Put the numbers of the appropriate illustrations in the sixth column of the chart.

	1	2	3	4	5	6
Type of easel	*Manufactured or homemade*	*Cost*	*Use*	*Adjustability of height*	*Variability of tilt*	*Illustration*
A						
B						
C						
D						
E						

1

4

2

5

3

6

Aural Test: Answer Book   2

PART ONE

In this part of the Test you will hear part of a radio programme. The speakers are discussing the Registry Mark illustrated on the loose sheet. You will hear the discussion first, then you will hear the main points again. As you listen you should make notes about the Mark. Write your notes on the blank marks provided on this page. In the boxes provided on this page complete the letters required to make notes about *years* and *months*. The first 4 boxes have been started for you. You will later have time to use your notes to complete the marks on Page 3.

For rough work while listening to the tape.

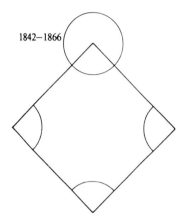
1842–1866

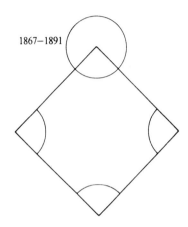
1867–1891

For rough work before completing your answers—

	a	b	c	d							

A	B	C	D																				

JOINT MATRICULATION BOARD

TEST IN ENGLISH (OVERSEAS) AURAL TEST   MARCH 1985

THIS SHEET IS FOR USE IN ANSWERING PART ONE OF THE AURAL TEST

Registry Mark.

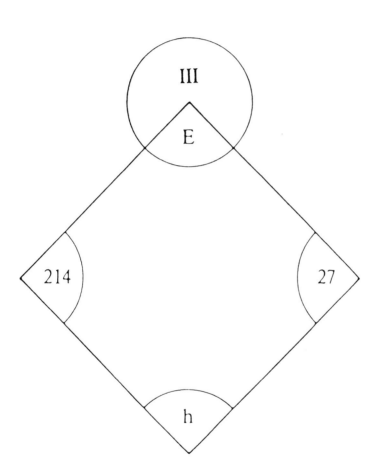

Complete the registry marks below using your notes.

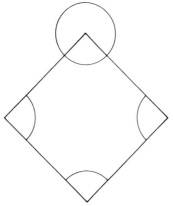

1. An earthenware object made on 14 January 1843 by manufacturer 327.

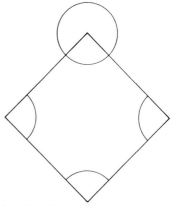

2. A wooden object made on 2 April 1858 by manufacturer 513.

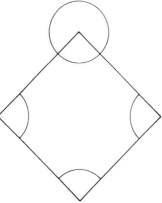

3. An earthenware object made on 10 June 1870 by manufacturer 134.

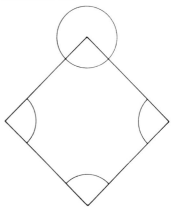

4. A metal object made on 28 July 1873 by manufacturer 179.

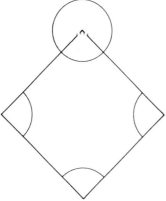

5. A wooden object made on 19 May 1882 by manufacturer 117.

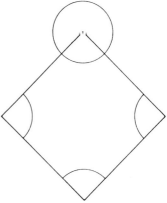

A glass object made on 6 September 1860 by manufacturer 996.

PART TWO

Section 1.

In this part of the Test you will hear a short talk on the subject of *cotton*. As you listen to the first section of the talk you should look at Figure 1 and shade in the months from *planting to harvesting cotton in the USA*.

You will hear Section 1 of the talk only **once**.

Section 2.

You will hear the second section of the talk **twice**. As you listen

(i) choose the *eight* correct sentences from a–j below;

(ii) put them in the correct order in the column labelled a–j, in Table 1;

(iii) complete Table 1 by writing the stage of the process in the other column. The names of the stages are— Classing, Coating, Ginning, Growing, Harvesting, Planting, Pressing.

Note that *two* of the sentences below refer to the same stage.

For rough work

a. The seeds are separated from the bolls.

b. The seeds are chemically treated.

c. The bolls are classed.

d. The plants are sprayed.

e. The fibres are chemically treated.

f. The soil is weeded.

g. The seeds are classed.

h. The bolls are picked.

i. The fibres are pressed.

j. The seeds are sown.

a–j	Stage
1.	
2.	
3.	
4.	
5.	
6.	
7.	
8.	

Figure 1

Table 1

a—j	Stage
1.	
2.	
3.	
4.	
5.	
6.	
7.	
8.	

Appendix V

The International English Language Testing System (IELTS)

Background to the International English Language Testing System

The International English Language Testing System (IELTS) supersedes the earlier English Language Testing Service (ELTS) test. The ELTS test was originally designed as a test for prospective postgraduate students but a growing demand from other student groups and receiving institutions, especially in Australia, as well as new developments in testing theory, has resulted in this up-to-date, completely revised and flexible testing system.

IELTS provides a readily available method of assessing the English language proficiency of non-native speakers who intend to study or train in the medium of English. The System offers an "on-demand" test which measures the skills needed for effective study and training. Whilst measuring candidates' general English language proficiency IELTS takes account of differences in subject specialisms and course types.

IELTS is jointly managed by the British Council, the University of Cambridge Local Examinations Syndicate (UCLES) and the International Development Program of Australian Universities and Colleges (IDP) and administered by UCLES. The British Council has wide experience in test administration around the world and a long-standing record of student placement in many disciplines. UCLES is an internationally recognised body in the provision of examinations of all kinds; in the field of English as a Foreign Language alone, it examines well over 100,000 candidates every year. IDP operates an Educational Information and Counselling Service for students in Asia and the Pacific who intend to study in Australia.

Why is a comprehensive testing system necessary?

A recent survey of 600 overseas students at British Universities found that nearly 20% were perceived to be handicapped in their studies by insufficient English language proficiency. On the other hand, of the 80% of students who were doing well in their studies many had attended pre-sessional courses on the basis of detailed and reliable English language test results.*

The number of overseas students studying in Australia has increased rapidly in the past few years. Experience has shown that in a substantial number of cases information regarding the English language proficiency of overseas students has been incomplete. Australian institutions have requested an English test which provides an indication of students' level of English skills in listening, speaking, reading and writing. Such an approach allows for appropriate pre-course English and concurrent English to be provided in conjunction with the student's main study programme.

For a large number of overseas students an accurate assessment of their English, followed by recommended amounts of tuition to remedy areas of weakness, can make the difference between success and failure – or at least between an enjoyable or a stressful learning experience.

*C Criper & A Davies (1988).
ELTS Validation Project Report
ELTS Research Report 1(i), The British Council and University of Cambridge Local Examinations Syndicate, Cambridge.

What does the test consist of?

The IELTS test is divided into four subtests. Each candidate takes two general subtests, Listening and Speaking, and a module comprising two specialised subtests, Reading and Writing. The general components test general English while the modules test skills in particular areas suited to the candidate's chosen course of study.

The tests are taken in this order – Reading, Writing, Listening, Speaking – and timed as follows:

Reading	55 minutes
Writing	45 minutes
Listening	30 minutes
Speaking	11-15 minutes

Total Test Length – 2 hours 25 minutes

Reading and Writing

Four modules are available. These modules test reading and writing in an academic or general training context. Texts and graphic material are drawn from the candidates' broad field of study.

In the Reading section (55 minutes) the skills and functions tested include following instructions, finding main ideas, identifying the underlying concept or theme and identifying relationships between ideas in the text. Item-types include gap-filling, short-answer questions, sorting events into order and a minimum of multiple choice.

In the Writing section (45 minutes) the skills and functions tested include organising and presenting data, listing the stages of a procedure, describing an object or event or sequence of events, evaluating and challenging ideas, evidence and argument.

Candidates are asked to complete two tasks, one involving information transfer or reprocessing (15 minutes) and the other requiring candidates to draw on information from a variety of sources and their own experience to present an argument or solve a problem (30 minutes).

Writing test papers are marked by qualified examiners, trained in IELTS test procedures. Ratings are monitored by UCLES on a regular basis to ensure that uniform standards are maintained.

Listening
This is a test of listening comprehension in the context of general English proficiency. The earlier sections deal with social survival topics – travel, accommodation, health and welfare – and the later ones with topics in the area of education and training. The test is based on a tape recording and item-types include controlled note-taking, form filling, gap-filling and short-answer questions. As in the Reading subtest, extensive use of multiple choice questions is avoided, so that guessing does not become an important factor in IELTS.

Speaking
The Speaking Test is a structured oral interview, designed to encourage candidates to demonstrate their ability to speak English. The emphasis is on general speaking skills, rather than those related to students' own fields of study. The test is rated according to a global proficiency scale. In making their assessments, interviewers take account of effective communication and appropriate and flexible use of grammar and vocabulary. All interviews are recorded so that ratings given by interviewers can be monitored on a regular basis.

How are the results reported and interpreted?

Reporting of Results

On-the-spot marking ensures that test results are available very soon after the test is taken. A *test report form* will normally reach the receiving institution within two weeks of the candidate sitting the test.

The *test report form* gives details of the candidate's nationality, first language, date-of-birth and proposed subject of study and qualification as well as the date and results of the test and the module taken.

The nine Academic Bands and their descriptive statements are as follows:

Expert User. Has fully operational command of the language: appropriate, accurate and fluent with complete understanding.

Very Good User. Has fully operational command of the language with only occasional unsystematic inaccuracies and inappropriacies. Misunderstandings may occur in unfamiliar situations. Handles complex detailed argumentation well.

Good User. Has operational command of the language, though with occasional inaccuracies, inappropriacies and misunderstandings in some situations. Generally handles complex language well and understands detailed reasoning.

Competent User. Has generally effective command of the language despite some inaccuracies, inappropriacies and misunderstandings. Can use and understand fairly complex language, particularly in familiar situations.

Modest User. Has partial command of the language, coping with overall meaning in most situations, though is likely to make many mistakes. Should be able to handle basic communication in own field.

Limited User. Basic competence is limited to familiar situations. Has frequent problems in understanding and expression. Is not able to use complex language.

Extremely Limited User. Conveys and understands only general meaning in very familiar situations. Frequent breakdowns in communication occur.

Intermittent User. No real communication is possible except for the most basic information using isolated words or short formulae in familiar situations and to meet immediate needs. Has great difficulty understanding spoken and written English.

Non User. Essentially has no ability to use the language beyond possibly a few isolated words.

Did not attempt the test. No assessable information.

Form of results

Each subtest is reported separately in the form of a *Band Score*. The individual subtest scores are added together and averaged to obtain an *Overall Band Score*. Each Band corresponds to a descriptive statement which gives a summary of the English of a candidate classified at that level. The scale of Bands ascends from 1 to 9 for the Academic Modules and from 1 to 6 for the General Training Module.

The General Training Module is not designed to test the full range of language skills required for academic purposes. Candidates taking this module are unlikely to demonstrate the upper range of such skills and will not be able to score higher than Band 6. Admission to undergraduate or postgraduate courses should **not** then be based on performance on the General Training Module.

Interpretation of Results

The interpretation of test results by receiving institutions involves relating course requirements to the candidate's proficiency in English as indicated by the *Overall Band Score* and by individual subtest scores. The appropriate level required for a given course of study or training is ultimately something which institutions/faculties/course tutors must determine in the light of knowledge of their own courses and their experience of overseas students taking them.

The British Council has, however, used its long experience of placing overseas students to establish certain guidelines. Courses are categorised into four types:

Category A: linguistically exacting academic courses.

Category B: linguistically less-exacting academic courses.

Category C: linguistically exacting training courses.

Category D: linguistically less-exacting training courses.

Minimum levels of acceptability are generally regarded as:

Category	Acceptable Band	Probably acceptable Band
A:	7.5	7.0
B:	7.0	6.5
C:	6.0	5.5
D:	5.5	5.0

It is important to note, however, that these judgements are frequently modified to take into account the individual scores on the different subtests, the requirements of a particular course and details of the candidate's background. Institutions may wish to apply additional criteria regarding acceptance of candidates for particular courses.

Such variables also affect recommendations for language tuition. Experience has shown that the speed of learning, as expressed by the number of hours required to improve one band, can vary from person to person between 100 hours and over 200 hours, with a tendency for more rapid rates of progress at the lower levels.

The General Training Module is not designed to test the full range of language skills required for academic purposes. Candidates taking this module are unlikely to demonstrate the upper range of such skills and will not be able to score higher than Band 6. Admission to undergraduate or postgraduate courses should **not** then be based on performance on the General Training Module.

What do receiving institutions need to know?

The *Overall Band Score,* which is the average of the
component *Band Scores,* provides a summary
assessment of the candidate's proficiency in
English. For some receiving institutions this may be
a sufficient guide to the adequacy of the candidate's
English for the proposed course of study. Other
receiving institutions may require a particular level
in one or more subtests as well as a specific *Overall
Band Score.* Each institution is clearly in the best
position to decide which *Band Scores* it requires for
its own courses, relating *Band Scores* in the
individual subtests to language skills of greatest
relevance to particular courses.

For example, a course which places heavy demands
on listening and reading skills but requires little
writing and oral interaction, will call for higher
rating on the Listening and Reading tests than on
Writing and Speaking. On the other hand, a
training attachment with heavy oral demands may
well call for higher rating on the Speaking and
Listening tests than on the Reading and Writing. As
an institution becomes familiar with the IELTS
results and their interpretation, it develops a policy
with regard to each of the subtests.

The individual *Band Scores* provide information
about the candidate's language ability in the four
skills Reading, Writing, Listening and Speaking,
thus permitting remedial tuition when necessary.
Each institution can decide whether such tuition
should be before or concurrent with the main
course. It is, therefore, useful to test candidates well
in advance so that pre-course tuition can be
recommended where appropriate. Reporting of the
individual *Band Scores* means that the receiving
institution can also recommend the type of pre-
course tuition needed. For example, if a receiving
institution is dissatisfied with the candidate's
reading and writing scores, it can recommend pre-
course tuition which concentrates on those skills.

How is the test monitored and developed?

The International English Language Testing System is continuously monitored by the British Council, the University of Cambridge Local Examinations Syndicate and the International Development Program of Australian Universities and Colleges.

Analyses of the test are concerned with such matters as the mechanical accuracy of clerical procedures, the internal reliability of the subtests, the reliability of subjective marking, the behaviour of individual test items, the relationship between the various subtests and the evaluation of profile reporting. Data analysis built up on the *Rapid-access management information system* programme at UCLES in Cambridge provides computerized access to information on the following:

• the relationship between *Band Scores* and common criteria such as fluent/good or adequate/inadequate;

• the relationship between Bands derived from the Test and Bands as reported by pre-course and main course tutors;

• notions of adequacy in IELTS Band terms for particular courses and subjects.

Further specific studies are planned, involving all academic and technical aspects of IELTS.

The revision of ELTS

Feedback from ELTS test centres both overseas and in the UK and from other ELTS users was collected and collated by the ELTS Revision Project. This feedback, together with the results of the *Edinburgh Validation Study* and the suggestions for further research and improvement proffered by participants at a conference held in London in July 1987 to consult language testing researchers, contributed to the data which formed the basis of the major ELTS Revision Project which was completed in 1989 (for further details see IELTS Research Reports, forthcoming). During the Revision Project, specialists in English for Academic Purposes, subject specialists in a wide range of academic disciplines, language testers, language test researchers and applied linguists commented on developing test specifications and draft test items. After extensive revision, tests were piloted in September – November 1988 in the UK and Australia, and were further revised in line with the revised specifications. Thereafter widespread trialling took place world-wide from January – May 1989. In addition, sections of the new and old tests were tried in tandem so that the current test could be standardised and calibrated against the old. A full range of statistical and content analyses were undertaken, and the results of these analyses are separately available in the *Professional Test Manual*.

Studies of the concurrent and predictive validity of the test battery are under way to ascertain to what extent the new test is able to predict and identify the problems that overseas students might have because of language in their study or training setting, in an English medium. This research is being conducted collaboratively with a variety of institutions and will be reported on at professional conferences and in the IELTS Research Report series.

What the Test Contains

MODULAR SECTION

Reading

Time allowed: 55 minutes

Number of questions: about 30 - 40

You will be given a Test Booklet which contains three or four reading passages related to your own subject area and questions on these passages. In some cases the questions appear before the relevant reading passage; in other cases they appear after the reading passage. You will record all your answers in the Test Booklet, following the directions given.

There is a wide variety of different question types. Here are some examples of the kinds of text and questions you may meet. (Please note the texts are only extracts; the actual reading passages are mostly at least one page long.)

EXAMPLE 1 (MODULE A)

A section of the text reads as follows:

> Harmful ultraviolet radiation may reach the surface of the Earth in increasing quantities in the 1990s as the ozone layer thins - yet biologists still cannot predict the effects. Scientists have now established that the springtime "hole" in the ozone layer above Antarctica is a direct effect of chlorine compounds produced by the breakdown of chlorofluorocarbons (CFCs), compounds that do not occur naturally and have lifetimes of scores of years in the atmosphere. Some evidence suggests that a smaller ozone hole may be developing over the Arctic, and that CFCs have depleted the ozone in the stratosphere by a few per cent over the past decade.

The text is accompanied by some questions. For example:

> 1. CFC stands for *Chlorofluorocarbon*

You answer the question by writing "chlorofluorocarbon" in the space provided.

EXAMPLE 2 (MODULE A)

A later section of the same passage reads:

> The ozone then absorbs ultraviolet in the band between 200 nm and 300
> nm, known as "far" UV (or hard UV). The radiation in the band from
> 300 nm to 400 nm, which does reach the ground, is known as near UV.

You are provided with a table which has some missing information:

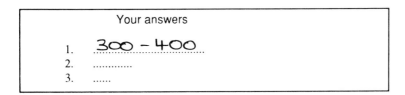

	Near UV	Far UV	Extreme UV
wavelengths/nm	1.	3.	5.
effect on atmosphere	no information given	4.	
effect on humans/life	2.		

You have to complete the boxes in the table by writing the missing information in the spaces provided:

```
         Your answers
    1.   300 - 400
    2.   ............
    3.   ......
```

The text says that radiation in the band from 300 nm to 400 nm is known as near UV and so for Question 1 "300 - 400" has been written in the appropriate space underneath the table.

EXAMPLE 3 (MODULE B)

A section of the text reads as follows:

> Fluoridation consists of raising the concentration of the fluoride ion F in
> water supplies to about 1 part per million with the aim of reducing dental
> caries (tooth decay) in children. In fluoridated areas, there are now many
> longitudinal studies (studies over time) which record large reductions in
> the incidence of caries. The results of these and of fixed time surveys
> have led to the 'fluoridation hypothesis', namely that the principal cause
> of these reductions is fluoridation.

The text is followed by a summary of the passage. You have to complete the summary by writing
ONE or TWO words in each space.

For example:

	Your answers
Fluoridation is the addition of ..1.. to the water supplies. The ..2.. that	1. fluoride 2. ....

You write "fluoride" in the first space to the right of the summary.

EXAMPLE 4 (MODULE C)

A section of the text reads as follows:

> What are the purposes of continuing career education? Some people think about the matter very simplistically, but most people realize that several goals must be sought simultaneously and that the process of doing this is difficult. We may identify at least eight purposes of continuing professional education.
>
> The first of these is to keep up with the new knowledge required to perform responsibly in the chosen career. Just think, for example, how much has happened in the various professions in ten years. At the start of the decade, we had just learned how to keep a man in orbit around the earth; at its end, we had sent many men to the moon.

You are provided with a list of fourteen "Aims of continuing education" and you are asked to choose which of these fit each of the eight aims described in the passage:

> **Aims of continuing education**
>
> ......
>
> L. Contemplating theory
>
> M. Preparing for career change
>
> N. Staying in touch with developments in professional knowledge
>
> ......

The first purpose of continuing professional education is to keep up with new knowledge, so you select N from the above extract of alternatives.

> Your answers
>
> Aim 1   ..N........
>
> Aim 2   ......

EXAMPLE 5 (GENERAL TRAINING MODULE)

An extract of the text reads as follows:

WHERE TO FIND HELP IN THE COLLEGE

Here is the location of some important college services and facilities.
Rooms numbered 100-130 are on the first floor and those numbered
200-230 on the second floor of the main college block.

Examinations Office	**125**
Self Access Language Learning Centre Students can attend on a drop-in basis from 9.00 am to 4.15 pm.	**203**
Finance Office Payment of fees.	**124**
General Staff Room	**225**

You have to write down the room number you should go to in order to find various college services.
For example:

	Room
Question 1: You want to pay your fees.	.124
Question 2: You ...	

You pay fees at the Finance Office so you write "124" in the appropriate space.

EXAMPLE 6 (GENERAL TRAINING MODULE)

An extract of the text reads as follows:

STUDENTS' INSURANCE SCHEME

WHAT IS COVERED UNDER CONTENTS?

Under the 'Contents' section your possessions - which do not have to be itemised - will be protected on a 'new for old' basis where items will be replaced as new - IRRESPECTIVE OF THEIR AGE OR CONDI- TION.

'Contents' includes clothes, books, radios, audio and video players, TVs, jewellery, home computers, furniture, household goods, domestic appliances, other electrical equipment and sports equipment.

You are asked to say whether, according to the extract, some statements are correct. You circle A if the statement is correct, B if it is incorrect and C if the information is not given.

	Correct	Incorrect	No Information Given
1. You are not insured if your cassette-recorder is stolen.	A	(B)	C

According to the text audio players *are* insured so you circle B, "Incorrect".

Writing

Time allowed: 45 minutes

Number of questions: 2 writing tasks.

There are two writing tasks, both of which must be completed. You are advised to spend 15 minutes on Task 1 and 30 minutes on Task 2.

MODULES A, B AND C

In the first task you will be asked to look at a diagram, a drawing, or perhaps a piece of text and to present the information in your own words. For example, if your subject of study is in the field of Technology, you might see a diagram of a physical process; you would then have to write a description of the equipment or process. This must **not** be written in the form of notes.

The second writing task is rather longer. You will be asked to consider one of the points raised in the reading passages which you studied earlier, and then to write about it, perhaps presenting arguments for and against, relating it to your own experience or your own country etc.

GENERAL TRAINING MODULE

For Task 1 you will be asked to write a letter. This will be related to life as a student in an English-speaking country. You might, for example, have to write to a shop to complain about something you have bought, or you might be asked to write to a college officer asking about accommodation.

For Task 2 you have to write a description or a report. This might, for example, be a report for a course supervisor. It will **not** take the form of a letter. You might be asked to list the stages in a procedure, or to explain why something is the case, or to provide general factual information. The task may be related to one of the passages in the reading test.

GENERAL SECTION

Listening

Time allowed: 30 minutes

Number of questions: about 30 - 35

The Listening Test has four sections, all of which are recorded on tape. As you listen, you will have in front of you a test booklet with a number of different types of exercise. When you hear the recording you should answer each question, following the directions given. There will be time for you to read the instructions and questions, and you will have a chance to check your work.

All the recordings will be played once only.

EXAMPLE 1

In one section you may hear a conversation between one or more people. In your test booklet you will see a series of pictures. You have to choose which of the pictures gives the correct answer to the question, according to the information you hear on the tape.

For example, you hear the following conversation:

> Speaker 1: Hello, Mrs Baxter?
>
> Speaker 2: Yes?
>
> Speaker 1: I'm Gerry Richardson er I hope you've er been expecting me.
>
> Speaker 2: Oh yes you're the new student, aren't you? Yes, I've been expecting you ... please come in.
>
> Speaker 1: Thank you.

You then read the question "Who is at the door?" and look at the pictures below:

Gerry Richardson, a young man, is at the door, so for Question 1 you circle 'D' beside the picture of a man.

EXAMPLE 2

In another section of the test you may have to complete a form according to the information you hear. For example, you hear:

Speaker 3: Good afternoon, can I help you?

Speaker 1: Yes ... er I've just arrived and I want to register er for er...

Speaker 3: Ah yes ... right ... well first of all we need some details [Pause] ... you're Mr er

Speaker 1: Richardson.

Speaker 3: Richardson, and your first name?

Speaker 1: Gerry.

Speaker 3: Gerry - umm - how do you spell that?

Speaker 1: G - E - R - R - Y.

In the form (part of which is shown below), you have to write "Gerry" in the space for First Name.

COLLEGE LANGUAGE CENTRE

STUDENT REGISTRATION FORM

SURNAME ....*Richardson*.........

① FIRST NAME ....*Gerry*..........

MALE [✓]   FEMALE [ ]

EXAMPLE 3

In another section of the test you may hear a lecture being given to college students. In the following example, you hear a professor giving an introductory talk to some new students. You have to fill in details in a timetable. You hear:

Speaker 4: Now I'd better tell you exactly what you'll be doing for the rest of this term. We're now in the first week of term. The most important thing you have to do this week, as I said, is see your course tutor. He or she will give you details of your placement.

You have to write ''See course tutor'' beside WEEK 1 in the timetable.

TIMETABLE

WEEK 1   *See course tutor*

WEEK 2   ....

Speaking

Time allowed: 11 - 15 minutes

The Speaking Test consists of an oral interview, that is a conversation between you and the examiner.

The test is divided into five Phases:

1. Introduction	The examiner introduces him/herself and you have a brief discussion about your life, home, work and interests.
2. Extended Discourse	You are expected to speak at some length about one or two familiar topics.
3. Elicitation	The examiner will give you a card with some information on it. You have to ask the examiner questions relating to what you read on the card.
4. Speculation and Attitudes	You will be asked questions about your future plans and your proposed course of study.
5. Conclusion	The examiner will bring the interview to an end.

The examiner will use detailed guidelines to rate your performance according to a 9 - Band proficiency scale.

Each interview will be recorded.